Tree Fruit
PHYSIOLOGY:
Growth and Development

A comprehensive manual for
regulating deciduous tree fruit
growth and development

Tree Fruit PHYSIOLOGY:
Growth and Development

*A comprehensive manual for regulating
deciduous tree fruit growth and development*

Edited by
Karen M. Maib
Dr. Preston K. Andrews
Dr. Gregory A. Lang
Dr. Kent Mullinix

Contributors include
Brent Black
Dr. Frank Dennis
Dr. Don Elfving
Dr. John Fellman
Dr. Duane Greene
Dr. Scott Johnson
Dr. Norm Looney
Dr. Jim Mattheis
Dr. Stephen Myers
Dr. Curt Rom

Published by
Good Fruit Grower
Yakima, Washington

Published by Good Fruit Grower
a division of Washington State Fruit Commission
105 S. 18th Street, Suite 217
Yakima, Washington 98901-2149
509-575-2315, Fax 509-453-4880

First printing December 1996

Library of Congress Cataloging-in-Publication Data
    Tree fruit physiology : growth and development : a comprehensive manual
    for regulating deciduous tree fruit growth and development /
    edited by Karen M. Maib...[et al.].

         p.   cm.

    Includes bibliographical references.
    ISBN 0-9630659-6-3 (alk. paper)
    1. Fruit trees—Physiology. I. Maib, Karen M. (Karen Marie),
    1957-   .

    SB357.28.T74   1996   96-46960
    571.8'2373--dc21   CIP

™ ∞ *The paper used in this publication meets the minimum requirements*
of American National Standard for Information Sciences—Permanence
of Paper for Printed Library Materials, ANSI Z39.48-1984.

Printed and bound in the United States of America

Preface

A sincere thank you to the many contributors to *Tree Fruit Physiology: Growth and Development*. It was the editors' privilege to work with so many talented pomologists. Their efforts in making the shortcourse a valuable learning experience and this book a worthy reference is greatly appreciated.

And, as always, the staff at Good Fruit Grower is to be applauded for setting and maintaining the quality standards under which this project was completed. *Tree Fruit Physiology* is the latest in a series of collaborations between Washington State University and Good Fruit Grower that has produced quality resource materials for the tree fruit industry.

Karen Maib, Editor

Table of Contents

PART III: Regulation of Reproductive Growth and Development

PART IV: Regulation of Fruit Quality

Introduction

Higher plants are sophisticated, complex, biological systems. Not static objects, they are well-organized, living systems capable of processing matter and energy in their environment. One of the most fascinating things about living organisms is their ability to grow and develop. Studying and understanding the physiological functioning of plants, including plant growth and development, are essential to the serious pomologist. While we must integrate knowledge from entomology, pathology, soil science, plant nutrition, economics, and other fields, an understanding of the basic physiological processes involved in growth and development is necessary if we are to regulate effectively vegetative and reproductive growth and development and fruit quality.

This book is the outcome of a three-day shortcourse that focused on the regulation of vegetative, reproductive, and fruit growth of pome and stone tree fruits.

The book is divided into four major sections. Part 1, "Physiology and Regulation of Tree Fruit Growth and Development," lays the foundation in Chapter 1, with an overview of the physiological processes, and the coordination and interconnectedness of the many processes involved in whole tree growth and development. Chapter 2 discusses how growth is regulated with light, water, temperature, photosynthesis, and nutrients. Chapter 3 introduces the main families of plant hormones and their role in the normal functioning of higher plants. Part 1 concludes with an important discussion on the essential components for getting desired results from spray applications of plant growth regulators.

Chapters 5 and 6 in Part 2 explore the coordination of root and shoot growth and the interactions between roots and shoots, with emphasis on rootstocks, root growth, pruning, root restriction, and branch and canopy manipulation. Chapter 7 discusses the manipulation of vegetative and reproductive growth with water and nitrogen.

Regulation of flower development, fruit development, and fruit ripening and maturity are the subjects discussed in Part 3. The many factors, including cultural, that influence flower bud formation, fruit size and shape are discussed in Chapters 8, 9, and 10. The role of ethylene and the physiology of quality changes during maturation and ripening is covered in Chapter 11. A basic discussion of how and why fruit grows is included in this section.

The final section, Part 4, is devoted to the regulation of fruit quality. The first two chapters discuss fruit quality in relation to environmental stresses; pome fruits are covered in Chapter 12 and stone fruits in Chapter 13. Specific disorders and implications regarding postharvest life and quality are addressed. The last two chapters are discussions on the effects of gibberellin-based plant bioregulators (PBRs) and the ethylene-based preharvest growth regulators, ethephon and aminoethoxyvinylglycine (AVG), on fruit quality.

This book will be a useful reference for orchard consultants, fruit growers, instructors, Cooperative Extension faculty, and other students of deciduous whole tree physiology and the regulation of growth and development.

KAREN MAIB
Editor

part I
Physiology and Regulation of Tree Fruit Growth and Development

DR. DON ELFVING
Tree Fruit Research & Extension Center
Washington State University
1100 North Western Avenue
Wenatchee, WA 98801
phone: 509-663-8181; fax: 509-662-8714

DR. CURT ROM
Department of Horticulture
University of Arkansas
316 Plant Science Building
Fayetteville, AR 72701
phone: 501-575-7434; fax: 501-575-8619
crom@comp.uark.edu

DR. NORM LOONEY
Agriculture and Agri-Food Canada
Pacific Agri-Food Research Centre
Summerland, B.C. V0H 1Z0, Canada
phone: 250-494-6361; fax: 250-494-0755
looneyn@em.agr.ca

MR. BRENT BLACK
Department of Horticulture
Oregon State University
Ag and Life Science 4017
Corvallis, OR 97331-7304
phone: 503-737-5443; fax: 503-737-3479
blackb@bcc.orst.edu

Physiological Processes and the Coordination of Vegetative and Reproductive Plant Growth and Development

Don C. Elfving
Washington State University
Tree Fruit Research and Extension Center
Wenatchee, Washington

Plants have evolved in a very different way from animals. Their sessile mode of life imposes significantly different requirements for survival. In order to survive and reproduce, sessile organisms have developed strategies to tolerate or circumvent unfavorable environmental extremes and to take as full advantage as possible of more favorable conditions (Trewavas, 1981). Plants do not possess the high degree of cellular specialization typical of animals; plant cells display a high degree of developmental plasticity, characterized by the ability of many types of plant cells to regenerate new plant organs or even complete plants under appropriate conditions.

In the wild, plants, including tree fruits, developed physiological and morphological adaptations to overcome vagaries of the environment, the negative effects of pests and diseases, and the competitive pressures from other species (Schwabe, 1978). Some of these adaptations are not necessary or desirable in an agriculturally managed ecosystem, where the environment is optimized with the aim of maximizing agricultural production.

Among other characteristics, agriculturally optimized fruit trees would not require pollination for fruit set, would not experience biennial bearing, would not require thinning, would not experience preharvest fruit drop, and would partition a greater proportion of photosynthetically produced assimilates into fruit as opposed to vegetative tissues (Luckwill, 1977).

In cereals and vegetables, the plants themselves have been extensively modified through genetics and breeding, because generation time is short and genetic diversity is sufficient to make this strategy practical. In contrast, modification of fruit trees through breeding is complicated by difficulties of very long generation times and complex, poorly-understood genetics. Therefore, other strategies have been sought to overcome characteristics of fruit trees that do not favor sustained maximum production of fruits.

The use of plant growth regulators (PGRs) has become important in tree-fruit culture, because many chemical materials have been discovered that profoundly affect the growth and development of fruit trees, and because practical techniques for their use have been developed rapidly as compared to the time required for genetic modification and development (Davis, et al., 1988; Looney, 1980, 1983a, 1983b, 1993; Miller, 1988).

Plant growth substances in fruit trees

When the first discoveries were made of naturally-occurring chemical substances in plants that could profoundly affect their growth, the concept of plant hormones was born (Trewavas, 1981). This idea, transferred to plants from developments in mammalian hormone physiology during the same time, implied that these substances were locally synthesized in plants, exerted their action at a distance from the site(s) of production, and controlled growth through changes or differences in concentration.

The concept of naturally-occurring plant growth substances as hormones is being altered by growing evidence that the role of growth substances in plants is not strictly hormonal, but rather that these compounds act to coordinate or integrate growth by stimulating or inhibiting processes so that groups of cells behave in concert (Trewavas, 1981, 1982).

Concentrations of growth substances vary enormously in plant tissues over the growing season. Luckwill (1970) showed that the content of auxin-like and cytokinin-like substances in apple xylem sap reached a maximum concentration in the spring, and tended to decline over the rest of the season.

How such changes are related to specific growth processes is still unclear. Treharne et al. (1985) described problems in relating growth-substance content in fruit tissues with fruit growth and development. Much remains to be learned about naturally-occurring growth substances and their function in plants.

Exogenous applications of PGRs have been used to influence many growth processes in fruit trees. Undesired side effects associated with the use of PGRs on fruit trees have always presented potential or real problems. These side effects may be avoidable, but their possible occurrence often limits the degree of response that can be economically achieved with PGR applications (Davis, et al., 1988; Miller, 1988; Tromp and Wertheim, 1980).

Examples include the former use of daminozide (Alar) to reduce the vigor of shoot growth. In this case, undesirable reductions in fruit size limited the amount of Alar that could be applied for this purpose. Undesirable carryover effects the following season also limited the amount of Alar that could be applied during the growing season.

Similar responses have been reported when paclobutrazol was used to control apple tree shoot growth. The use of ethephon (Ethrel) for fruit loosening can be accompanied by gummosis in *Prunus* species and/or leaf abscission. Again, limiting the concentration and timing of such applications largely or completely overcomes these side effects. The use of auxins such as naphthaleneacetamide (NAD) or naphthaleneacetic acid (NAA) for fruit thinning can result in the formation of pygmy fruit in Delicious.

The multitude of effects on both vegetative and reproductive growth observed from the exogenous application of PGRs supports the idea that growth substances in plants are much more general in their effects on cells and tissues than the analogous, but quite distinct, hormones that influence specific tissue and organ behavior in animals.

The competition theory of fruit-tree growth

Fruiting decreases vegetative growth. Maggs (1963) showed that the presence of fruit reduced the dry-weight increment in vegetative tissues of apple trees. He further demonstrated that the proportional reduction in the growth of various parts of the tree was greater for plant parts more distant from the leaves, the sources of photosynthetically produced assimilates. In his trials, the root system experienced the greatest reduction in growth due to fruiting. These observations are consistent with the concept that various parts of the tree grow by competing for the products of the leaves.

The mean fruit weight of a crop of apples is inversely proportional to the number of fruit on the tree (Forshey and Elfving, 1977). This inverse relation between crop load and the size of the apples making up that crop supports the concept that the fruits themselves are in competition with each other for resources required for their growth and that their growth is resource-limited.

The various vegetative parts of an apple tree do not accumulate dry weight (i.e., grow) at the same rate nor at the same times throughout the growing season (Forshey et al., 1983). Some factor or factors regulate the sites where growth occurs in the tree over the course of the growing season. These observations strongly suggest that growth is not strictly governed by competition for resources alone.

For example, scaffold limbs do not enlarge more rapidly than the trunk, despite their being closer to the sources of photosynthetic assimilates. Roots, most distant from the leaves, experience their second flush of growth in the late summer and fall, when accumulation of dry weight in aboveground wood is reduced. Shoots terminate their extension in length, their dry-weight accumulation, and the production of shoot leaves in early to midsummer, despite the ready availability of photosynthates produced nearby.

So what controls growth—growth substances or resources? Evidence from the above-mentioned studies and many others supports a clear distinction between control of the location of growth versus the rate of growth. A growing body of evidence supports the concept that growth substances dictate where growth occurs, while resources (water, nutrients, carbohydrates, etc.) limit the rate or extent of growth (Abbott, 1977; Trewavas, 1981).

The well-known concept of limiting factors and their effect on growth, originally articulated by Liebig nearly 200 years ago, lends credence to this idea. A link between growth substances and processes directly affecting assimilate production and distribution has not been established (Lenton, 1984; Morgan, 1980).

Physiological processes as models

SHOOT GROWTH

Exogenous PGRs can both stimulate (cytokinin, Promalin) or inhibit (auxin, daminozide, paclobutrazol) shoot growth (Davis et al., 1988; Elfving, 1984, 1985; Forshey and Elfving, 1977; Miller, 1988). The timing of the application may be critical to obtaining a satisfactory response. For example, studies of the induction of shoot growth in field-grown apple trees with cytokinins indicated a change from maximum induction to no response within one week (Elfving, 1984). Many responses to exogenous PGR applications occur only within a relatively narrow time window; such rapid changes in response may reflect internal changes in the balance of naturally-occurring promoters and inhibitors and/or altered sensitivity of cells to growth substances (Trewavas, 1981, 1982).

Heading cuts in one-year-old wood stimulate shoot growth in apple branches (Forshey and Elfving, 1989). The typical response involves the growth of several very vigorous shoots from near the heading cut. When NAA was applied to the cut ends of dormant-headed apple branches before growth resumed in the spring, the auxin treatment had a strong effect on where new shoot growth took place on the limb, but did not alter the stimulating effect of the cut itself (Elfving and Forshey, 1977).

In a companion study, summer heading new shoots in June stimulated the maximum amount of regrowth (Elfving, unpublished). When NAA was applied to the cut ends following summer heading, the normal stimulation of shoot growth was inhibited for the remainder of the growing season. However, when growth resumed the following spring, nearly a year after heading, branches headed the previous summer and treated with NAA produced the increased shoot growth characteristic of summer-headed limbs. These studies showed clearly that a single exogenous auxin application could affect where growth occurred in a headed limb, but had no effect on the amount of that growth. This concept was applied to the training of young apple trees, using NAA applications to redirect the enhanced shoot growth in newly-planted and headed freestanding apple trees into potential scaffold limbs (Elfving and Forshey, 1977).

In another study of pruning effects on shoot growth, competing shoots were removed from previously headed limbs on young Empire apple trees very early in the growing season to physically restore a single terminal growing point on headed limbs. Despite this attempt to recreate a morphologically normal limb, total shoot growth still showed the stimulative effect of the heading cut (Elfving, 1990). In this trial, reduced trunk enlargement during that growing season suggested that the vigorous shoot growth resulting from heading produced a measurable change in the allocation of dry weight from secondary growth of limbs and trunk to new shoots in those young trees.

In a study conducted from 1982 to 1987, profound changes in growth and productivity were observed in Northern Spy apple trees treated annually with either Alar shortly after flowering to reduce shoot growth or Alar+Ethrel in midsummer to stimulate flowering (Elfving and Cline, 1990). Over the five years of this study, total yield from PGR-treated trees was 35% greater than controls. Shoot growth was substantially reduced, thereby reducing pruning requirements and significantly improving economic value of the crop (Elfving, 1988).

The detailed data taken during this study suggested the following scenario for how the PGR applications resulted in the many changes in tree behavior observed (Elfving and Cline, 1990). The annual applications of either Alar alone or Alar+Ethrel increased the density of spurs in the canopy. The increases in spur density were followed by

increased flowering, which, in turn, resulted in increased yields. Much, if not most, of the reduced vegetative vigor observed appeared due to the consequences of larger yields.

Northern Spy apple trees are notoriously biennial. There was no change in bienniality during this study, suggesting no consistent direct effect of PGR applications on flower formation itself. There were no consistent changes in fruit set directly attributable to the PGR treatments.

The evidence suggests that the primary direct effect of these annual PGR treatments was to somehow encourage more buds to develop into spurs. From that point on, the cascade of events leading to increased yields and reduced vegetative vigor was mediated mainly by natural processes in the trees themselves, with little or no direct effects from the PGR applications.

THINNING AND FRUIT GROWTH

Chemical thinning with PGRs is characterized by the narrow time window for a response (Williams, 1979). This narrow window may reflect rapid internal changes in growth-substance balance and/or rapid changes in tissue sensitivity to the thinning compounds. The mechanism by which chemical thinners reduce fruit set is not known precisely, but is thought to involve alteration in the supply of assimilates to fruitlets.

The consequence of greater limitation on the supply of photosynthates to fruitlets is that a larger proportion of the fruitlets is unable to sustain sufficient growth and eventually abscises. This concept that fruit set depends heavily on an adequate supply of assimilates is supported by experimental evidence that substantial fruit-set reductions can be produced by shading the canopy for only a few days during the first few weeks after flowering (Byers et al., 1990).

Blossom thinners cause physical damage to flowers, thereby impeding fertilization, and will not be considered further here. Several different classes of chemical compounds are in commercial use for accomplishing postbloom thinning. Auxins, cytokinins, ethylene-generating compounds, and carbamates, although differing substantially in their chemistry and effects on plant tissues, are all capable of reducing fruit set when applied during a short time interval after flowering.

Return bloom the next year is improved by chemical thinning. This well-known relationship is thought to be related to the effects of gibberellic acid (GA) produced by the endosperm of developing apple seeds. The endosperm of apple seeds develops very rapidly in the first weeks following fertilization. Production of gibberellic acid by the growing endosperm results in the movement of GA from the seeds into the tissues of the spur to which the fruitlet is attached.

The presence of GA in spur tissues at that time is thought to result in inhibition of flower induction in the lateral meristem of the spur. Chan and Cain (1967) reported classic experiments that demonstrated the involvement of seeds in the inhibition of flowering on apple spurs.

Exogenous applications of GA following flowering can inhibit flower formation in apple trees (Miller, 1988). The presence of fruitlets at the time of GA application greatly enhances the inhibitory response to that treatment. Application of GA to non-flowering trees may produce little inhibition of flowering unless sufficiently high concentrations are used to produce significant morphological modifications in lateral buds.

These observations suggest that exogenous GA applications may promote the inhibition of flower formation by supplementing the natural internal balance of GA such that much more inhibition of flower formation becomes possible. In addition, the observed responses of flowering to exogenous GA support the idea that exogenous PGR applications may stimulate or inhibit a single process, the consequences

of which may have major effects on subsequent tree growth and productivity.

Fruit growth in apple reflects both the number of cells in the fruit and the size of those cells. In apple, the cell-division phase of fruit growth precedes, and is almost completely separate in time from, the cell-enlargement phase. Cell division in apple fruitlets is the dominant growth process for the first 35 to 45 days following fruiting (Schechter et al., 1993).

After that time, growth in apple is almost exclusively the result of enlargement of cells already present in the young fruitlet. Growth in fresh and dry weight of apples takes place at a constant rate from the onset of cell enlargement until harvest (Blanpied, 1966), or for up to a few weeks after harvest if the fruit is not removed at the normal harvest time (Schechter et al., 1993).

Recent evidence demonstrates that altering cell division in the young fruitlet can have a more profound effect on final fruit size than a simple reduction in fruit load (Wismer et al., 1995). In this study, the thinning effects of benzyladenine (BA, Accel) were compared with those of NAA and carbaryl (Sevin). All three materials produced the same level of thinning.

However, BA induced a greater rate of cell division in treated fruits, resulting in a larger number of cells per fruit. Both NAA and carbaryl produced a comparable reduction in fruit load to BA and larger cells than in BA-treated fruit, but had no effect on cell division. Nevertheless, BA-treated fruit were significantly larger, suggesting that increased cell numbers can affect final fruit size to a greater extent than simply reducing competition among fruits on the tree.

The sensitivity of fruitlets to postbloom thinners coincides with the period of maximum cell division. In the study described above, postbloom application of BA increased the rate of cell division but not the duration of the process. What controls cell division in apple fruitlets? Can we develop better controls over this process to improve fruit size even further? Can we learn to extend the period of cell division as well as increase the rate of the process? Would extending the duration of cell division affect the time that fruit reach maturity? The development of chemical tools to control the fruit cell-division process offers the prospect of significant advancements in our ability to improve fruit quality in an economically beneficial manner.

Conclusions

The role of growth substances in plants is still unclear. There is little evidence that the concentrations of growth substances measured in plant tissues have much influence over rates of growth of plant organs. The evidence presented here supports the idea that exogenous PGR applications have immediate and direct stimulatory or inhibitory effects that produce a chain of subsequent responses that can result in significant changes in both vegetative and reproductive growth and development.

We need to learn much more about both naturally-occurring growth substances and the responses of both trees and the fruits themselves to exogenously-applied PGRs.

We need more knowledge about how growth is regulated internally, about the nature and behavior of the receptors of PGR signals, about how and when cells change their sensitivity to chemical signals, and about the genetic bases for these responses.

I believe that there are still many opportunities for the development of economically beneficial PGR effects in tree fruits, and that PGRs will continue to represent an important tool for the management of both fruit trees and the fruits they produce.

Literature cited

Abbott, D.L., "Supply and demand in the apple tree," *Scientific Hort.* 29 (1977): 19-24.

Blanpied, G.D., "Changes in the weight, volume, and specific gravity of developing apple fruits," *Proc. Amer. Soc. Hort. Sci.* 88 (1966): 33-37.

Byers, R.E., J.A. Barden, R.F. Polomski, R.W. Young, and D.H. Carbaugh, "Apple thinning by photosynthetic inhibition," *J. Amer. Soc. Hort. Sci.* 115 (1990): 14-19.

Chan, B.G. and J.C. Cain, "The effect of seed formation on subsequent flowering in apple," *Proc. Amer. Soc. Hort. Sci.* 91 (1967): 63-68.

Davis, T.D., G.L. Steffens, and N. Sankhla, "Triazole plant growth regulators," *Horticultural Reviews* 10 (1988): 63-105.

Elfving, D.C., "Factors affecting apple-tree response to chemical branch-induction treatments," *J. Amer. Soc. Hort. Sci.* 109 (1984): 476-481.

Elfving, D.C., "Comparison of cytokinin and apical-dominance-inhibiting growth regulators for lateral-branch induction in nursery and orchard apple trees," *J. Hort. Sci.* 60 (1985): 447-454.

Elfving, D.C., "Economic effects of excessive vegetative growth in deciduous fruit trees," *HortScience* 23 (1988): 461-463.

Elfving, D.C., "Growth and productivity of Empire apple trees following a single heading-back pruning treatment," *HortScience* 25 (1990): 908-910.

Elfving, D.C. and R.A. Cline, "Growth and productivity of vigorous Northern Spy /MM.106 apple trees in response to annually applied growth control techniques," *J. Amer. Soc. Hort. Sci.* 115 (1990): 212-218.

Elfving, D.C. and C.G. Forshey, "Effects of naphthaleneacetic acid on shoot growth of apple trees," *J. Amer. Soc. Hort. Sci.* 102 (1977): 418-423.

Forshey, C.G. and D.C. Elfving, "Fruit numbers, fruit size, and yield relationships in McIntosh apples," *J. Amer. Soc. Hort. Sci.* 102 (1977): 399-402.

Forshey, C.G. and D.C. Elfving, "The relationship between vegetative growth and fruiting in apple trees," *Horticultural Reviews* 11 (1989): 209-287.

Forshey, C.G., R.W. Weires, B.H. Stanley, and R.C. Seem, "Dry weight partitioning of McIntosh apple trees," *J. Amer. Soc. Hort. Sci.* 108 (1983): 149-154.

Lenton, J.R., "Are plant growth substances involved in the partitioning of assimilate to developing reproductive sinks?" *Plant Growth Regulat.* 2 (1984): 267-276.

Looney, N.E., "Growth regulator use in commercial apple production," 409-418, 1980, edited by F. Skoog, In: *Plant Growth Substances*, New York: Springer Verlag, 1979.

Looney, N.E., "Growth regulator usage in apple and pear production," 1-26, edited by L.G. Nickell,. In: *Plant Growth Regulating Chemicals*, Vol. 1. Boca Raton, Fl: CRC Press, Inc., 1983a.

Looney, N.E., "Growth regulator use in the production of *Prunus* species fruits," 27-39, edited by L.G. Nickell, In: *Plant Growth Regulating Chemicals*, Vol. 1. Boca Raton, FL: CRC Press, Inc., 1983b.

Looney, N.E., "Improving fruit size, appearance, and other aspects of fruit crop quality with plant bioregulating chemicals," *Acta. Hort.* 329 (1993): 120-127.

Luckwill, L.C., "The control of growth and fruitfulness of apple trees," 237-254, edited by L.C. Luckwill and C.V. Cutting, In: *Physiology of Tree Crops*, New York: Academic Press, 1970.

Luckwill, L.C., "Growth regulators in flowering and fruit development," 293-304, edited by K.R. Plimmer, In: *Pesticide Chemistry in the 20th Century*, Symposium Series 37, American Chemical Society, 1977.

Maggs, D.H., "The reduction in growth of apple trees brought about by fruiting," *J. Hort. Sci.* 38 (1963): 119-128.

Miller, S.S., "Plant bioregulators in apple and pear culture," *Horticultural Reviews* 10 (1988): 309-401.

Morgan, P.W., "Synthetic growth regulators: Potential for development," *Bot. Gaz.* 141 (1980): 337-346.

Schechter, I., J.T.A. Proctor, and D.C. Elfving, "Reappraisal of seasonal apple fruit growth," *Can. J. Plant Sci.* 73 (1993): 549-556.

Schwabe, W.W., "Growth regulators and the control of development in fruit trees," Proc. Joint BCPC and BPGRG Symposium Opportunities for Chemical Plant Growth Regulation, 1978.

Treharne, K.J., J.D. Quinlan, J.N. Knight, and D.A. Ward., "Hormonal regulation of fruit development in apple: A mini-review," *Plant Growth Regulat.* 3 (1985): 125-132.

Trewavas, A.J., "How do plant growth substances work?" *Plant, Cell and Environm.* 4 (1981): 203-228.

Trewavas, A.J., "Growth substance sensitivity: The limiting factor in plant development," *Physiol. Plant.* 55 (1982): 60-72.

Tromp, J. and S.J. Wertheim. "Synthetic growth regulators: Mode of action and application in fruit production," 137-150, In: *Physiological Aspects of Crop Productivity, Proc.* 15th Colloquium of the Intl. Potash Institute, Bern, Switz., 1980.

Williams, M.W, "Chemical thinning of apples," *Horticultural Reviews* 1 (1979): 270-300.

Wismer, P.T., J.T.A. Proctor, and D.C. Elfving, "Benzyladenine affects cell division and cell size during apple fruit thinning," *J. Amer. Soc. Hort. Sci.* 120 (1995): 802-807, 1096.

2 Environmental Factors Regulating Growth: Light, Temperature, Water, Nutrition

Curt R. Rom
Department of Horticulture
University of Arkansas
Fayetteville, AR

"The change in motion is proportional to the motive force impressed."
(For every action, there is an opposite and equal reaction.)
—Sir Isaac Newton, 1729

As discussed in the previous chapter, the growth and development of fruit trees is a regulated process. It does not carry on willy-nilly, but rather it is controlled by internal and external forces.

The internal forces include differences in tissue water and solute content, and differences in plant hormone content. The external forces include the physical manipulation (pruning, training, fruit harvest, etc.) by the orchard operator, the application of exogenous plant growth-regulating substances or hormones, and the orchard's physical environment.

It is the goal of the modern, efficient orchardist, to harness the growth processes by understanding what factors and parameters affect both the type and rate of growth of the tree and to manage those processes to their greatest economic end. Thus, the statement of laws of physics by Sir Isaac Newton can be applied to orcharding. Every action or inaction the orchardist takes, has an effect on the growth and development of the tree.

During the last century, and particularly in the past four decades, an immense body of knowledge of the factors regulating growth of plants has been learned. Now, the individual pieces of the growth puzzle are fitting together.

In the first chapter of this book, a holistic review of the interactions and intricacies of fruit tree growth and development was presented. In subsequent chapters, the effects of plant growth hormones and their related growth-regulating substances will be presented and discussed. Further, several chapters will detail specific techniques to control growth with chemicals, and other chapters will explain biological processes of growth such as fruit maturity and how it can be manipulated.

This chapter discusses how the fruit tree plant, a biological organism, responds to the environment in which it is grown. Only a few years ago, we let nature take its course or Mother Nature have her way with fruit tree growth and productivity. However, with the knowledge of how the environment regulates growth, orchardists can now better manage tree growth and development by controlling or modifying the environment, taking an action to elicit a desired response from the tree.

Many of the horticultural practices followed in an orchard are done to directly or indirectly affect the orchard environment.

For example, tree training and pruning may be practiced to change light relations within the orchard and tree, irrigation is controlled to modify orchard water relations and temperature, and nutrients are applied to alter the natural or seasonal availability of naturally available nutrient elements.

The goals of this chapter are to review and inform the readers of environmental factors or parameters which regulate fruit tree growth and development and how that regulation occurs. Also, it is hoped that by highlighting some fundamental physiological processes in fruit trees, orchardists, or orchard consultants may be able to see how these processes can be managed in order to maximize fruit production.

This chapter will review some of the environmental factors which control or affect the rate or the extent to which fruit trees grow and their ability to produce large yields of high quality fruit.

The orchard environment— a managed ecological system

The orchard is an ecosystem. Different from surrounding temperate forest or desert ecosystems, the orchard ecosystem is highly controlled and managed. The population of the vegetation, primarily fruit trees and ground cover, are controlled. The density of and population dynamics, of animals (including vertebrates [voles, gophers, deer, etc.], arthropods [insects, spiders, etc.], and some fungi and bacteria are manipulated, controlled, or at least different than the orchard-surrounding ecosystems.

By definition, understanding the term ecosystem means that we understand no single part of the orchard systems exists in isolation, but rather, the various components of the orchard interact extensively as a system. Changing one aspect of the system has effects which ripple throughout the entire system. New concepts in orchard management, including integrated pest management or integrated orchard management, are predicated on the fact that chang-ing one element of the system has impacts on all aspects of the system. Practically, modern orchard managers should consider that they are actually involved in the total integrated orchard system management.

In the orchard ecosystem, the environment is an important component. The environment is also a component which can be managed to the benefit of the grower. In fact, it may be a mistake to consider not managing the orchard environment, or at least that which can be managed, and leaving the environment to its own may be tempting fate. Thus, to manage the orchard ecosystem efficiently, we must know how the environment regulates growth of the fruit trees and consider how we can manage the orchard environment.

ENVIRONMENTAL FACTORS AFFECTING GROWTH AND PRODUCTIVITY OF FRUIT TREES

The orchard environment is composed of light, temperature, water, nutrition, humidity, wind of the orchard atmosphere, and rhizosphere (soil root-zone). All of these are growth-regulating factors which can be managed to some extent.

Light provides fundamental energy for growth. It provides the physical impetus for the production of sugars, and it may control fundamental biochemical reactions in fruit plants. Light may trigger the initiation of plant organs such as flowers, control the direction of growth, or cause mutations (by certain wavelengths at certain energy levels).

Temperatures, both low and high, can minimize growth or cause injury. Temperatures in an "appropriate" range allow growth to proceed. Temperatures affect fruit size and quality, and thus, ultimately, their value and the economic return of the crop. Water is important in the ability of the plant to stand erect and turgid, to cool itself, and to move nutrients from the soil throughout the plant.

Wind can affect plant temperature, and water loss, and damage tissues through dehydration or mechanical friction. Growth cannot progress without the nutrients needed to produce the chemical components of the plant. These environmental factors regulate fruit tree growth and development by affecting the fundamental metabolic processes in the plant. These processes can be broken down into two general categories: primary metabolism and secondary metabolism. Primary metabolism includes the processes of carbon assimilation and production of carbohydrates through photosynthesis, and the process of chemical demolition of carbohydrates to release chemical energy and oxygen by respiration.

Secondary metabolism uses carbohydrates, proteins, and other key biological constituents to manufacture more complex structures such as pigments, phenolics, tannins, flavinoids, etc. Both primary and secondary metabolic pathways are nothing more than long series of biochemical reactions occurring within the living plant cells of leaves, stems, buds, and fruits.

The environment controls these biochemical reaction factors by two general means. First, the environment may affect the amount of "raw products" available for the reactions, and secondly, it may affect the rate and/or extent to which the reactions proceed.

To understand how plant metabolism is affected by the environment, we must first remember some fundamental plant chemistry. Thus, in the following section, the fundamental aspects of plant metabolism, chemical reactions, will be briefly reviewed.

An orchardist's review of introductory biochemistry
CHEMICAL REACTIONS

A chemical reaction is the combination of two or more atomic ions (or molecules) to form a new molecule as exemplified here:

$$[A + B \rightarrow C] \qquad \text{eq. 1}$$

where A, B, and C are atomic ions or molecules. In this very simplistic chemical reaction, ions [A] and [B] combine to form a new molecule [C]. In this case, [A] and [B] are considered the reactants and [C] the product. The reaction may proceed backward or be reversible as well:

$$[C \rightarrow A + B] \qquad \text{eq. 2}$$

In this example, the reactant [C] breaks down into the products [A] and [B].

Chemical reactions can absorb or give off energy, depending upon the energy state of the reactants and the products. But, because of the relation of energy and mass, energy is neither created by the chemical combination or lost during the chemical reaction. The rate at which the reaction occurs can vary. Typically, simple ionic reactions can occur more rapidly than those involving complicated molecules. Reaction rates increase as the concentration of the reactants increases. Typically, the chemical reaction rate is increased as the temperature of the reaction environment increases.

Energy is required for the chemical reactions to occur; an external source of energy is needed to join atoms together to form new, stable molecules. This energy needed is called activation energy. In many chemical reactions, this energy is contained in the reactants through their normal energy state and motion.

Reactions that give off energy as heat when reactants are combined in excess of the activation energy are called exothermic reactions, while those which absorb more heat energy during the reaction are called endothermic reactions. Typically, endothermic reactions require greater activation energy to begin the chemical reaction and proceed at a slower rate than exothermic reactions.

Some chemical reactions proceed faster or can only occur if a third group of atomic ions or molecules are present as *catalysts*. A catalyst participates in the reaction by lowering the activation energy necessary for the reaction to occur but does not become part of the products. Very simplistically, a catalyst may be thought of as a reaction mediator.

Because most chemical reactions are reversible, and the rate and extent of a reaction is dependent upon the concentration of both the products and reactants, chemical reactions tend to attain a chemical equilibrium. If eq.1 and eq.2 are combined showing a reversible reaction, it is apparent that the chemical equilibrium occurs where the concentration of the reactants [A] and [B] achieves an equilibrium to the concentration of the product [C]:

$$[A + B] \leftrightarrow [C] \qquad \text{eq. 3}$$

The chemical system reaches equilibrium when the rate of the forward and backward reactions are equal. However, changes in reaction temperatures or the presence of catalysts may alter the equilibrium and favor one set of reactants or products. If the concentration of either products or reactants changes, so does the chemical equilibrium until a new equilibrium is established.

BIOCHEMICAL REACTIONS

The chemical reactions discussed above may be thought to occur in a laboratory beaker in a solution under the careful attention of the chemist's eye. But these reactions also occur on the farm as the iron of a plow blade combines with oxygen to form iron-oxides or rust; or as the orchardist puts two incompatible sprays into a spray tank, and it agglomerates and gels. These are somewhat different than the chemical reactions which occur inside of the biological system of a fruit tree. These chemical reactions within living organisms are called biochemical reactions or *reactions of life*.

Biochemical reactions are a specific type of chemical reaction and thus have many of the same characteristics. There are reactants and products. In most cases, in biochemical reactions, the reactants may be relatively large molecules (or macromolecules), which are relatively energy stable. The reactions are typically endothermic and have very large activation energies. This is biologically good, because with the relatively large concentrations and number of biochemical reactants in the cell sap reactions could occur wildly or willy-nilly. But, instead, biochemical reactions are quite ordered.

A typical biochemical reaction can be somewhat distinguished from regular chemical reactions in that the reactants are relatively stable and will typically not react to form new products on their own, but instead they need to be catalyzed. The catalysts of biochemical reactions are enzymes, special protein molecules which bring the reactants together, lower the activation energy necessary for a reaction to occur, and allow the reaction to proceed, forming new products:

$$
\begin{array}{c}
[A + B \rightarrow C] \\
\uparrow \\
[\quad \boldsymbol{d} \quad] \qquad\qquad \text{eq. 4}
\end{array}
$$

In eq. 4, [A] and [B] are biochemical reactants, and [C] is the biochemical product of the reaction. The molecule [$\boldsymbol{d}$] represents a protein enzyme which catalyzes the reaction. The enzyme [$\boldsymbol{d}$] is essentially unaffected by the reaction and is retained after the reaction; it is **not** part of the product [C]. The enzyme controls the rate and equilibrium of the reaction and thus can control its direction (eq. 5).

$$
\begin{array}{c}
[A + B \leftrightarrow C] \\
\uparrow \\
[\quad \boldsymbol{d} \quad] \qquad\qquad \text{eq. 5}
\end{array}
$$

More than a single enzyme may control a reaction as well (eq. 6), where the enzyme [$\boldsymbol{d}$] combines the biochemicals [A] and [B] to form product [C]. However, the enzyme [e] causes the biochemical [C] to break down and form biochemical products [A] and [B], in the reverse reaction.

$$\begin{array}{c} [\quad e \quad] \\ \downarrow \\ A + B \leftrightarrow C \\ \uparrow \\ [\quad d \quad] \end{array} \qquad \text{eq. 6}$$

Enzymes also control the rate of the biochemical reaction. However, unlike chemical reactions which tend to increase in rate proportionally to the increase in temperature, enzyme-dependent biochemical reactions respond differently. Typically, the biochemical reaction rate increases up to a specific temperature, the optimum temperature, after which the reaction rate decreases because of the effects of the temperature on the stability of the protein enzyme. Thus, biochemical reactions are very temperature-dependent.

Some biochemical reactions use energy or require energy to form chemical bonds of the product. The energy is given by chemical bond energy donors. These are endergonic, or energy-requiring biochemical reactions. The energy may be chemical energy, as indicated by the energy donor [x] in eq. 7, or it may be energy provided by light, as in the initial stages of the photosynthesis biochemical reactions.

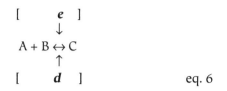

$$\begin{array}{c} A + B \leftrightarrow C \\ \uparrow \\ [\quad d \quad] \end{array} \qquad \text{eq. 7}$$

Other chemical reactions give off chemical energy as reactants break apart in reaction to form new compounds (eq. 8). These are called exergonic, or energy-producing reactions. Several of the biochemical reactions of the respiration pathway are exergonic and release chemical energy for use in other metabolic pathways in the plant.

In this case, the energy acceptor [z] accepts the chemical energy from the reaction of [C] breaking down into products [A] and [B] in the enzyme [d]-mediated reaction.

$$\begin{array}{c} [\; z^- \, z^+ \quad] \\ C \leftrightarrow A + B \\ \uparrow \\ [\quad d \quad] \end{array} \qquad \text{eq. 8}$$

Lastly, for many enzymes to be "activated" and thus able to participate in the biochemical reaction, co-factors or messenger ions, typically ions like calcium (Ca), magnesium (Mg), potassium (K), or phosphorus (P), plus other molecular co-factors must interact with the enzyme. These co-factors allow the enzyme to "recognize" the reactants or allow the reaction to occur.

Fundamental plant metabolic processes

With an understanding of plant biochemical reactions, the fundamental plant metabolic processes can be explored to understand how environmental factors affect growth. Primary plant metabolic processes include photosynthesis, the production of carbohydrates, and respiration, the consumption of photosynthetic carbohydrates for the release of chemical energy.

PHOTOSYNTHESIS

Photosynthesis is a series of biochemical reactions in which carbon dioxide from the air is combined with water in the plant cells to produce sugars ($C_6H_{12}O_6$), oxygen, and energy (e):

$$CO_2 + H_2O \rightarrow C_6H_{12}O_6 + O_2 + (e) \qquad \text{eq. 9}$$

Actually, this is a very simplified reaction expression of photosynthesis because a number of intermediate steps occur to chemically bind carbon dioxide and water, and ultimately have a sugar molecule produced.

The photosynthetic process is endergonic and thus requires the input of energy. The energy is derived from sunlight. As sunlight strikes the green chlorophyll pigment molecule in the cells of leaves, the chlorophyll pigments become "excited" by the increase in energy they have absorbed. It is the natural order of a chlorophyll molecule to "de-excite," or go to a lower energy level. They do this by giving off some of the absorbed energy as heat, some as low, glowing fluorescent light, and the remainder of the energy is given to energy acceptors as electron energy.

These energy acceptors convert electron energy to chemical bond energy and in later steps of the process, the energy is used in the biochemical reactions which build the sugar molecules. The production of the sugar requires a relatively large input of chemical bond energy from energy donors.

Thus, sugar is thought to be a high energy-carrying molecule. When the sugars are consumed or broken down by subsequent reactions, the energy is once again given off; it can be carried by other energy carriers or used to provide energy for chemical reactions to occur, building new biochemicals. The net result of photosynthesis is the production of energy-carrying acceptors and the production of high-energy sugar molecules.

Once the sugars are produced in the leaf cells, they can move from cell to cell by diffusion and ultimately into the transport tissues of the phloem for translocation to other plant tissues such as shoot tips (meristems), fruits, trunks, or roots. The carbohydrates may be further metabolized into more complex carbon structures such as starch for carbohydrate storage, as cellulose and related compounds which provide the structure of cell walls, or as complex flavinoids which provide color and aroma for the fruits.

In other tissues, they are metabolized into smaller molecules to release the chemical energy so that it can be used to build other biochemicals such as proteins or lipids (oil-like substances).

RESPIRATION

Respiration is a series of chemical reactions which are chemically almost the reverse of photosynthesis. Carbohydrates (sugars) are broken down into smaller molecules and ultimately back into carbon dioxide and water and chemical bond energy (*e*) (eq. 10). The carbon dioxide is then released back into the atmosphere, and the energy (*e*) released by the reactions is used in other metabolic reactions.

$$C_6H_{12}O_6 + O_2 \rightarrow CO_2 + H_2O + (e) \quad \text{eq. 10}$$

The respiration pathways are exergonic or result in the release chemical energy. The net result of respiration is the release of chemical energy stored in the carbohydrates and smaller carbon molecules, which can be used in other metabolic pathways for the production of other metabolites.

In both photosynthesis and respiration, the availability of reactants and the concentration of products can affect the rate of the reaction. Photosynthesis cannot occur without the input of light energy and the availability of carbon dioxide and water. Although atmospheric carbon dioxide is rarely limiting in field production, drought stress can result in an inability of the leaves to allow carbon dioxide to enter the leaves and participate in the reaction.

Thus, no matter how sunny it is, a droughted plant does not have the ability to photosynthesize. In cloudy conditions or in the interior of a dark, shady canopy, although there may be ample carbon dioxide available for the reaction, the water status of the leaf allows for the absorption of carbon dioxide, and leaves may be green and able to intercept light, the absence of light limits the photosynthetic process.

If the flow of carbohydrates out of leaves for use in other tissues or organs of the fruit trees is interrupted (as by harvesting fruit, severe summer pruning, trunk girdling, etc.), the carbohydrate content starts to build up within the leaf, disrupting the chemical equilibrium and thus slowing the rate of photosynthesis.

Similarly, if there are insufficient carbohydrates available for respiration in tissues which are highly respirationally active, respiration decreases, and no chemical energy or carbon molecule products are released; growth slows or nearly stops. A decrease in available oxygen (such as in flooded soils) will slow respiration.

Increasing the carbon dioxide content of the environment around the respirational tissue will slow respiration. As the energy from respiration carried in energy donors is "partitioned" to primary metabolism first and then to secondary metabolism, if there is a small carbohydrate supply for respiration, the production of secondary metabolites such as fruit aromas, flavors, and colors may be reduced.

In both respiration and photosynthesis, if the key enzymes are not available because of shortages in plant proteins, or the enzymes are not activated because of the absence of co-factors, the processes may slow or stop.

Environmental factors regulating growth

As mentioned in the introduction, several meteorological environmental factors regulate fruit tree growth and development. Of specific mention here are the factors light, temperature, water, and nutrition. These factors affect growth because of the direct effect on biochemical reactions and metabolic processes.

LIGHT

Much has been written recently on the importance of light in orchards. Light has several important functions in fruit trees, including photosynthesis, photomorphogenesis, phototropism and photoperiodism. As mentioned above, photosynthesis is the synthesis of carbohydrates after the interception of light energy. Photomorphogenesis is the direct control of growth by

light. Phototropism is the directional response of growth towards or away from a light source. Photoperiodism, is the seasonal response of plant growth and development to changes in day length.

Photomorphogenic effects in plants occur naturally and frequently but are often overlooked by tree fruit growers. Light is necessary for the production of plant pigments such as chlorophyll and anthocyanins, leaf expansion is promoted by light, stem elongation is typically inhibited by light, and seed germination is light-dependent. The light does not carry photomorphogenic information, but is absorbed either by special pigments in the plants or directly modulates the effectiveness of enzymes in biochemical systems.

To the fruit grower, photomorphogenesis is important. It is readily apparent that leaves in the shaded portions of tree canopies are smaller and have less chlorophyll. Thus, summer pruning to alleviate within-tree shading may not be completely satisfactory, as the inner-canopy leaves are small and will not grow further and do not have sufficient chlorophyll to elicit a maximum photosynthetic rate. This knowledge may affect decisions about timing of summer pruning.

Fruit in the middle of the tree are often small and poorly colored. Summer pruning or training to improve light penetration into the trees can correct this situation.

A clear indication of the power of light in morphogenesis is the dependence upon light for bud differentiation. Typically, buds remain vegetative until they are induced to become reproductive. Numerous studies have indicated that flower bud differentiation in fruit trees does not occur at light levels lower than 10 to 30% of the full ambient sunlight; typically, light is more important for pome fruits than stone fruits for flower formation. Even if the flower bud is initiated and developed, the quality of the bud, using indicators such as bud size, spur leaf size, bourse shoot leaf area, or fruit set, are all directly dependent and proportional to the amount of light shining directly on the spur.

In phototropism, where meristems grow toward or away from light, there is a complex relationship between light receptors in cells and the hormone auxins which cause cell elongation. It is thought that the light intercepted in some cells causes the transport of auxin laterally in the meristem toward the shaded side or away from the light.

When the auxin reaches those cells and tissues and attains an active concentration, the cells expand, causing a curvature on the dark side of the plant, bending it toward the light. When light is equally distributed to all sides of the meristem, the auxin concentration in the meristem balances itself. Inhibitors produced by the light receptors on the illuminated tissues have also been proposed. This theory may account for the inhibition of stem elongation in well-illuminated conditions. Thus, in dark, shaded canopies there is protrusion of long, leggy watersprouts. In a well-pruned canopy with good light distribution shoots are shorter, thicker, and have more lateral development.

In photoperiodism, photoreceptors in tissues recognize the relative duration of the light and dark cycles of the day, and thus mediate biochemical pathways in response. The result includes shoot elongation in response to lengthening days or long days (days longer than the night), changes in branching patterns with day length, flower formation in some plants in response to shortening days, leaf fall, and the onset of dormancy in response to short days.

The rate of photosynthesis is directly related to the amount of light intercepted by leaves *(see Figure 1)*. In complete darkness, the photosynthetic reaction does not occur, but actually, it proceeds in reverse or respiration occurs. At about 2 to 5% of full sun, the photosynthetic process reaches the compensation point where photosynthesis equals respiration. Photosynthesis contin-

---

FIGURE 1

The relationship of light intensity to fruit tree photosynthetic rate. [A] dark respiration, [B] compensation point (respiration = photosynthesis), [C] light saturation point of photosynthesis.

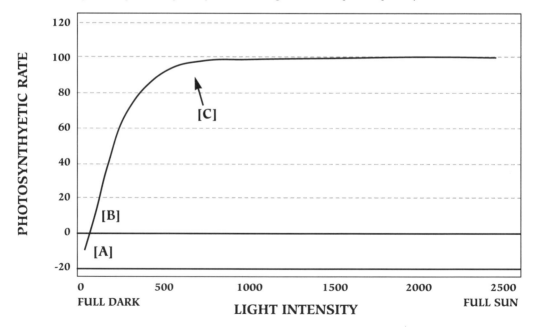

ues to increase with more light until about 35 to 50% of full sunlight, at which point it levels off or becomes saturated with light.

Leaves that are grown initially in low light and then are moved to high light conditions, do increase in their photosynthetic rate but never achieve the maximum rate of photosynthesis of a leaf developed in full light *(see Figure 2)*. If the availability of carbohydrates is a determinant in fruit tree growth, then light directly regulates both the rate and amount of growth which can occur during the season.

When the effects of light on fruit trees are taken together, there is a direct relationship between the amount of light intercepted by an orchard and its yield potential *(see Figure 3)*. It has been demonstrated that yield of an orchard system, especially in the early or establishment years, increases with increasing light interception. Others have shown that early yields are closely related to the amount of light intercepted by the spur leaf canopy and the whole canopy early in the season. Orchards planted at low densities with wide spacing, do not intercept sufficient light or have sufficient bearing surface to produce an economic crop early in the life of the orchard.

There appears to be an upper limit of light interception at 70 to 80% of total sunlight for maximum economic production. As light interception continues to increase above this limit, such as with multiple-row bed systems, total yield and economic yield may be reduced because of tree-to-tree shading reducing flowering, fruiting, and fruit quality.

Also, there are limitations imposed by the availability of orchard equipment; there is a need to move both equipment and people into and out of the orchard for management operations such as spraying, pruning, and harvesting. Some leaning canopies, such as a "A" or "V" shaped systems, may allow for higher light interception with less intra-tree shading, and allow for equipment movement underneath the canopy.

FIGURE 2

The relative photosynthetic rate of apple leaves grown in low light, low light then moved to high light, or grown in high light conditions (after Barden, 1978).

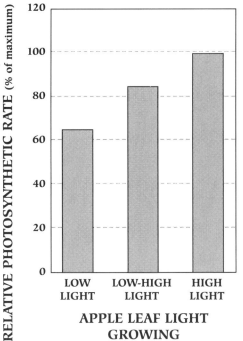

APPLE LEAF LIGHT
GROWING
ENVIRONMENT

FIGURE 3

The relationship of light interception across a season or several seasons during the establishment of an orchard and yield of the orchard system (after Robinson, Lakso, Rom, and Allen, and others).

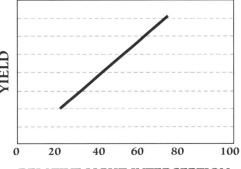

RELATIVE LIGHT INTERCEPTION
(% OF TOTAL AVAILABLE LIGHT)

In summary, to maximize production, it is important to maximize light interception early each season and early in the life of the orchard. This is typically accomplished by high density plantings of trees on size-controlling, precocious rootstocks with proper tree training (tree shape and size) to allow for maximum light interception by the tree. Light interception increases with both increasing tree height and reduced between-row spacing. However, both tree height and between-row spacing also can contribute to intra-tree shading.

Although light interception is critical for maximum yield potential, the economic yield of an orchard can be variable, dependent upon the light distribution within the tree *(see Figure 4)*. In tall, wide, or thick trees, light can become limited as the amount of light in the canopy diminishes as a function of the distance it travels through the leaf canopy. Fruit color and soluble solids of apple start to be reduced at light levels less than 70 to 80% full sun. Photosynthesis, flower formation, and fruit development are limited at light levels below 25 to 40% full sun.

In the inner portions of big tree canopies, photosynthesis can be reduced and fruit formation, size, and quality minimized. Thus, growers train and prune trees to allow light to penetrate to all quarters of the tree in order to allow the entire canopy to maximize its productive potential. The trade-off between maximum light interception and optimum light distribution with canopies has resulted in the development of systems with tree canopies that have a narrow profile, either in narrow, tall conical shapes or narrow "A" or "V" shapes.

TEMPERATURE

Temperature effects on plants are somewhat confounded by interactions with other environmental factors, including light and water

FIGURE 4

The relationship of light intensity within an apple tree canopy and the distance the light has to travel through the canopy. Light levels below 80% full light may limit fruit size and quality; light below 30% may limit photosynthesis and flower formation.

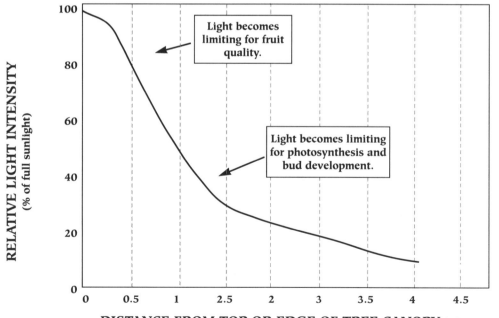

stress of the plants, and temperature tolerance is dependent upon the concentrations of carbohydrates and nutrient ions. However, some generalizations about the temperature reaction of fruit trees can be drawn.

Because of the relation of temperature to the biochemical reaction processes, temperature has a significant regulating role in fruit tree growth and development. Three "cardinal temperatures," the *minima, optima,* and *maxima,* are important regulating benchmarks in fruit tree biochemical reactions. Typically, there is a base or minima temperature below which chemical reactions (or growth) does not occur in the fruit tree *(see Figure 5).* As temperature increases, the rate of reaction increases until the optima temperature, at which point the reaction rate is at its maximum. As temperatures continue to increase, the reaction slows and eventually stops, as the enzymes become inactivated by the high temperature at the reaction maxima temperature.

For instance, in photosynthesis, there is very little photosynthetic activity at orchard temperatures below about 1 to 3°C. However, as temperatures increase, the photosynthetic rate increases until the reaction reaches its maximum rate at the temperature optimum of 25 to 30°C *(see Figure 6).* Above that temperature, photosynthesis starts to decrease. However, in some plants, the photosynthetic process acclimates to continued exposure to temperatures higher than the optimum, and thus, the optimum temperature shifts to a higher temperature. Thus, the plants can continue to grow at relatively high temperatures.

In the field, photosynthesis of fruit trees has been observed to occur at temperatures higher than the reported optimum, implying that fruit trees may acclimate. However, in

FIGURE 5

The relationship of temperature to the relative rate of growth or enzymatic reactions in plants. [A] temperature minima, [B] temperature optima, [C] temperature maxima.

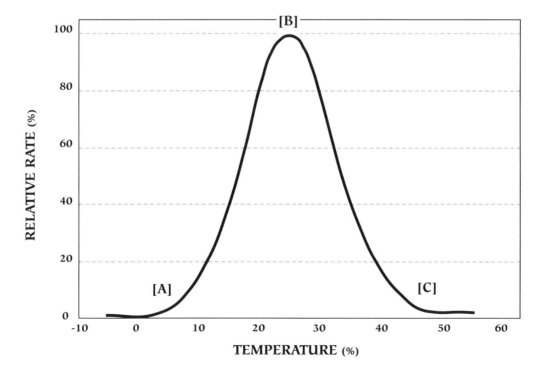

studies of this phenomena, true acclimation was difficult to observe. Although the photosynthetic mechanism did not acclimate, other plant processes adjusted to compensate.

For instance, it has been observed that after continuous exposure to high temperatures, the conductance of gases from apple leaves increases at higher temperatures. Thus, transpiration occurs at a higher rate than expected at high temperature, compared to leaves of trees grown in cooler temperatures. The result of the more rapid transpiration is leaf cooling. Thus, if an apple tree has been exposed to durations of daily temperatures of 35°C, the increased transpiration cools the leaf 2 to 3°C, keeping the leaf within the optimum temperature range for photosynthesis (see Figure 7).

This clearly exemplifies the point made earlier about how temperature and other environmental influences interact. Even though there has been some compensation for trees grown at temperatures of 30 to 35°C, at higher temperatures (>38°C), photosynthesis decreased. Orchards grown in regions or seasons of high temperatures require extra attention to their water requirement so that the leaves can compensate for the high temperatures with increased transpiration.

Presumably, small water stresses would cause dramatic leaf temperature effects and significantly reduce photosynthesis. If temperatures are very high (>38 to 40°C), orchard managers must intervene to cool the orchard using air circulation from wind machines or utilize evaporative cooling effects of irrigation.

The processes of respiration are also affected by temperature. In summary, as temperatures increase, the respiration processes increase almost linearly.

FIGURE 6

The response of relative apple leaf photosynthesis to air temperature. Maximum photosynthesis typically occurs in a a range of 23 to 28 (after Moran).

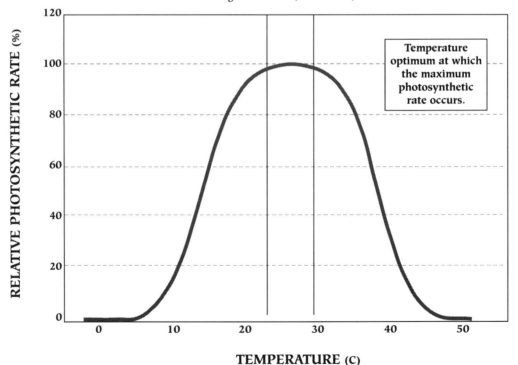

In hot conditions, carbohydrates are rapidly consumed. One of the most compelling reasons to maintain orchard temperature by evaporative cooling and to hydrocool harvested hot fruit is to reduce the reaction rate of respiration and thereby preserve the carbohydrates in the tissues.

As a result of reduced carbohydrates produced in high temperatures, and a higher percentage of carbohydrates being utilized to maintain the high respiration rates in high temperatures, secondary metabolites in fruits such as color and flavor can be reduced. It has been demonstrated that the evaporative cooling effect of sprinkler irrigation during the final third of the growing season may improve fruit color, presumably by reducing both fruit and leaf temperature. Also, fruit temperature is related to the incidence of sunburn and internal breakdown of the fruit. Reducing orchard temperatures may reduce yield losses to sunburn and internal breakdown.

Cold temperatures also have regulating effects on fruit trees. Fruit trees need exposure to temperatures between 5 to 7°C for five to eight weeks or 500 to 1,400 chill units (1 chill unit is approximately 1 hour at 5°C) to overcome physiological dormancy. Temperatures below 1°C do not affect the chill requirement and cannot contribute to overcoming dormancy. Also, temperatures greater than 15 to 20°C during the winter do not contribute to overcoming dormancy. Extremely low temperatures may lead to either winter injury caused by ice crystal formation penetrating through and disrupting cell membranes, or tissue dehydration by the slow freezing of tissues and the removal of water.

Orchard temperature can be managed by the orchardist. Of course, the orchard location and site are important factors controlling the temperature. The exposure (south versus north, or west versus east) may affect average daily orchard temperature and the temperature at various times of the day.

The relation of the orchard to surround-

FIGURE 7

Temperture difference between air (TA) and leaf (TL) for apple leaves grown at 25 and 35°C for 20 days. Leaves grown at 35°C were more able to cool themselves by evapotranspiration due to higher conductance rates at high temperatures (after Moran, 1996).

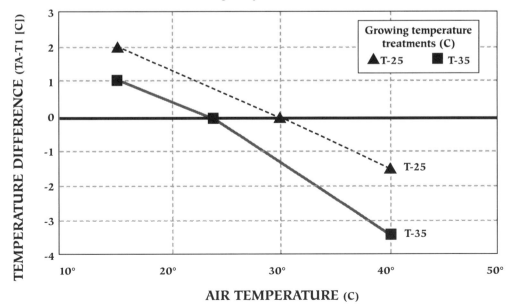

ing topography can affect temperature, as cool air either drains onto the orchard or away from the orchard, or an adjacent large body of water ameliorates rapid temperature fluctuations. If winter or spring temperatures threaten to be too low and the potential of tissue freeze damage occurs, the orchardist may add heat to the orchard and lower the inversion ceiling, may utilize orchard fans to recapture and recirculate radiative convection heat, or may use overtree sprinkler irrigation to maintain tissue temperatures close to freezing due to the phenomena of heat from ice nucleation.

If the summer orchard temperatures exceed optimum for growth, development, and fruit quality, it becomes more important to maintain ideal water status of the tree, so that it can efficiently transpire and cool itself. Additionally, irrigation, either undertree or overtree, may be used to take advantage of the phenomena of the absorption of heat from water evaporation and thereby lower orchard and tissue temperatures. Orchards with complete cultivation of the orchard floor tend to have higher orchard temperatures than those with some ground-cover vegetation.

WATER

Water is another environmental factor which has regulatory activity in the orchard system. Several examples of the role of water interacting with the utilization of light by fruit trees and the maintenance of fruit tree temperature have already been given above.

The vast majority of water utilized by a fruit tree is taken up from the soil by the tree roots and moved through the plant xylem in response to the transpiration pull of water lost by evapotranspiration. Inside of the fruit tree, water has several important functions. It is the medium in which all of the biochemical reaction of fruit trees occurs; it is the cell sap in all of the cells of the plant. It is a reactant in some biochemical processes such as photosynthesis, where the hydrogen and oxygen ions are

split from each other and combined with carbon dioxide to form sugars.

Water keeps cells, tissues, and organs turgid by exerting pressure on the cell membranes and cell walls. After water induces turgidity in combination with other processes, cell expansion can proceed. It is this cell expansion and the addition of new cell wall material in turgid cells which can be fundamentally termed as "growth." Water is the medium through which nutrients move from the soil around the roots, up through the plant, and into the various tissues and organs.

Lastly, water is lost by evapotranspiration; water evaporates from the sunken stomatal pores on the bottom of leaves (transpiration) or directly from the leaf surface. As water undergoes the chemical phase change from the liquid to the gaseous state in evaporation, it absorbs heat energy and carries it away with the water vapor. Thus, with evapotranspiration, there is leaf cooling, allowing the biochemical processes within the leaves to occur at or near their optimum reaction temperatures.

The need for careful attention to the water status of the tree should be self-evident. In modern orchards, there is very seldom debate about the need for irrigation, but there is considerable discussion and study about the when, how, and how much of water application. It is difficult to measure the water status of the tree because there is a continuum of water from the soil, through the plant, and into the atmosphere. Thus, it is often necessary to measure the soil, the plant, and the atmosphere to get the most accurate picture. Soil water content is measured to determine the water reserve or water available to the plant.

These measurements are predicated on the knowledge that as water disappears from the soil due to run-off, gravity, or use by plants, water tension (or increased suction) starts to occur within the plant. As plant water tension increases due to the difficulty in attaining water from the soil, growth slows. Some aspects of growth such as leaf expansion are very sensitive to very small soil water deficits. Thus, there is an optimum range of soil water content to maintain the tree at a low tension level which does not adversely impact growth.

Measurements can be made directly of the plant water tension or water content. Water tension of stems can be measured, and it is related to the conductance of water vapor in evapotranspiration *(see Figure 8)*.

As stem water tension increases, the conductance of water out of the leaf decreases. This is an indication that stomates are closing, and the movement of water out of the leaf and carbon dioxide into the leaf is reduced. As a result, photosynthesis may decrease and respiration increase as leaf temperature also increases with reduced conductance.

Recently, there have been developments in infrared thermography, where the temperature of the plant relative to the ambient temperature can be measured and inferences about the plant water status can be drawn. Other water use and status estimates can be made by calculating the loss of water from the plant by evapotranspiration based upon air temperature and water content. All of these methods strive for the same goal of maintaining soil water in an "optimum" range so as not to flood or limit the plant, so the fruit tree has an adequate amount of water to maintain growth, development, and maximum product quality.

Water stress at critical periods of growth in some species has been used to control vegetative growth and enhance return cropping. For instance, small, short-lived water stresses during stage II of peach fruit development (pit hardening) may limit vegetative growth. When water is returned to the system during stage III or final swell, fruit continue to develop normally.

In arid regions, this has been a practice well utilized to control the vigorous growth of peach trees in the absence of an adapt-

able size-controlling rootstock. However, it has not worked well in more humid areas where sporadic and unpredictable rainfall occurs during the fruit growing season. Although some successes have been observed in using deficit irrigation strategies in apples, many adverse fruit size effects have also been reported.

The method of irrigation affects both the orchard environment and tree growth. Because of the effects of orchard cooling due to sprinkler irrigation, some of the effects of sprinkler versus trickle irrigation are difficult to interpret. Also, the frequency and duration of watering, and variation in soils among various trials, makes the reports of irrigations effects on growth and fruit quality inconsistent.

Reports have indicated better shoot growth control and spur formation under trickle irrigation, while other reports have noted better lateral shoot growth with microsprinkler irrigation compared to trickle irrigation. It has been reported that applesauce made from apples under controlled trickle irrigation was more viscous and less watery than apples grown under sprinkler irrigation.

NUTRITION

The supply and uptake of chemical elements from the environment, particularly

---

FIGURE 8

The relationship of stem water tension (plant water stress) and leaf conductance rates.

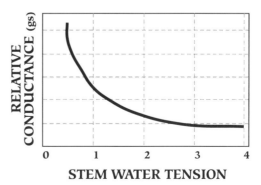

STEM WATER TENSION

the air and soil, and the subsequent utilization of the elements in plant metabolism and growth can be considered plant nutrition. Thus, the elements themselves would be considered nutrients. Some mineral elements are considered essential for growth because they fulfill three defined requirements of essentiality:

1) The elements are directly involved in metabolic processes of the plant as a constituent of a metabolite or required for the action of an enzyme,

2) A deficiency of the essential element results in plant death and an inability to complete its life cycle, and

3) A deficiency is specific for an individual element; no element can substitute for another element.

The essential elements are absorbed as nutrient-containing compounds, which are then metabolized to release the essential element ion which may be metabolized further into organic compounds. But, it is the single element, not the compound absorbed or metabolized, which is essential to the tree. Based on the criteria for essentiality, several elements are considered essential (see Table 1).

The definition of essential elements generalizes their function in plants (see Table 2). The essential elements take part in the biochemical processes in fruit trees, are important in regulating the osmotic potential and turgor of cells, and become part of the biochemical molecules that make up all of the structural components of cells, tissues, and plant organs as well as the sugars, acids, flavors, aromas, and colors of fruits. The nutrient ions have regulating roles in acting as "messengers" relating the physiochemical conditions of tissues, act with enzymes as co-factors, or may participate in biochemical reactions as chemical catalysts.

Each nutrient element can exist in a range of concentrations within the plant. Knowing their involvement in the biochemical processes, these concentrations can be considered as being in a deficient range (limiting biochemical activity, growth, and productivity), an adequacy or sufficiency range (optimum concentration for maximum biochemical activity, growth, and productivity), or a toxicity range where they act as biological "poisons." These ranges and the appropriate concentration for each element and selected groups of elements is the basis for foliar analysis based fertilizer recommendations.

Some elements have specific roles which clarify their importance in regulating fruit tree growth (see Table 2). Nitrogen is the key constituent of proteins in plants—the proteins which are the enzymes regulating biochemical reactions. An estimated 70 to

TABLE 1

Essential nutrient elements for fruit trees.

Elements with tissue concentrations of 0.1 to 3.0% (leaf dry weight)		Elements with tissue concentrations of 1-1000 ppm (leaf dry weight)	
Element	Symbol	Element	Symbol
Carbon	C	Iron	Fe
Hydrogen	H	Manganese	Mn
Oxygen	O	Copper	Cu
Nitrogen	N	Zinc	Zn
Phosphorus	P	Boron	B
Potassium	K	Molybdenum	Mo
Calcium	Ca	Chlorine	Cl
Magnesium	Mg	Sodium	Na
Sulfur	S		

80% of all foliar N is in the protein enzyme RuBisCo, ribulose biophosphate carboxylase. This protein is the enzyme which assimilates CO_2 from the air, splits it, and incorporates it into the precursors of sugars in the photosynthetic process.

Four N atoms are used in the production of each green chlorophyll pigment molecule, which absorbs light and releases the electron energy for the activation of the photosynthetic biochemical pathway. Magnesium is the central ion in each chlorophyll pigment molecule. A lack of N or Mg will result in reduced photosynthetic rates.

Nitrogen is very mobile and moves to areas of the canopy with high light. As a result, N will move out of older and more shaded leaves in the interior of shaded canopies. Eventually, the leaves with very low N will turn pale, yellow, senesce, and abscise.

Phosphorus is incorporated into compounds with ester (P) bonds, or P is reduced from phosphates and acts as an individual element. Phosphorus and several P-containing compounds are energy-carrying acceptors and donors in biochemical reactions. Like N, P is very mobile and moves to areas with high metabolic activity. Limitations in plant P may result in reduced photosynthesis, respirational problems, and the inhibition of other primary metabolic pathways.

Potassium (K) is found only in its ionic form in plants. It is an activator of enzymes used in primary metabolism such as the production of carbohydrates and proteins. As an ion, it is an active buffer in the cell solution, neutralizing organic acids and providing a near neutral environment in which biochemical reactions occur. Potassium is an osmotic agent especially important in the movement of water into and out of stomatal guard cells; thus, it helps regulate both transpiration and photosynthesis. A deficiency of K may result in "sluggish" guard cells which lose water unnecessarily, or do not open to allow maximum transpiration cooling and

photosynthetic absorption of carbon dioxide. Thus, a deficiency symptom of K is often leaf scorch, similar to drought stress.

Orchard nutrition is managed by annual soil and foliar sampling and analysis in coordination with visual observation of tree growth, and quantitative records of fruit yield and quality.

Together, these data can be used to construct a fertilizer application program to maintain the nutrients in the sufficiency ranges for optimum growth and maximum yield and fruit quality. Recently, there has been significant development in the technologies of applying nutrients, including fertigation and foliar nutrient "feeds;" however, at this time, the scientific literature on these technologies is very limited.

Nutrients can be absorbed into the plant in two general methods. First is passive uptake in which the nutrients move either by mass flow or diffusion. Mass flow of nutrients occurs when the elements are dissolved in the soil water solution, and move into the plant with the water pulled through the plant by transpiration. Second is active uptake,

TABLE 2

The role of essential nutrients as chemical constituents or regulating factors in plants.

Elements used as plant constituents[z]	Elements which have biochemical regulating roles[x]	
C	P	K
H	Ca	Mg
O	Fe	Mn
N	Cu	Zn
P	B	Mo
K		
Ca		
Mg		
S		

[z] *Elements used as chemical constituents function as part of biochemicals or macromolecules which are metabolically active or used in plant structure, including sugars, proteins, cellulose, cell walls, lipids, membranes, etc.*

[x] *Elements with regulating roles are elements that act as ions or as small molecules to be energy donors, acceptors, buffering agents, osmotic agents, co-factors or messengers, and thereby function to affect biochemical processes.*

where energy is required to absorb the elements across the root cell membranes.

It is obvious then that for passive mass flow uptake of nutrients by plants, several conditions must occur. The nutrients must be available in the soil. The soil must have sufficient soil water to allow the nutrients to dissolve into it. And, the plant must have active transpiration to move water into the plant system. Factors affecting transpiration, such as shading, dysfunctional stomates, or damaged leaves, may result in limitations to nutrient uptake.

For active uptake of nutrients, respiration must occur in the roots. Thus, the root zone must be in an appropriate temperature range for adequate respiration, and there must be adequate carbohydrates available to supply the root respiration pathways. Also, roots must have adequate oxygen for respiration to occur. Anything that affects the photosynthetic production and transport of carbohydrates in leaves and stems may limit the rate of root respiration and, therefore, nutrient uptake, by active mechanisms.

Managing the orchard ecosystem to regulate orchard growth and productivity—summary

The orchard is a unique ecosystem of interacting environmental factors such as light, temperature, water, and nutrition. Although these factors are the parameters within which fruit are produced, and they may impose the limits of potential fruit production, these environmental factors must now be managed to allow the orchard system to achieve its productive potential. Leaving nature to *run its course* can be a costly mistake.

The environmental factors affect growth by affecting the fundamental biological processes of fruit trees—the metabolic biochemical reactions and pathways such as photosynthesis and respiration. The environmental factors interact, and their management must consider how they interact.

For instance, increasing light interception by orchard systems and improving light distribution within canopies with a higher proportion of the orchard canopy illuminated will result in greater plant water use. Small water stresses may reduce leaf size and thereby limit light interception. Plant water stresses may result in reduced transpiration and thus increased plant temperatures and increased respiration rates.

Proper nutrition is needed for the plant to regulate its water balance and have functional stomates, to intercept light and convert the solar energy into electrochemical energy, and to provide the chemicals which constitute plant growth by cell expansion, tissue growth, and organ development.

Poor light utilization due to shading or high temperatures may limit carbohydrate resources for growth or the active uptake of essential nutrient elements. Thus, the modern grower must think about how the management of one environmental factor affects all elements of the orchard ecosystem.

In very simplified terms, several rudimentary points can be seen. Tree fruit growers should manage light interception by developing orchards with systems that intercept light early in their life by filling their allotted space quickly and developing a strong spur canopy early in the season. Light penetration and distribution within the tree is controlled by tree size and shape and managed with training and pruning techniques.

Orchard temperature should be managed to keep the trees at an optimum temperature range for photosynthesis and development of product quality by carefully selecting orchard sites, using wind circulation, and the evaporative cooling effects of irrigation.

Water within the orchard system should be monitored by soil and plant evaluation systems and plant water status maintained in a range where conductance and growth is not limited, but the soil is not flooded. Nutrients should be monitored annually by soil and foliar analysis and nutrients applied to the soil system or directly to the plant by foliar application to maintain nutrient element levels in the adequacy range.

Truly, what Sir Isaac Newton observed about physics can be applicable to the orchard. For every environmental occurrence in the orchard, the tree responds. It is the conscientious orchardist's objective to control the environment (as much as possible) and thereby control the tree response to meet the goals of the orchard operation.

Literature cited and additional reading

Barden, J.A., "Apple leaves, their morphology and photosynthetic potential," *HortScience* 13(6) (1978): 6544-646.

Faust, M., *Physiology of Temperate Zone Fruit Trees*, John Wiley & Sons, NY, 1989.

Flore, J., "Stone Fruit," In *Environmental Physiology of Fruit Crops*, 223-270, edited by B. Schaffer and P.C. Anderson, Boca Raton, FL: CRC Press, 1994.

Flore, J.A. and A.N. Lakso, "Environmental and physiological regulation of photosynthesis in fruit crops," *Hort. Rev.* 11 (1989): 111.

Jackson, J.E., "Light interception and utilization by orchard systems," *Hort Rev.* 2 (1980): 208-267.

Jones, H.G., *Plants and Microclimate*, Cambridge, MA: Cambridge Press, 1992.

Lakso, A.N., "Apple," *Environmental Physiology of Fruit Crops*, 3-42, edited by B. Schaffer and P.C. Anderson, Boca Raton, FL: CRC Press, 1994.

Moran, R.E., "Acclimation of net CO_2 assimilation and vegetative growth of apple," PhD dissertation, Univ. of Arkansas, 165 pages.

Moran, R.E., "Growth, fruiting, and photosynthesis as affected by the diurnal course of light," MS thesis, Univ. of Arkansas, 161 pages.

Muromtsev, I.A., "Active parts of roots systems of fruit plants," 1969, Moscow, Russia: Kolos Publishers, [translated from Russian, USDA, 1984].

Rom, C.R., "Bud development and vigor in fruit trees," *Flowering and Pollination Shortcourse*, edited by B. Peterson, WSU Extension Publication, Pullman, WA, 1987.

Rom, C.R., "Light thresholds for apple tree canopy growth and development," *HortSci.* 26(8) (1991):9 89-992.

Rom, C.R., "Pomology 101: Basics of fruit tree training, " *Compact Fruit Tree* 26 (1993): 35-45.

Rom, C.R., "Fruit tree growth and development," edited by B. Peterson and R. Stevens, *Tree Fruit Nutrition, 1994,* Yakima, WA: Good Fruit Grower, 1-18.

Rom, C.R., "Balancing growth and cropping: Which comes first, the canopy of the crop, " *Compact Fruit Tree* 27 (1994): 53-59.

Rom, C.R. and B.H. Barritt, "Light interception and utilization in orchards," *Intensive Orcharding,* 1989, edited by B. Peterson, Yakima, WA: Good Fruit Grower, 41-58.

Westwood, M.N., *Temperate Zone Pomology; Physiology and Culture* (3rd edition). Portland, OR: Timber Press, 1993.

3 Role of Endogenous Plant Growth Substances in Regulating Fruit Tree Growth and Development

N.E. Looney
Agriculture and Agri-Food Canada
Pacific Agri-Food Research Centre
Summerland, British Columbia

Earlier presentations in this section have looked at the basic raw materials of life and at some of the processes that use these materials to produce fruit trees and fruit crops. An important aim of these articles is to call attention to the fascinating interconnectedness of these processes.

Obviously, higher plants contain the genetic information required to coordinate these resource gathering, elaboration, distribution, and development phenomena. Less obvious, however, is how this genetic information is translated into the myriad of growth and development processes characteristic of each species.

An important part of the answer to this intriguing question seems to involve the chemicals we call plant hormones, plant bioregulators, or simply plant regulators.

These interesting chemicals both promote and inhibit organ formation; profoundly influence the nature and direction of growth of organs and tissues; and control a wide range of physiological processes, including abscission, fruit ripening, fruit set, transpiration, dormancy, and germination. Additionally, they even play a key role in distributing the products of photosynthesis.

This chapter will introduce the concept of plant hormones, briefly describe those chemicals or families of chemicals known to be important in fruit tree physiology, and give some examples of their effects.

THE GENERAL NATURE OF PLANT HORMONES AND A HISTORICAL CONTEXT FOR MODERN RESEARCH

Plant hormones are quite diverse in their chemistry but, unlike animal hormones, are generally not proteins or polypeptides. Furthermore, they are not produced by a specialized organ and are not circulated through a cardiovascular system. Nonetheless, they are essential elements in plant biology and have been a prominent theme in plant physiology research for nearly a century.

It was late in the 19th century that Charles Darwin (1880) suggested that the mechanism by which plants position stems and roots in response to gravity and light involves a transportable signal. In 1911, Boysen-Jensen demonstrated, by grafting, that the movement of shoots toward a light source was indeed caused by a "material," a chemical substance.

A contemporary of Darwin, Julius Sachs (1880) also applied the laws of causality to organ development. He assumed the existence of root-forming and flower-forming substances that move in different directions in the plant.

Thus, the stage was set for the discovery

in the 1920s of the first plant hormone, auxin. It was isolated and its biological activity demonstrated by re-application to shoot tips (Went, 1928). A very few years later, this chemical was specifically identified as indoleacetic acid (IAA) and the "Golden Age" of plant endocrinology was born.

THE HORMONE CONCEPT AS IT APPLIES TO PLANTS

While plant growth substances do not totally fit the hormone concept as it has been developed for animal biology, most scientists agree that there are enough similarities to justify the term plant hormone. Some general characteristics of plant hormones are discussed below. The hormones mentioned are discussed in greater detail in a later section.

Transport—Despite the abovementioned original work that strongly suggested transport is a key ingredient of how plant hormones work, we now know that some actions of plant hormones do not involve organ-to-organ transport and may not even require transport within tissues.

For example, a hormone prominently involved in the regulation of water status in plants, abscisic acid (ABA), is both produced by and utilized within the cells that regulate the opening and closing of stomata.

Still, there are many situations where organ-to-organ transport is important. Root-produced cytokinins are believed to signal the status of the root system to the shoots.

Abscisic acid appears to communicate the energy requirements of developing seeds or fruit to nearby leaves; and auxin, moving from a new leaf toward the root system, stimulates the formation of new conductive tissues.

Concentration and sensitivity—Like animal hormones, plant hormones are active at very low concentrations. However, much has been written in recent years about the fact that the biological responses to plant hormones are not always proportional to the concentration of the hormone in the

organ or tissues being affected.

There are many explanations for this, but the concepts of sensitivity and receptivity are probably the most relevant. Lack of sensitivity is sometimes explained by one hormone counteracting the action of another. Cells or tissues may cease to respond to a hormone because the number of "receptor sites" is limited, and these sites are quickly saturated.

Hormone metabolism and compartmentalization—As suggested above, plant hormones are relatively simple molecules when compared to the protein and polypeptide hormones found in animal physiology. It is argued, probably correctly, that they therefore have less potential to convey information. On the other hand, they can function in unique ways that improve their utility and flexibility as biological effectors.

—Some are readily conjugated with sugars to form inactive sugar esters, raising the possibility that effective hormone concentration can be modulated by the activity of a key enzyme.

—Plant hormones, being relatively small molecules, can move readily through cellular membranes and into and out of subcellular organelles. Furthermore, their chemistry is such that they can become compartmentalized or be released from a compartment, thus becoming available or unavailable to act over critical periods of time.

—Finally, water-soluble plant hormones move rapidly in the nonliving conductive system of plants (apoplastic transport); for example, cytokinins move in this manner from roots to shoots. Other hormones are transported primarily in the phloem (symplastic transport). Auxin falls into this category.

THE NATURAL PLANT HORMONES

Other chapters will focus on the natural and synthetic plant bioregulating chemicals (PBRs) and their importance in modern tree fruit production. However, to properly understand the effects and the potential benefits of PBRs, it is necessary to review the classes of natural or endogenous plant hormones and how they influence normal growth and development.

Unfortunately, we can only hope to introduce the topic here. For those with a special interest in this subject, the book *Plant Hormones and Their Role in Plant Growth and Development* (Davies, 1987) is suggested reading. This book has been recently revised and retitled as *Plant Hormones–Physiology, Biochemistry and Molecular Biology* (Davies, 1995).

Auxin. As already mentioned, natural auxin, indoleacetic acid *(see Figure 1)*, was the first plant hormone to be fully characterized. It is synthesized from the amino acid tryptophan in young leaves, especially by the cells present in leaf primordia at the shoot apex (well before these leaves are visible to the naked eye). Another rich source of auxin is the developing seed.

Auxin diffuses from cell to cell, stimulating stem growth through cell enlargement and cell division. Leaf-produced auxin always moves down the stem, can move long distances, and always moves in the "living" transport system of plants, the phloem. Notable effects of auxin on plant growth and development phenomena include:

Apical dominance—Auxin diffusing from shoot tips suppresses the growth of lateral buds. It is now known that the control of apical dominance also involves other growth substances. Still, this role of auxin is very important and of practical concern when devising pruning strategies for fruit trees.

Early fruit growth and fruit set—Auxin arising from developing seeds stimulates cell division and cell enlargement in fruit tissues. This physiological activity enhances the competitiveness of these young fruits, increasing their chances of continued development. Those that continue to develop are said to have "set."

Root initiation—While the precise role of IAA in root development of whole trees is still unclear, low levels of synthetic auxins in tissue culture systems promote root branching and development. The synthetic auxin indolebutyric acid (IBA) is routinely used to promote rooting of cuttings.

Fruit ripening and leaf senescence; abscission—It is strongly suspected that natural auxin functions to delay both fruit ripening and leaf senescence. Certainly, applied auxinic PBRs (i.e., synthetic auxins) such as naphthaleneacetic acid (NAA) and 2,4,5-trichlorophenoxypropionic acid (2,4,5-TP) delay senescence of the cells in the abscission zone.

Unfortunately, however, these chemicals also stimulate whole fruits to ripen by promoting the production of ethylene. These contradictory effects are explained by the differences in surface-to-volume ratios of stems and fruit. Auxin is able to override the effects of ethylene at the abscission zone but not in the much more bulky fruit.

Vascular tissue (xylem and phloem) differentiation—Perhaps the most fundamentally important role of auxin produced by young leaves is to stimulate the formation of the vascular connections to the rest of the plant. Vascular element formation is always in the direction of the root system, the only direction that auxin can move.

Promotion of ethylene production—Ethylene production induced by applications of synthetic auxins can enhance "femaleness" in cucumber and other plants that produce both male and female flowers; promote flower formation in pineapple and many other tropical fruit crops; and inhibit root growth. This suggests that the relationship between natural auxin and ethylene production may be quite important and indeed, many effects originally attributed to auxin alone are now believed to be caused by auxin-induced ethylene production.

However, as stated above, auxin can also "protect" some tissues from some specific effects of applied ethylene, most notably the senescence of cells in the abscission zone.

Ethylene, at least in chemical structure, is the simplest of all plant hormones *(see Figure 1)*. It is also the only hormone that exists normally as a gas. Ethylene is synthesized from the amino acid methionine, usually in response to some external stress applied to the whole plant or to a single plant organ such as the fruit. It can be synthesized by virtually all plant cells and, being a gas, it moves by gaseous diffusion. It is unique among plant hormones in being able to stimulate its own production.

While it is still not clear that there is an absolute requirement for ethylene to achieve normal plant growth, it is involved in many developmental processes that are exceed-

FIGURE 1

Key molecules in the plant hormone biology of most higher plants.

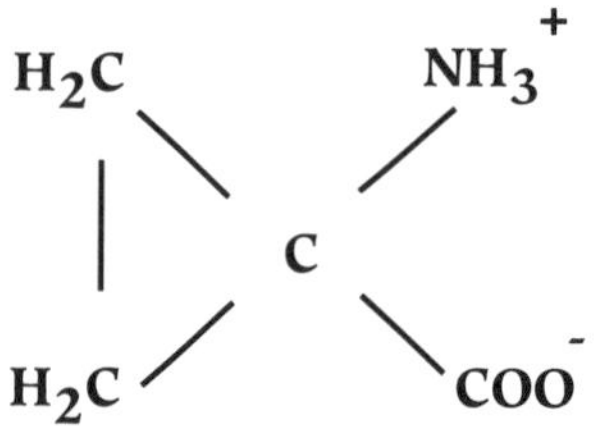

1 Amino Cyclopropane
1 Carboxylic Acid (ACC)
(Ethylene Precurser)

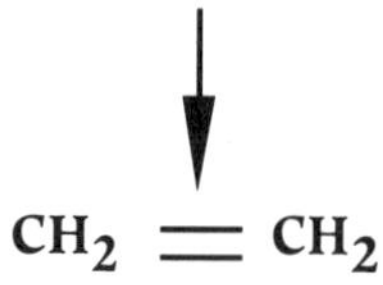

Ethylene

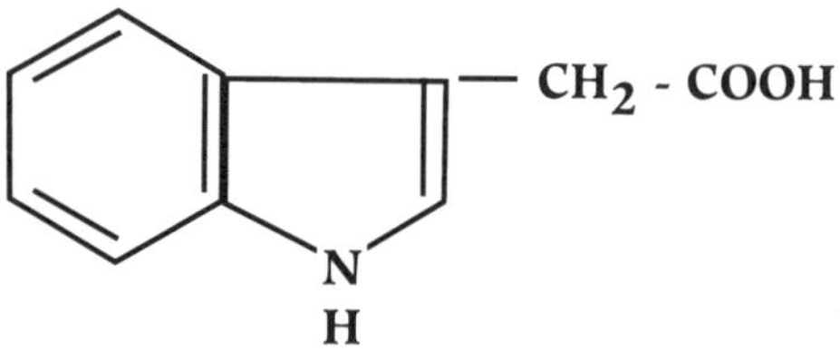

Indoleacetic Acid

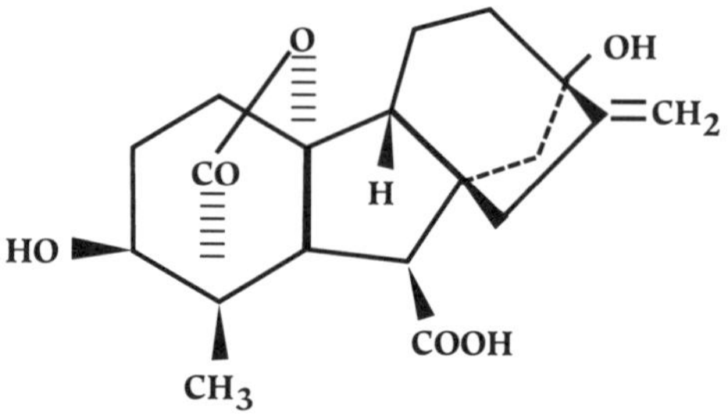

Gibberellin A₁

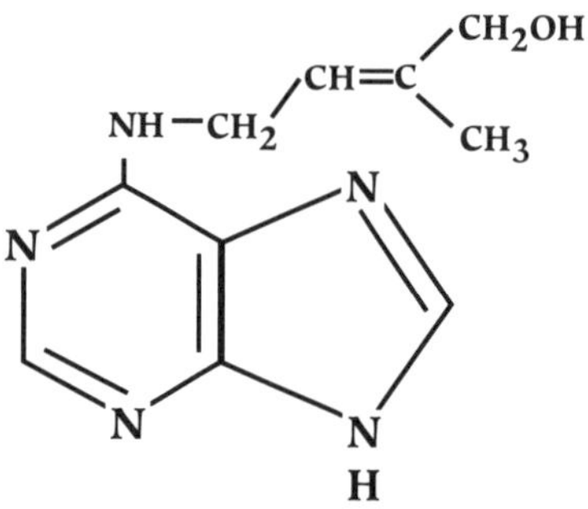

Zeatin

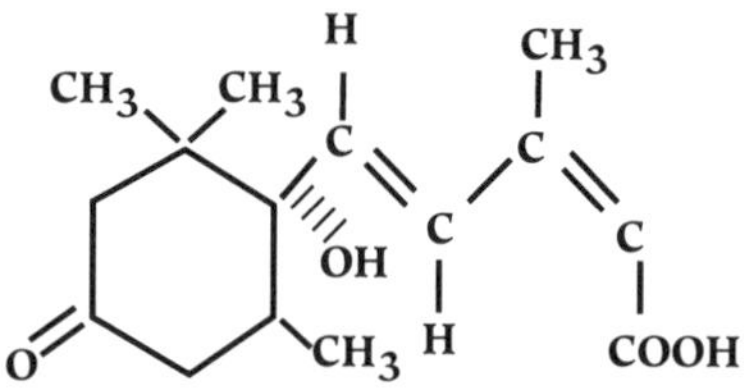

Abscisic Acid

ingly important in production horticulture.

Fruit ripening and abscission—Ethylene is produced in high quantities by ripening apples, pears, peaches, and apricots. These "climacteric" fruits undergo rather dramatic changes during ripening and a few parts per million of ethylene gas will initiate the ripening process. Interestingly, immature fruit or fruit attached to the tree are much more resistant to ethylene induced ripening. Nonclimacteric fruits (e.g., cherries, grapes) are relatively unresponsive to ethylene.

The process of fruit and leaf abscission also involves ethylene; senescence of cells in the abscission zone is promoted by this hormone. Ethylene arising from the PBR chemicals we classify as ethylene generators (e.g., ethephon), applied a week or two before harvest, is the basis for the mechanically harvested sour cherry industry of Michigan.

Flower and leaf senescence—Like fruits, leaves treated with ethylene will yellow and eventually fall from the tree. However, leaves are generally more tolerant of ethylene than are fruit, possibly because of higher levels of auxin or other anti-senescence hormones in leaves. Flower petal senescence is often triggered by pollination; the mechanism seems to be a burst of ethylene that occurs with pollination.

Releasing bulbs and tubers from dormancy—A good example of this phenomenon is the sprouting of potato tubers following ethylene treatment.

Epinasty and other shoot and root growth phenomena—There are many examples of ethylene affecting growth and development of plants. Leaf-droop (epinasty) of waterlogged plants is mediated by the immediate precursor of ethylene (a nongaseous chemical we call ACC; *see Figure 1*) transported from the roots to the aboveground stem. Low levels of ethylene promote root extension growth in rice, and ethylene stimulates shoot elongation in many aquatic plants. Stems of higher plants thicken in response to physical stresses such as wind movement, a phenomenon believed to be medi-

ated by stress-induced ethylene.

Flower induction—Very dramatic effects are evident on pineapple and some other tropical fruit crops. However, the role of ethylene in flowering is less clear on deciduous fruit trees.

Sex expression—As is the case with auxin, ethylene or its immediate precursor (ACC) promotes femaleness in cucumber and other dioecious plant species.

Gibberellins. There are many closely-related chemicals in the "family" of plant hormones called the gibberellins (GAs). Most plant species contain several different GAs. On the other hand, only a few GAs possess significant biological activity. Gibberellic acid (GA_3) is the most widely used GA in horticulture, but it is not found naturally in most higher plants. GA_1 *(see Figure 1)* is believed to be the primary "growth" gibberellin in higher plants, but other GAs may function to control flowering, seed germination, etc.

The biosynthesis of GAs in some fungi and all higher plants involves a complicated series of steps starting with mevalonic acid. Arguably, the elucidation of this biosynthetic pathway is one of the most important and impressive achievements of modern-day plant biology.

The sites of GA biosynthesis, in order of certainty, are developing fruits and seeds, shoot tips, and roots. The latter possibility is far from certain. Transport appears to occur in both the phloem and the xylem, but long-distance transport may not be important.

Gibberellins cause cells to elongate, and for this reason, they are primarily thought of as shoot elongation hormones. However, the effects of GAs are quite diverse, and new involvements are discovered every year. Some of the many phenomena involving GAs in higher plants include:

Stem elongation—GA-induced stem elongation appears to involve both cell elongation and cell division. Other plant hormones, most notably auxin, are also involved in this phenomenon. GAs are also involved in the elongation of fleshy fruits such as apples and grapes.

Seed germination—Seeds that normally require a cold treatment for germination can be induced to germinate by applications of a GA. The energy required for germination comes from the conversion of stored starch to sugars, and GAs are known to induce the formation of the key enzymes required in this metabolic pathway.

Promotion and inhibition of flowering—Some coniferous trees can be induced to form cones by GA treatment, and various herbaceous plants that require long days to flower can be induced to flower under short days by GA treatment. With most fruit trees, the expected response to applied gibberellins is an inhibition of flower formation. However, this does not mean that all GAs are equally inhibitory. Furthermore, it is likely that endogenous gibberellins, in concert with other hormones, play a positive role in flower initiation and development.

Induction of maleness—GAs have the opposite effect to that described for auxin and ethylene in plants with a dioecious flowering habit.

Breaking dormancy of buds—Applied GAs can be used to estimate the degree of dormancy of fruit tree buds in midwinter. Applied to dormant crowns moved from the field to forcing sheds, GA_3 treatment advances the production of hothouse rhubarb by several weeks.

Suppression of fruit ripening—GA_3 treatment is known to delay fruit ripening of sweet cherries and maintain peel chlorophyll in citrus; however, not all fruits are affected in this way.

Cytokinins are defined as substances which, in combination with auxin, stimulate cell division in plants and interact with auxin to determine the direction of tissue differentiation. Their discovery followed the observation that plant tissues cultured *in vitro* would not undergo cell division unless a "growth factor" contained in coconut milk was added to the system. Eventually, it became known that all plants produce such a factor, and these chemicals were called cytokinins.

All natural cytokinins are closely related to the nucleic acid bases that are the building blocks of RNA and DNA. The most common cytokinin in higher plants is zeatin *(see Figure 1)*, originally isolated from corn seeds. It occurs as a free base and as a sugar conjugate (zeatin riboside). In addition to developing seeds, cytokinins are produced by root tips. Root-produced cytokinins move in the xylem, along with water and mineral elements, to the leaves and shoot tip.

While the precise mode of action of cytokinins is still poorly understood, synthetic cytokinins are now known that have a remarkable ability to stimulate growth in plant tissue culture systems and, more recently, of organs in whole plant systems. Two good examples of these "high activity" cytokinins are thidiazuron and forchlorfenuron, both urea-based cytokinins *(see Figure 2)*. A few parts per million of either chemical, applied during the cell division stage, will stimulate fruit enlargement of kiwifruit and several other fruit species.

Here are some physiological phenomena that appear to be controlled by cytokinins in higher plants.

Stimulation of cell division in fruits and shoots—As indicated above, this function requires the presence of auxin and is easily demonstrated in rootless plant culture systems. Gall formation on roots and stems is caused by high localized cytokinin production.

Release of lateral buds from apical dominance—This effect forms the basis of successful tissue culture-based fruit tree propagation systems where proliferation of growing points is a key requirement. The situation is less clear in whole plants, but it is likely that root-produced cytokinins counteract shoot-produced auxin to define the contrasting growth habits of trees and shrubs.

Leaf expansion via cell enlargement—It is widely suspected that this is how root-produced cytokinins "adjust" leaf area to match the capacity of the root system to take up water and nutrients.

Chloroplast development and delay of leaf senescence—In a phenomenon probably related to the above, cytokinins are known to stimulate the formation of chloroplasts from the proplastids of plants grown in the dark. They also counteract ethylene-induced leaf senescence. The overall effect of cytokinins is to promote and retain leaf "greening."

Stomatal opening—Reduced levels of root-produced cytokinin "signal" the leaf to conserve moisture; high levels indicate strong root activity, and the stomata react accordingly. The strongest evidence for this scenario is that applied cytokinins promote stomata opening in model systems.

Abscisic acid *(see Figure 1)*, discovered in the early 1960s, was originally thought of as a natural growth inhibitor that played an important role in sustaining dormancy of seeds, buds, and even whole trees. An early name given to this chemical was "dormin." Later it was suggested to have a role in promoting leaf abscission and was called abscisin II. The name abscisic acid (ABA) was introduced in 1968 and is now firmly established, even though we now know that neither dormancy nor abscission is specifically controlled by ABA.

Abscisic acid is classed as a sesquiterpene and, like the gibberellins, arises from mevalonic acid. It is synthesized in mature leaves, especially in response to water stress. Seeds are also rich in ABA and may also be a site of biosynthesis. However, many details of ABA biosynthesis are yet to be discovered.

Abscisic acid seems to move readily in both the xylem and the phloem of plants. It moves out of leaves and toward the root system via the phloem; movement toward the shoot tip is probably in the xylem.

Some key effects of ABA in plant biology include:

Regulation of water status—Achieved by stomatal closure and perhaps by a general slowing of growth processes during stress periods.

Preventing premature sprouting of seeds—By counteracting gibberellins in the promotion of α-amylase activity.

Promotion of storage protein synthesis in seeds—As well as inhibiting germination, ABA actually stimulates protein accumulation by developing embryos.

Facilitating carbohydrate "unloading"—In this manner, ABA facilitates the transport of the products of photosynthesis to seeds and other storage organs.

FIGURE 2

Synthetic cytokinins: 6-benzyladenine (a cytokinin widely used in tree fruit horticulture) and two highly active urea-based cytokinins, thidiazuron and forchlorfenuron.

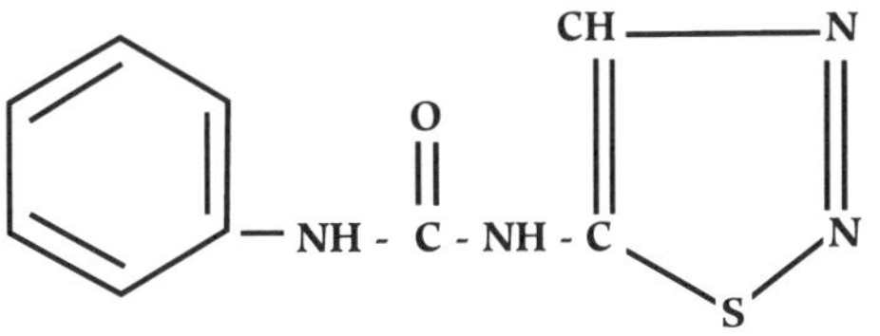

Thidiazuron

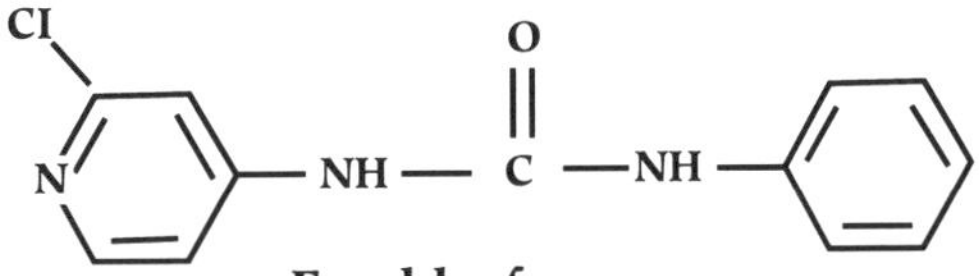

Forchlorfenuron

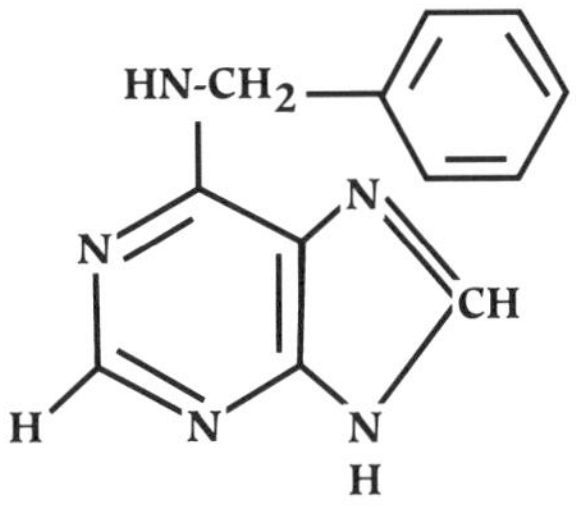

Benzyladenine

It is of interest to note that, unlike all of the other hormones mentioned above, no commercial PBR has yet to arise from what is known about ABA chemistry. This may change in the near future since several very active research teams are presently searching for bioactive ABA analogs. The aim of these teams is to identify chemicals that could be used to improve stress tolerance in a wide range of crops.

Other hormones. There are several other chemical "families" suspected of possessing hormonal activity in plants. However, there is ongoing debate about whether they should be classed as hor-

mones, "second messengers," or simply as chemicals with intriguing biological activity.

The family of chemicals known as polyamines *(see Figure 3)* is a good example. These chemicals seem to be widespread in plant biology and are found in all cells, often at concentrations higher than normal for a plant hormone. They are thought to play a role in tissue differentiation and may protect plant tissues from senescence (Evans and Malmberg, 1989). There is as yet no commercial role for the polyamines in horticulture.

Brassinolide *(see Figure 3)*, extracted from rape pollen, has very high activity and

FIGURE 3

Brassinolide and the polyamines, are naturally-occurring chemicals with documented bioregulatory activity in plants. However, there is ongoing debate about the classification of these chemicals as plant hormones.

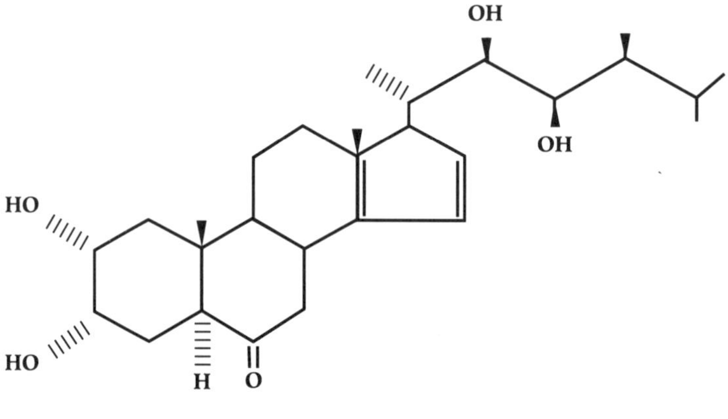

Brassinolide

Putrescine $H_3\overset{+}{N}\text{-}CH_2\text{-}CH_2\text{-}CH_2\text{-}CH_2\text{-}\overset{+}{N}H_3$

Spermidine $H_3\overset{+}{N}\text{-}CH_2\text{-}CH_2\text{-}CH_2\text{-}CH_2\text{-}\overset{+}{N}H_2\text{-}CH_2\text{-}CH_2\text{-}CH_2\text{-}\overset{+}{N}H_3$

Spermine $H_3\overset{+}{N}\text{-}CH_2\text{-}CH_2\text{-}CH_2\text{-}\overset{+}{H_2}N\text{-}CH_2\text{-}CH_2\text{-}CH_2\text{-}CH_2\text{-}\overset{+}{N}H_2\text{-}CH_2\text{-}CH_2\text{-}CH_2\text{-}\overset{+}{N}H_3$

Polyamines

a few parts per billion will enhance the effectiveness of auxin. However, it is not yet clear that this chemical plays a natural role in plant growth and development (Cutler et al., 1991).

CONCLUDING REMARKS

The bioregulating chemicals described in this chapter, whether we call them plant regulators or plant hormones, are, with a few exceptions, found only in plants. Furthermore, they are not known to have significant biological activity in animal systems.

While we still do not know precisely how these molecules achieve their effects on growth and development, we do know that they are critically important to plant life. We also know that while each hormone is involved in a different array of "primary" functions, most growth and development phenomena require several hormones in a beautifully orchestrated fashion.

Even a general appreciation of the sophisticated nature of these endogenous control systems should help us to succeed in the nursery, orchard, and packing house. It is often stated that success in commercial horticulture is achieved by those who learn to work with, rather than against, the natural processes and tendencies of plants. Many of these processes and tendencies are explained by the activity of the natural biochemicals we call plant hormones.

Finally, the study of plant endocrinology has already resulted in many products and practices of great value to tree fruit horticulture. Modern techniques for clonal propagation, promoting or inhibiting flowering and fruit set, improving various aspects of fruit quality, and promoting or suppressing fruit abscission, ripening, and senescence are but a few examples.

Other chapters will cover in more detail some of these PBR-based technologies.

Literature cited

Boysen-Jensen, P., "La transmission de l'irritation phototropique dans l'Avena," Bull. Acad. Roy. Denmark 1 (1911): 3.

Cutler, H.G., T. Yokota, and G. Adams (Eds.), *Brassinosteroids: Chemistry, Bioactivity and Applications.* Washington, D.C.: American Chemical Society, 1991.

Darwin, C. and F. Darwin, *The Power of Movement in Plants,* London: John Murray, 1880.

Davies, P.J., *Plant Hormones-Their Role in Plant Growth and Development,* Boston: Kluwer Academic Publishers, 1987.

Davies, P.J., *Plant Hormones-Physiology, Biochemistry and Molecular Biology,* Boston: Kluwer Academic Publishers, 1995.

Evans, P.T. and R.L. Malmberg, "Do polyamines have roles in plant development?" Annu. Rev. Plant Physiol. Plant Mol. Biol. 40 (1989): 235-269.

Sachs, J., "Stoff und Form der Pflanzenorgani," I. Arb. Bot. Inst. 2 (1880): 452-488.

Went, F.W., "Wuchstoff und Wachstum," Rec. Trav. Botan. 25 (1928): 1-116.

4 Plant Growth Regulator Application Technology, Uptake and Action

Brent Black
Department of Horticulture
Oregon State University
Corvallis, Oregon

M.J. Bukovac
Department of Horticulture
Michigan State University
East Lansing, Michigan

Growth regulators are applied to fruit trees to control vegetative growth and development, flowering and fruiting, and fruit development and ripening. For the most part, growth regulators represent naturally occurring plant hormones (e.g., gibberellins), analogs of naturally occurring hormones (NAA, BA), or other agents which may alter the internal levels of plant hormones (AVG, ethephon).

For any growth regulator to cause the intended response, it must be taken up by the plant and translocated to the organ, cellular, or sub-cellular site where the desired physiological response is induced.

The commercial effectiveness of growth regulator use depends on: 1) efficient delivery of the compound to the tree, 2) efficient uptake and translocation to the "active site," and 3) consistent and predictable response. Traditionally, growth regulators were delivered in high-volume foliar sprays. More recently, low-volume spraying has been widely adopted because of reduced applicator and equipment time.

Low-volume spraying involves applying an equivalent dose of active ingredient in a reduced carrier volume, resulting in a spray solution with a higher concentration of active ingredient.

Some commercial growth regulator formulations are relatively expensive. Efficient use of these compounds would also dictate accurate application of the necessary dose with minimal loss of material. Unfortunately, only about 35 to 65% of spray solution directed at fully-foliated trees by traditional air-blast spraying is retained by the foliage. With low-volume spraying, this can drop below 25% (Herrington et al., 1981).

A number of commercially available growth regulators are now in wide use, despite variable results. One example is the use of postbloom applications of NAA as a fruit thinning agent for apples. Aside from the risks of over- or under-thinning, undesirable side effects such as "pygmy" and "small fruit" problems periodically occur with cultivars like spur-type Delicious.

Despite over 40 years of research and commercial experience, obtaining desired results from NAA thinning sprays while avoiding the side effects is still considered more an art than a science. NAA fruit thinning is a useful model for illustrating various aspects of approaching efficient growth regulator performance.

Following is a discussion of factors affecting the delivery, uptake, and response processes involved in growth regulator application. The aim is to provide background information for a better understanding of factors which may detract from efficient growth regulator use.

Delivery

The primary method for delivering exogenous growth regulators is through foliar spray application using water as the carrier. Foliar spraying, as a delivery system, is also important for applying pesticides to control pathogens, insects, and mites. However, some attributes of growth regulators present unique problems and concerns which may not be normally encountered in the application of pesticides.

GROWTH REGULATORS DIFFER FROM PESTICIDES

As previously mentioned, growth regulators must be taken up by the plant to give the desired effect. With the exception of "systemic" pesticides and foliar nutrients, this is unique to growth regulators. However, significant distant translocation does not occur for many growth regulators, resulting in a localized response. For example, applying NAA as a fruit thinning agent to a single branch, results in fruit thinning on that branch.

Growth regulators are active at relatively low concentrations and have a fairly narrow acceptable dose range. The high degree of biological activity makes overdosing a common problem, and the difference between too little and too much is relatively small. Ethephon (at 2 to 3 pints per acre) is commonly used to induce fruit abscission in cherry. Overdoses (4 to 5 pints per acre) result in leaf abscission or permanent damage to fruiting wood by inducing gum formation (Olein and Bukovac, 1983).

Uniform spray coverage is desirable in all aspects of orchard spraying to minimize environmental risks and the unnecessary use of expensive compounds. However, it becomes more critical for growth regulators than for pesticides, due to the narrow acceptable dose range and the potential damage from over-dosing. Historically, this higher demand for uniform coverage was met by the use of high-volume sprays.

By applying the compound in a volume of water at or near the full retention capacity of the canopy, the potential over-dosing was minimized because excess spray solution dripped from the leaves and was lost. Low-volume spraying results in a large number of small droplets distributed over the leaf surface. Dose becomes proportional to the amount of spray which is delivered to the canopy and retained by the leaf surface. To approach efficient performance of applied growth regulators, we must first improve the uniformity of spray coverage.

COMPONENTS OF DELIVERY BY SPRAY APPLICATION

Delivering compounds by spray application is a complex process involving a number of interacting factors. To approach the high level of uniformity needed for growth regulator application, thereby minimizing the risk of undesired response, one must first understand the various factors affecting the spray application process. The components of orchard spraying have been defined as follows (Bukovac, 1988):

—Active ingredient
—Formulation
—Spray solution characteristics
—Droplet formation
—Spray pattern characteristics
—Transport of droplets to the target
—Target definition and characteristics
—Environmental conditions during spray application and drying
—Spray droplet:leaf surface interaction
—Deposit formation
—Penetration of active ingredient, and
—Translocation of active ingredient to reaction site.

SPRAY SOLUTION

The nature of the compound and its formulation can play a role in determining the amount of active ingredient deposited on the leaf surface and available for absorption by the plant. For example, photodegradation and volatility of compounds reduces the amount of material available for absorption by the plant. NAA is degraded by ultraviolet (UV) light (Crosby and Tang, 1969), which, under conditions of slow uptake, may account for significant losses of material, particularly under conditions of high light such as in the fruit-producing areas of the Pacific Northwest. With just a three-hour exposure to full sunlight (under Michigan conditions), 75 to 80% of the NAA may be lost (Bukovac et al., 1985).

The free acid or salt formulations of 2,4-D are volatile, and loss under field conditions is well documented (Marth and Mitchell, 1949). Loss of applied active ingredient from photodegradation or volatilization would have a marked effect on performance and is directly related to the chemical properties of the active ingredient and its formulation.

The physical characteristics of the spray solution (surface tension, viscosity) play a role in determining spray droplet size and spray droplet:leaf surface interactions, the importance of which will be discussed later. Commercial growth regulators often contain surfactants intended to optimize the physical characteristics of the spray solution for the conditions of recommended use.

SPRAYER DESIGN

The orchard sprayer affects efficiency of delivery by determining the size of spray droplets formed and transport of the droplets to the target tree. Spray droplet size influences spray penetration into the tree canopy, and whether or not the droplet will impact and be retained by tree leaves. Smaller droplets tend to go around leaves and end up contributing to spray drift. Smaller droplets also evaporate more quickly.

Larger droplets may fall out of the air stream or may strike the leaf and bounce off. To attain efficient spray coverage, the spray should be delivered in droplets of optimal size for impacting and being retained by tree leaves.

Many low-volume sprayers utilize air-shear nozzles. Droplet size from these nozzles is extremely variable and affected by a number of factors. The large number of small droplets produced present unfavorable conditions for precise spray coverage. Some of the newer low-volume sprayers use rotary or spinning disk nozzles, which provide more uniform droplet size, but droplet size is still small, making precise delivery difficult.

Transport of the spray droplet to the target is also determined by the sprayer. The important factors in droplet transport include spray pattern, and volume and velocity of carrier air. Traditional air-blast sprayers give a fan-shaped spray pattern where all the spray originates from essentially a point source near the bottom of the canopy. The limitations to this design are readily apparent in the inability to distribute spray evenly between lower branches near the spray alley, and branches in the top center of the tree, both important fruit-bearing areas.

Some estimations are that many sprayers distribute from three to five times more spray near the lower outside portion of the canopy than in the top center (Bukovac et al., 1985). This may be a conservative estimate in the case of more dense canopies and larger trees such as those found in sweet cherry cropping systems.

A significant advancement has come with the use of tower sprayers. With the spray source distributed uniformly along the vertical axis of the tree, the discrepancy between spray coverage of lower and upper portions of the tree is minimized. More recently, "tunnel sprayers" have gained some research interest and are in commercial use in Europe. The tunnel spray pattern involves nozzles directed at the target tree from both sides and above. The perceived advantages of this design include uniform coverage of the tree and reduced drift by containing the spray under a hood.

The speed and volume of air used to transport droplets to the target is another important consideration in developing an efficient delivery system. Low-volume sprayers which utilize air-shear nozzles require high velocity, low-volume air for these nozzles to function properly. Unfortunately, these conditions prove unfavorable for spray coverage. Low-volume, high-velocity air slows significantly within a short distance from the sprayer (Reichard et al., 1979) and is either insufficient to reach the center portion of the tree, or slows to the degree where droplets either fall out of the spray stream or have insufficient energy to impact on leaves.

It is believed that uniform spray coverage depends on a volume of air sufficient to displace the air in the canopy volume (Randall, 1971). Some low-volume sprayers are now designed with low-speed, high-volume air delivery systems for more uniform distribution of spray droplets through the canopy.

SPRAYER PERFORMANCE

Growers can make the greatest contribution to sprayer performance by properly calibrating, adjusting, and operating the sprayer according to manufacturer specifications. In a survey of (broadcasting and banding) field sprayer calibration, Grisso et al. (1988) reported calibration errors ranging from 40% under application to +60% over application. Only one-third of applicators surveyed were applying pesticides within 5% of the intended rate, and 75% of

commercial and 60% of private applicators were applying pesticides within 10% of desired rates.

The authors conclude that this is a significant improvement over the results of a previous survey. However, with growth regulator application, a margin of error as small as 10% could be the difference between desired performance and harmful overdose.

Orchard spraying has an additional degree of complexity compared to the field spraying just described. The dose which a tree receives from a foliar spray is proportional to the amount of leaf area available to intercept and absorb the compound. In tree fruit production systems, leaf area is not consistently reflected by land area, yet manufacturers continue to base label recommendations for growth regulator use on land area. To attain more efficient use of growth regulators, doses should be adjusted for the sprayed canopy area such as in the Tree Row Volume method (Byers et al., 1968; Herrera-Aguirre and Unrath, 1980).

Other factors affecting sprayer performance are ground speed and weather conditions. Ground speed is important in obtaining maximum sprayer performance. Randall (1971) reported a more uniform spray coverage with slower ground speed. Similar results have been reported elsewhere (Bukovac et al., 1985). Low-volume sprayers are more adversely affected by windy conditions than are high-volume

TABLE 1

Full bloom dates and fruit diameter measurements for Redchief Delicious apple fruit over three seasons at Clarksville Michigan (king fruit diameter, KFD; days after full bloom, DAFB).
Adapted from Black et al., 1996.

1991			1992			1993		
Date	KFD	DAFB	Date	KFD	DAFB	Date	KFD	DAFB
9 May	FB		16 May	FB		12 May	FB	
			21 May	4.6	5	25 May	6.6	13
22 May	10.6	13	28 May	8.0	12	6 Jun	12.1	25
			6 Jun	15.0	21	10 Jun	16.7	29
29 May	19.9	20	11 Jun	20.6	26	14 Jun	22.5	33

sprayers, due to smaller droplet size and lower volume of carrier air.

TARGET CHARACTERISTICS

Spray coverage uniformity is also influenced by the target tree. The orchard design, including tree form, size, and planting density all would influence distribution of spray through the canopy. Most efforts at developing tree-training systems are devoted to maximizing light exposure or fruit quality. Spray coverage is affected by tree form (Bukovac et al., 1985; Gaynor and Layne, 1979), suggesting one area for potential improvement of growth regulator efficiency would be to consider spray application requirements when developing training systems.

Certainly, the sprayer size should be matched to target tree size. It should also be noted that canopy density, which influences spray penetration and coverage, changes over the growing season.

SPRAY DROPLET:LEAF SURFACE INTERACTIONS

The nature of the leaf surface affects how the spray droplet interacts with that surface, affecting spray coverage and uptake. Leaf surface characteristics influence whether or not droplets which strike the leaf will be retained or reflected, and how well the retained droplets will wet the leaf surface to form spray deposits. From these spray deposits, the active ingredient must pene-trate into the leaf and trigger the desired response.

The characteristics of upper and lower leaf surfaces differ, and can change over the season. Leaf surface characteristics also differ among species and cultivars (Bukovac, 1982). The presence of a dense mat of leaf hairs (trichomes) on the lower surface of apple leaves (Black et al., 1995a) or heavy, plate-like wax deposits on the surface of pear leaves (Bukovac, 1980) affect retention, wetting, and uptake from spray solutions.

ENVIRONMENTAL CONDITIONS

Weather conditions during and shortly after spraying also influence the amount of material available for plant uptake. Warm, dry conditions result in rapid evaporation of water from spray droplets. This rapid drying of the spray drastically reduces the amount of material taken up.

Conversely, cool, humid conditions result in slower droplet drying and more material available for uptake. Rewetting of the dried deposits, either from light rain or dew, also increases the uptake of available active ingredient.

Uptake

In addition to eliminating the possibility of growth regulator overdose, high-volume sprays provide more ideal conditions for uptake than do low-volume sprays. High-volume sprays completely wet the leaf surface with a thin film of spray solution,

TABLE 2

The effect of NAA (15 mg l^{-1}) on fruit weight (grams) of Redchief Delicious at harvest in relation to intraspur fruit position (ISFP) and competition on a given spur (ISFC). From Black et al., 1996.

Fruit		Treatment		NAA effect
Position	Competition	Control	NAA	(%)
King	None	204	211	3
	Lateral	208	191	-8
Lateral	None	218	206	-6
	King	172	148	-14
	Lateral	200	181	-9

allowing for maximum contact with the leaf surface, and slow drying. Low-volume sprays result in a number of small, fast-drying droplets scattered across the leaf surface, which contain high concentrations of growth regulator.

Evidence suggests that the amount of growth regulator taken up is proportional to the number of spray deposits on the surface; in other words, an equal amount of spray distributed in more droplets of smaller size results in a greater response than fewer large deposits (Crabtree and Bukovac, 1980).

Other factors which influence the amount of growth regulator taken up through the leaf surface include temperature and leaf age. Aside from the effect on droplet drying, higher temperatures increase the uptake of NAA by apple (Black et al., 1995a) and pear (Greene and Bukovac, 1972) leaves.

A similar temperature effect is seen in the uptake of gibberellins by sour cherry leaves (Knoche et al., 1992). The age of the absorbing leaf also influences uptake, as older leaves have heavier waxy coatings, which present a more formidable barrier to penetration of foliar-applied compounds.

A large number of surfactants are commercially available, all of which effectively increase wetting of the leaf surface by the spray solution.

However, in some cases, addition of a given surfactant has no effect on growth regulator response (Bukovac, unpublished). In such cases, the added expense of the surfactant is not justified. For most surfactants, experimental data is either weak or nonexistent as to how much growth regulator performance is enhanced.

Response

It is difficult to measure or compare response directly due to the variability in growth regulator uptake, as observed activity is the net result of uptake and plant response. Following is a discussion of several factors known to affect plant response.

TISSUE SENSITIVITY

The sensitivity of a target tree or target tissue on a tree varies over the season. Depending on the process targeted for regulation, there may be a window of opportunity for application. For example, gibberellin applied to sour cherry trees effectively reduces flowering the following season. Bukovac et al. (1986) reported that a 25 ppm application of gibberellin at three or four weeks after bloom resulted in 60% inhibition of flowering, but applications at either two or five weeks after bloom caused only 20 to 30% inhibition.

Optimum sensitivity of target tissue does not correspond to a calendar date. In fact, due to seasonal variations in weather conditions, rate of physiological development varies greatly from season to season. Postbloom applications of NAA for fruit thinning are not effective unless applied when the target trees are responsive. Often, recommendations for postbloom thinners are based on days after full bloom (DAFB) (Hull, 1993). A comparison of king fruit diameter (KFD) measurements over three seasons illustrates this variation in rate of physiological development (see Table 1).

For example, timing a postbloom thinning application of NAA at 10 to 12 mm KFD would have corresponded to 13 DAFB in 1991 and 25 DAFB in 1993. A physiological index such as fruit diameter provides a more direct, and probably a more meaningful, basis for timing a growth regulator application to the physiological development of the tree.

Sensitivity may vary among different tissues on the same tree at the same time of year. For example, NAA differentially affects fruit size depending on the fruit's position on a spur, and whether or not there are other fruits present on the same spur. The greatest negative effect of NAA on fruit size at harvest occurs on lateral fruits competing with a king fruit on the same spur (see Table 2).

The sensitivity of the targeted tissue may

also be affected by exposure to other growth regulators. Tank mixing NAA and Accel to thin spur-type Delicious results in a drastic reduction in fruit size, with a major portion of the crop ending up as small fruit *(see Table 3*, Bukovac et al., 1995). This same interaction is seen when a king bloom application of Promalin is followed by an NAA thinning application at 10 mm king fruit diameter *(see Table 4,* Bukovac et al., 1995).

Accel and Promalin both contain the same growth regulator active ingredients (benzyladenine and gibberellins A_4A_7). It should also be noted here that tank mixing growth regulators with fungicide or insecticide sprays is not generally recommended.

Growth regulator sensitivity also varies among cultivars. For example, some cultivars are notoriously difficult to thin with growth regulator application, while others are easily over-thinned. This is reflected in different thinning recommendations for different cultivars (Hull, 1993).

The vigor of a tree, or branches on a tree, will also determine response. Less vigorous branches tend to be more sensitive to growth regulator applications for fruit thinning (Bukovac et al., 1985). Also, trees under stress, such as from winter injury or disease, respond differently than do healthy vigorous trees. Stressed trees are more easily thinned with growth regulator application, but may be less responsive to growth regulator applications for control of preharvest drop.

Efficient application of growth regulators to obtain a desirable response will depend on an accurate assessment of the sensitivity of the target tissue, which includes understanding the seasonal, tissue, and cultivar variation, as well as the physiological status of the target tissue.

EFFECT OF SPRAY VOLUME ON RESPONSE

Aside from the effects on coverage uniformity, the response to applied growth regulators may also be influenced by volume in which the active ingredient is applied. A constant dose of Alar to control preharvest drop of apple was more effective in a high-volume than in a low-volume application (Rogers and Krestensen, 1973). In contrast, ethephon applied in low-volume sprays is *more* effective than high-volume sprays for promoting fruit abscission in cherry (Bukovac, 1981), and enhancing pigment formation in apple (Luckwill et al., 1973).

Studies on the effects of spray volume on growth regulator activity are sometimes difficult to interpret, because differential response to spray volume may be due to differences in uniformity of spray coverage. This is particularly the case when different application techniques are used for each spray volume.

Thinning applications of NAA result in similar fruit size regardless of spray volume, when spray coverage is consistent.

TABLE 3

Interaction of NAA and Accel on fruit size and yield in spur-type Delicious

Treatment	Small fruit (% < 2.5")	Yield (kg/tree)
Nonthinned control	2.2	77.2
Hand thinned	0.2	60.3
NAA, 15 ppm	11.1	63.9
Accel, 25 ppm	2.8	55.4
NAA + Accel	22.2	71.2

TABLE 4

Interaction of NAA (15 ppm at 10 mm KFD) and Promalin (1.5 pt/acre at king bloom) on fruit size and yield in Redchief Delicious. (Clarksville, Mich., 1994)

Treatment	Small fruit (% < 2.5")	Yield (kg/tree)
Nonthinned control	6.7	88.3
Hand thinned	1.6	81.1
NAA, 10 ppm	4.9	65.5
Promalin, KB	9.9	85.1
Promalin + NAA	25.0	58.4

Black et al. (1995b) applied NAA at equivalent doses in high-volume to 1/8 high-volume sprays and measured both spray coverage uniformity and harvest fruit size.

All treatments were applied with a Kinkelder low-volume sprayer, and spray volume differences were obtained by adjusting flow rate of spray solution to the nozzles. Measurements of spray deposition at four points in the canopy indicated that spray coverage uniformity was consistent among volumes. Fruit size distribution at harvest was not affected by the volume in which an equivalent dose of NAA was applied (Black et al., 1995b).

ENVIRONMENTAL CONDITIONS

Besides the effect on the amount of material absorbed by the plant, weather conditions during the response period may also affect plant response. For example, warmer conditions during the response period have been shown to increase response to applied ethephon (Jones and Koen, 1985).

Summary

Although applying foliar sprays in the orchard is a common cultural practice, growth regulator application is unique. The requirement that growth regulators be taken up by the plant, the high degree of activity at low doses, and the narrow acceptable dose range, are unique characteristics that must be recognized in growth regulator application.

Growth regulator application requires a higher level of precision in uniform delivery. Efficient delivery requires selecting spray equipment best suited for the job, and calibrating and adjusting the equipment for maximum performance.

Obtaining consistent response requires attention to the physiological and environmental parameters which influence uptake of and response to applied growth regulators, and adjusting management practices accordingly.

Literature cited

Black, B.L., P.D. Petracek, and M.J. Bukovac, "The effect of temperature on uptake of NAA by Redchief Delicious apple leaves," *J. Amer. Soc. Hort. Sci.*, 120 (1995a): 441-445.

Black, B.L., J. Hull, Jr., and M.J. Bukovac, "Effect of spray volume and time of NAA application on fruit size and cropping of Redchief Delicious apple," *Scientia Hort.* 64 (1995b): 253-264.

Bukovac, M.J., "The performance of growth regulators when applied in low-volume sprays," John A. Hannah distinguished lecture. Annual Rep. Mich. State Hort. Soc. 110 (1980): 17-28.

Bukovac, M.J., "Performance of daminozide and ethephon when applied in low-volume sprays to sour and sweet cherry," *Acta Hort.* 120 (1981): 25-29.

Bukovac, M.J., "Low-volume application of plant growth substances to fruit trees," *Proc. 21st Int. Hort. Cong.* 1 (1982): 107-121.

Bukovac, M.J., "Spray application technology: A critical factor in pesticide performance," *Proc. Oregon Hort. Soc.* 79 (1988): 100-105

Bukovac, M.J., B.L. Black, and J. Hull, Jr., "Interaction of NAA with Accel and Promalin on fruit size in Delicious and Empire apples," *HortScience* 34 (1995): 765. (abstract)

Bukovac, M.J., J. Hull, Jr., C.D. Kesner, and R.P. Larsen, "Prevention of flowering and promotion of spur formation with gibberellin increases cropping efficiency in Montmorency sour cherry," *Annual Rep. Mich. Hort. Soc.* 116 (1986): 122-130

Bukovac, M.J., D.L. Reichard, and R.E. Whitmoyer, "The spray application process: Central for the efficient use of growth regulators in tree fruits," 5th International Symposium on Growth Regulators in Tree Fruits, *Acta Hort.* 179 (1985): 33-45.

Byers, R.E., K.D. Hickey, and C.H. Hill, "Base gallonage per acre," V.P.I. *Fruit Notes*, June 1968.

Crabtree, G.D., and M.J. Bukovac, "Studies on low-volume application of plant growth substances; part 1: ethylene production, induced by 1-naphthylacetic acid, as a means of evaluating spray parameters," *Pestic. Sci.* 11 (1980): 43-52.

Crosby, D.G., and C. Tang, "Photodecomposition of 1-naphthaleneacetic acid," *J. Agr. Food Chem.* 20 (1969): 76-79.

Gaynor, J.D., and R.E.C. Layne, "Captan deposition in peach orchard hedgerows," *J. Amer. Soc. Hort. Sci.* 104 (1979): 330-332.

Greene, D.W., and M.J. Bukovac, "Penetration of naphthaleneacetic acid into pear (*Pyrus communis* L.) leaves," *Plant and Cell Physiol.* 13 (1972): 321-330.

Grisso, R.D., E.J. Hewett, E.C. Dickey, R.D. Schnieder, and E.W. Nelson, "Calibration accuracy of pesticide application equipment," *Applied Engr. in Agric.* 4 (1988): 310-315.

Herrera-Aguirre, E., and C.R. Unrath, "Chemical thinning response of Delicious apples to volume of applied water,". *HortScience* 15 (1980): 43-44.

Herrington, P.J., H.R. Mapother, and A. Stringer, "Spray retention and distribution on apple trees," *Pestic. Sci.* 12 (1981): 515-520.

Hull, J., Jr., "Plant growth regulators," edited by J.W. Johnson, J. Hull and A.L. Jones, In: Fruit Spray Calendar. Michigan State University Extension Bulletin E-154, 1993.

Jones, K.M., and T.B. Koen, "Temperature effects on ethephon thinning," *J. of Hort. Sci.* 60 (1985): 21-24.

Knoche, M., N.K. Lownds, and M.J. Bukovac, "Factors affecting the absorption of gibberellin A_3 by sour cherry leaves," *Crop Prot.* 11 (1992): 57-63.

Luckwill, L.C., R.D. Child, and H. Campbell, "Effect of growth regulators on fruit quality," Rep. Long Ashton Res. Stn. 1973.

Marth, P.C., and J.W. Mitchell, "Comparative volatility of various forms of 2,4-D. Bot. Gaz. 110 (1949): 632-636.

Olein, W.C., and M.J. Bukovac, "The effect of ethephon-induced gum accumulation in sour cherry (*Prunus cerasus* L.) on shoot water relations and hydraulic conductance," *Acta Hort.* 137 (1983): 55-64.

Randall, J.M., "The relationships between air volume and pressure on spray distribution in fruit trees," *J. Agric. Engr. Res.* 16 (1971): 1-31.

Reichard, D.L., R.D. Fox, R.D. Brazee, and F.R. Hall, "Air velocities delivered by orchard air sprayers," *Trans. Amer. Soc. Agr. Engr.* 22 (1979): 69-73.

Rogers, B.L., and E.R. Krestensen, "Preharvest drop of Stayman apples as influenced by SADH in dilute and concentrate form," *HortScience* 8 (1973): 314-315

part II
Regulation of Vegetative Growth and Development

DR. CURT ROM
Department of Horticulture
University of Arkansas
316 Plant Science Building
Fayetteville, AR 72701
phone: 501-575-7434; fax: 501-575-8619
crom@comp.uark.edu

DR. STEPHEN MYERS
Head, Department of Horticulture
University of Arkansas
316A Plant Science Building
Fayetteville, AR 72701
phone: 501-575-2603; fax: 501-575-8619
scmyers@comp.uark.edu

DR. SCOTT JOHNSON
University of California
Kearney Agricultural Center
9240 South Riverbend Avenue
Parlier, CA 93648
phone: 209-891-2500; fax: 209-891-2593
sjohnson@uckac.edu

5 Coordination of Root and Shoot Growth: Roots and Rootstocks

Curt R. Rom
Department of Horticulture
University of Arkansas
Fayetteville, Arkansas

Roots are an often forgotten but critically important organ of the fruit tree system. They are forgotten because they are difficult to observe and are essentially "invisible" under the orchard floor.

Although difficult to view and observe, roots significantly regulate the growth and performance of fruit trees. Because of the difficulties of observation, information on tree fruit root systems is more limited than information on the aerial portions of the tree, and the management of roots has been studied less. Nonetheless, knowledge of root growth and development and the regulation of growth exerted by the rootstock will lead to better orchard management.

When the fruit tree in the orchard is considered, it must be remembered that they are really a compound genetic system; the tree is a combination of the aerial clonal plant cultivar (the scion) and a rootstock cultivar. Those roots must be managed just as the aerial portion of the tree is managed. The function and role of roots to fruit trees, and their relationship to shoot growth, will be presented in the chapter.

The function of roots to fruit trees

Roots perform several key functions to the tree. They interact with the soil and provide a structure for support of the tree. Roots are critical for water uptake and the assimilation of nutrient elements from the soil. Roots are an important storage organ for carbohydrates produced during the growing season and needed during the "dormant" seasons when biological activity of the tree continues.

Roots also exert some genetic control over the aerial portion of the plant and can influence plant development such as the date of bloom, amount of bloom on a tree, time to come into production, fruit size and quality, time of harvest, and winter hardiness. Rootstocks vary in adaptability to soil type (sand versus clay) or soil pH (acid versus alkaline).

Some rootstocks have resistances to orchard soil insects, vertebrate or disease pests, and thus allow an orchard to exist where these pests may have been limiting factors. One of the most prevalent reasons for the use of clonally propagated rootstocks is for the genetic size control the root system exerts on the aerial portion of the tree and their nature to induce precocity or early fruit production.

At present, there is no perfect or ideal rootstock, and there is great variation among rootstocks in their functions and regulation of tree growth. Rootstocks vary in their ability to support the tree. Some rootstock genotypes, by their genetic nature, tend to have brittle roots and break, while other rootstocks have more flexible roots.

Similarly, some rootstocks readily branch laterally, form roots from the root-stock shank, and/or have roots radiating out from the rootstock shank close to the plant surface, while others tend not to form lateral roots from the shank, tend to be relatively confined, and/or grow deeper into the soil.

When the characteristics of brittle roots, poor shank rooting, and/or deep roots are combined with a heavy crop load, heavy wet soils, and/or strong winds, trees may break off at the roots or lean to such an extent as to be unmanageable. In these cases, support is often needed to supplement the rootstock's inherent strength and allow the tree to carry a maximum crop load or withstand winds.

The uptake of water and nutrients by roots

ROOT GROWTH

The activity of roots varies throughout the season. Root growth is most active when soil temperatures are in the range of 15 to 25°C, and water is available (see Figure 1). Because of this, and their coordination with the aerial portions of the tree, roots tend to have two periods of growth, occurring in the early spring and in autumn during and/or after harvest (see Figure 2).

Root growth in the spring begins before bud break, as soon as soils warm to levels suitable for growth. As shoots begin their grand phase of growth and more of the carbon and nutrient assimilates are partitioned to shoot growth, root growth slows.

Also, high soil temperatures during the summer may reduce root growth. Although the roots are not growing, they are still actively absorbing nutrients and water as

---

FIGURE 1

Apple root growth (as percent of maximum rate) as affected by soil temperature.
Vertical lines indicate optimum growth temperatures at which growth is within 20% of the maximum rate.
Cardinal temperatures for root growth are: 3 to 7°C for the growth minima, 15 to 25°C for the growth optima, and 40 to 45°C for maxima (after Muromtsev, 1984).

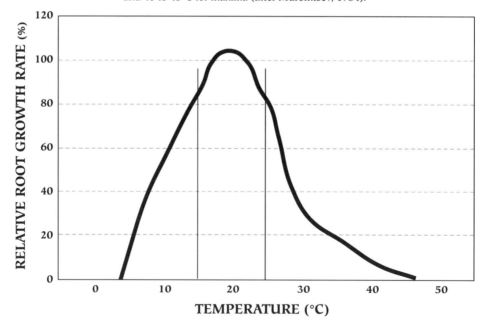

the requirement for shoots demands.

As shoot growth ends in late summer and fruit growth slows and the fruit are harvested, root growth begins again and continues as long as the soil is in a temperature range suitable for growth and carbohydrate supplies from photosynthetic leaves are available. This fall growth of roots is the basis for the successful application of nutrients in early fall and the nutrient uptake and partitioning into flower buds which will bloom next spring. It is clear that this is a coordination between root and shoot growth.

When roots grow, they extend from the root tip meristem. Young, actively growing tree fruit roots are about 1 to 10 millimeters in diameter and very white in their appearance. At the tip of the root is a group of cells called the root cap. These are thick-walled cells acting similar to a helmet or plow that clear the way as the root grows and extends through the soil. Behind the root cap is a meristematic area of rapidly dividing cells. Some of the dividing cells are added to the root cap as the root cap cells are lost due to the friction of moving through the soil. The vast majority of new cells are added behind the root cap and account for the extension of the root.

Directly behind the meristematic area is a very important region of the growing root. This is the area called the *zone of maturation;* this is where the cells are maturing by enlarging both longitudinally and laterally.

From the epidermal cells of the root in this zone come root hairs, fine protuberances of the epidermal cells which can extend several millimeters from the root. They increase the surface area of the roots more than 100 times and are very active in the uptake of water and nutrients.

The young, white, developing roots account for a significant amount of nutrient and water uptake for the plant. As the root "moves" through the soil and continues to expand laterally, the root hairs disappear,

FIGURE 2

The relative growth of various organs of an apple tree. *FB* = full bloom; *HARV* = date of fruit harvest.

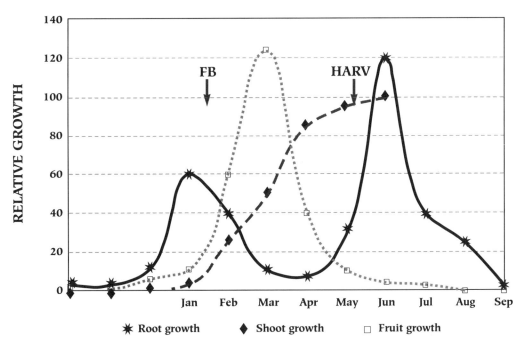

and the epidermal cells are sloughed off. Cracks and fissures along cell walls may become apparent. Within 30 to 60 days of forming, roots will start to change color from a white to tan or brown color as the lateral thickening occurs.

The root system of a fruit tree is very dynamic. Roots grow, die, and decompose continuously. Estimates have been made that anywhere from 25 to 50% of the total mass of a tree fruit root system turns over each year. Old roots die, wither, and decay while new roots appear. Roots are heterotropic: they do not produce their own carbon supplies for respiration but rather rely on carbohydrates translocated from photosynthetically active leaves via the phloem.

Conversely, leaves have no ability to absorb mineral nutrients or water from the atmosphere and must rely on roots as their sole source of nutrient elements and water, which moves upward through the plant in the conductive tissue, xylem.

ROOT DISTRIBUTION

The distribution of roots in the soil is varied, depending upon the soil profile and the orchard system. Most studies indicate that the majority of tree fruit roots are found in the top 25 to 50 centimeters of the soil profile. However, in light, gravelly, or rocky soils, tree fruit roots may penetrate the profile several meters deep. It has been reported that it is the oxygen concentration of the soil profile, in combination with adequate moisture, which controls the depth to which roots will grow. In heavy soils with poor gas exchange, roots may be found closer to the soil surface due to the sufficient oxygen concentrations there.

Lighter soils may have better oxygen content and exchange and allow deeper root growth. Frequent flooding of soils tends to result in root development closer to the soil surface, but in soils with good percolation or available water tables a few meters below the surface, there may be tree fruit roots penetrating to greater depths.

Because of the necessity of water, oxygen, and nutrients for tree fruit root growth, they are not exceptionally good competitors with grass and weed roots. Several scientists have reported that there may be extensive surface proliferation and branching of tree fruit roots in the weed-free tree-dripline strip. However, when the tree roots confront the drive-row grass strip, roots will become less dense, branch less, and tend to penetrate deeper into the soil, thus avoiding extensive interplant competition.

Roots will move into moist and nutrient-rich mulches placed upon the soil surface below a tree. Flooding, heavy soils, and hot soils may increase the amount of root suckers or aerial shoots arising directly from the root system. Suckering is a genetic trait of some rootstocks, and rootstock breeders are conscientiously looking to avoid this trait.

WATER UPTAKE BY ROOTS

Water from the soil can move into the plant in several ways. It can move along the cell walls and membranes in the developing/growing young roots. This is called apoplastic movement of water. The water moves along the cell walls until it enters the xylem and the pull of the transpirational stream. Water can move due to osmotic forces as well. In the root hairs and epidermal cells, the concentration of ions and compounds such as sugars "attracts" water from the soil profile. Water moves across the semipermeable membrane from the soil, where there is a lower concentration of dissolved solutes, into the cell, where there is a higher concentration of solutes.

Then, this water moves from cell to cell in much the same manner and finally moves into the xylem and the transpirational stream. The movement of water into cells and from cell to cell is called symplastic movement. In old roots, more water moves by mass flow and apoplastic means as water flows into the fissures and cracks on the root surface, and then, due to the adhesive attractiveness between water molecules and the cell wall surface, it binds to the cell wall. The cohesive strength of water molecule to water molecule bonds pulls the water into the transpirational stream.

The differences in rootstock water relations and their effects on tree growth has not been thoroughly studied. However, practical experience has filled in some of the knowledge gaps. Differences in the efficiency of uptake of water due to rootstock differences is unclear. Some rootstocks tend to have reduced resistance to the movement of water once inside the root, but this does not necessarily relate to improvements in water extraction from the soil.

Typically, rootstocks that have wide spreading roots which tend to grow downward have a wider soil area from which to extract water and therefore appear to be more drought tolerant. Other rootstocks tend to be relatively confined in their soil exploration and have many fine "feeder" roots which are important in water uptake. These root systems are often thought to be drought prone; not because they are any more sensitive to drought, but because they are so efficient at extracting water from their confined root zone.

Some generalizations may be made at this point that many dwarfing apple rootstocks, such as M.9, B.9, M.27, P.22, P.16, P.2, and Mark, appear to be more drought sensitive. This reputation may be derived from the fact that the root systems of these stocks are relatively confined, and they efficiently remove water from that root zone. Even though there may be moisture in the tractor drive row, the tree row soil is dry.

Thus, these stocks appear to be sensitive to droughts that orchardists don't expect. Actually, several of the stocks have been shown to tolerate and physiologically adjust to dry soil and move water through their xylem with low resistance; they are not technically drought-sensitive but rather more susceptible to mismanagement of orchard soil moisture.

Conversely, very vigorous rootstocks

which are widely spreading and deeply penetrating, such as M.7, and M.111 apple rootstocks, tend to be considered more drought tolerant. In actuality, trees which have more spreading root systems can "harvest" water from a wider area of the orchard soil profile; they can "avoid" small droughts. Thus, in high density orchards with size-controlling rootstocks, water management is critical because drought conditions can occur between irrigations in the tree row. Using older, low density systems with vigorous rootstocks may lessen the intensity of soil moisture management requirements.

NUTRIENT UPTAKE BY ROOTS

Nutrients move into roots by two general mechanisms; passive uptake and active uptake. Passive uptake does not require any expenditure of energy from the root cells. The nutrients dissolved in the soil water will move with the soil water by mass flow, typically apoplastically. Some nutrient ions may move directly into root cells by diffusion because the concentration of the nutrient ion in the soil water is greater than in the cell sap.

Active uptake requires energy for the absorption of nutrient ions (see Figure 3). The energy is provided by respiration. Roots have high respiration rates breaking down the carbohydrates produced by leaves and transported to the roots via the conductive phloem tissues. Active uptake can occur either with the facilitation of carrier proteins or by energy and/or ion balance pumping mechanisms. In the membranes of root cell walls are specialized proteins which can attract and bind specific nutrient ions.

When activated, the carrier proteins in the membranes bind a specific nutrient ion on the outside of the cell, then rotate and release the nutrient ion on the inside of the cell. It has also been demonstrated that ions may be pumped outside the cell to create differences in energy balance across the cell membrane.

Thus, nutrient ions will move across the cell membranae to balance the energy differential. In the case of active nutrient uptake, leaves must be respirationally active. There must be carbohydrates produced in leaves from photosynthesis transported to the roots for their degradation via respiration. Any factor (e.g., shade, temperature, insect or disease damage, etc.) which reduces foliar photosynthesis may reduce active uptake. Because respiration requires oxygen, respiration is reduced in flooded soils, as is the active uptake of the nutrients.

Rootstock effects on the scion

TREE SIZE AND SHOOT EXTENSION

The genetic growth control provided by rootstocks is important to orchardists. It is this characteristic, especially when combined with characteristics which confer precocity to the scion cultivar of the tree, which has allowed the development of modern high density orchards. Rootstocks can cause variation in tree size ranging from mature trees which are only 1 to 1.5 meters tall to trees that are 10 meters tall (*see Figure 4*). Although a number of rootstocks have been identified with size-controlling characteristics, and some of the genetic basis of this character is understood, the mechanism which confers size control of the scion is not clear.

The effect of rootstock on shoot growth may be a factor relating to the ultimate tree size. It has been reported that rootstocks can cause variation in limb angle of the scion cultivar (*see Figure 5*). Presumably, limbs which are more horizontal than vertical may have different growth characteristics due to apical dominance and gravimorphic effects (*see Chapter 6*). More horizon-

---

FIGURE 3

This illustrates a schematic representation of active uptake of nutrients from the rhizosphere soil water solution into root cells. Active uptake requires energy from respiration to active carrier proteins and/or to pump protons across the membrane to balance ion concentrations and energy. XX = nutrient ion.

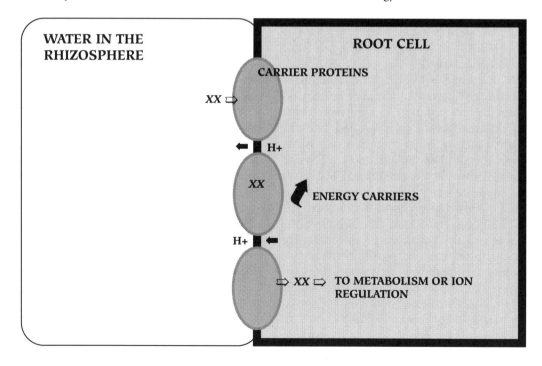

tal, or angled, limbs may grow slower, have more lateral branching and produce more fruit compared to vertical limbs.

Many observers have reported that shoot length varies with rootstock. The question then arises, is the difference in shoot length due to differences in the rate of growth (cm/day) or the duration of growth (number of days)? In a four-season study of ten rootstocks with Delicious as the scion cultivar, several conclusions were drawn (see Figures 4, 6, 7).

The peak growth rate of shoots on all rootstocks occurred two to four weeks after bloom in each season after, which the shoot growth rate decreased (see Figures 6 and 7). There were some differences in maximum growth rates among rootstocks; very size-controlling stocks such as P.22 and M.27 had lower maximum growth rates than many other stocks, including B.9, M.26, C.6, M.7, and M.4, which all had similar maximum growth rates. Most notably, however, was when extension growth of the various stocks stopped. Shoots on very dwarf-ing stocks (P.22, P.16, M.27) terminated in 40 to 60 days after bloom, intermediate size stocks (B.9, M.26, C.6) terminated 50 to 70 days after bloom, while vigorous stocks (M.7, M.4, and seedling) continued growth for 100 to 120 days.

The duration of shoot growth was better correlated to final shoot length than the maximum growth rate. Shoot length was also correlated to the total number of nodes or potential bud sites on the shoots (see Figure 8); in other words, shoots that grew longer during the season had more nodes, more leaves and total leaf area, and more buds which could form spurs in subsequent years. When two-year-old shoot segments on these trees were evaluated, the longer shoots had a greater number of lateral buds which developed into spurs and lateral shoots.

However, the percentage of the spurs which developed fruit buds was inversely correlated to the duration of growth; shoots that continued to grow longer into the season had a lower percentage of buds form

FIGURE 4

Apple rootstocks influence tree height and pruning time. As tree height exceeds 2.75 to 3.0 m, pruning time per tree increases dramatically.

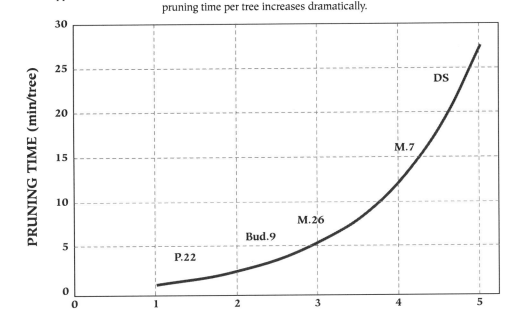

fruiting spurs. Total shoot length as affected by the rootstocks, was closely correlated to trunk diameter and cross-sectional area—an indicator of the total vegetative growth increment of the canopy. But, the longer the shoots grew during the season, the lower the tree's yield efficiency (kg fruit per square cm of trunk).

FIGURE 5

Rootstocks have been shown to affect the angle of limbs of the scion cultivar. In this study, rootstocks resulted in three distinct angles of scaffold limb formation from the main axis of the tree (after Warner, 1991).

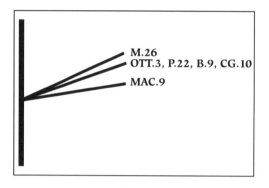

This indicates that rootstocks that induce shoots to continue growth for longer periods of time during the season tend to partition more of the photosynthetic carbohydrates to vegetative growth, compared to size-controlling rootstocks, which terminate growth and partition carbohydrates into fruit growth. Therefore, it is observed that size-controlling rootstocks affect the yield efficiency of the tree and the patterns of partitioning carbon.

OTHER ROOTSTOCK EFFECTS

Rootstocks also affect tree growth and productivity in other ways. Rootstocks can affect the time of bud break and bloom either causing early bud break and bloom or some slight delays in bloom. Following that pattern, rootstocks can affect the date of fruit maturity and leaf fall of the tree. Rootstocks, through their effect on shoot growth and canopy density, can cause differences in light distribution within trees and thus fruit quality (red color and soluble solids content).

Some rootstocks have better or worse

FIGURE 6

The effect of rootstock on shoot growth rate and duration. Each line represents the average of several stocks—dwarfing rootstocks: P.22, P.2, P.16; semi-dwarfing: B.9, M.26, C.6; vigorous stocks: P.1, M.7, M.4 seedling.

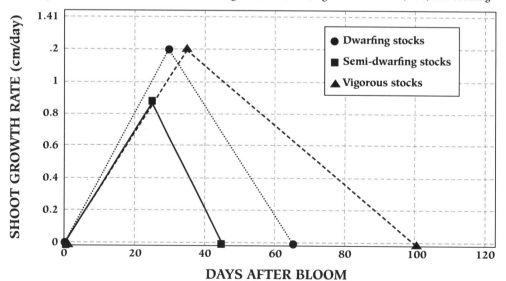

abilities to absorb and transport some cations such as calcium (Ca), magnesium (Mg) , and boron (B). Thus, rootstocks directly affect fruit quality by inducing susceptibility to corkspot or foliar Mg deficiency and reduced growth. It has been reported that fruit from Mark rootstock tend to have higher Ca content and therefore be firmer at harvest and after short storage periods.

Rootstocks can differ in winter hardiness and thereby affect the survivability of the tree. Reports have indicated that rootstocks potentially have a winter chill requirement and may vary in this requirement among various genotypes. This may relate to both their winter hardiness and the impact on time of bud break and bloom.

Rootstocks have indirect effects on management costs in the orchard. It has been shown that trees on vigorous rootstock which grow taller than 2.5 to 3.0 meters require longer to prune than smaller trees, due to the need to use ladders *(see Figure 4)*. On a whole orchard basis, small trees planted in high densities not only require less pruning time per tree but also less pruning time per acre.

In our studies, we have observed that rootstocks which cause a tree size that would be planted between 500 and 800 trees per acre require less pruning time than tree sizes which would be planted at 250 to 300 trees per acre *(see Figure 9)*. At extremely high densities (>1500 trees/acre), pruning time increases. When pruning time was evaluated as minutes of pruning per bushel of fruit produced, trees with high yield efficiencies (kg fruit/trunk cross-sectional area) have lower pruning requirements per bushel. This makes intuitive sense; vigorous trees require more pruning and produce relatively less fruit per increment of vegetative growth. When the effect of pruning on yield is considered (pruning tends to reduce yield by stimulating vegetative growth and inhibiting flower formation, *see Chapter 6*), the more a tree requires pruning, the more it must be pruned and the less fruit it will produce. It has been said "pruning begat pruning."

FIGURE 7

Rootstocks have little effect on the date of maximum growth rate but significantly affect the date of termination of shoot growth (data are means of shoot growth rates, 1991-1993).

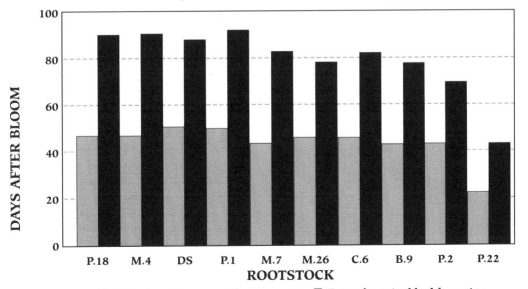

MODELS OF GROWTH CONTROL

The cause of rootstock effects has been theorized but not well proven. Several hypotheses about the growth control include nutrient transport limitation models, hormone transport inhibition models, hormone feedback models, and combinations of all these models *(see Figure 10)*.

Several scientists have shown, with varying degrees of success, that rootstocks vary in their uptake of nutrients and the transport of the nutrients across graft or bud unions. However, reports of the effect of rootstock on foliar nutrient content over long periods have demonstrated that although there are differences in nutrient content among rootstock genotypes, they are relatively small compared to seasonal effects. In fact, many of the differences can be accounted for due to the variation in crop load and crop-to-leaf area ratios also induced by the rootstocks. No good correlation between foliar nutrient content of any essential element or combination of elements to tree size and growth rates has been found.

Hormone models of growth control are based upon the interrelation of auxins and cytokinins. As mentioned in early chapters, auxins are produced in shoot tips and developing leaves. These move downward through the phloem in some part in response to gravity. Auxins "active site" where they incite a growth response is in root tips.

To simply state the theory, auxin moving from shoot tips into roots would stimulate root growth and development. With the increased root growth and development, there would be a concurrent increase in the absorption and utilization of water and nutrients, thus stimulating aerial growth. The developing and rapidly growing roots would produce the hormone cytokinins, which would move to leaves and shoot tips, stimu-

---

FIGURE 8

Rootstock influences both the number of spurs formed on shoots and the likelihood that those spurs develop flower buds and fruit. The longer shoots grew during the season, the more lateral buds developed, but fewer of the buds developed flowers.

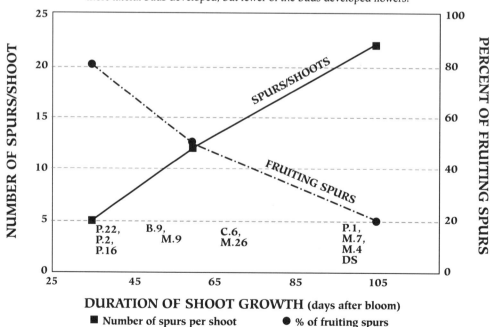

DURATION OF SHOOT GROWTH (days after bloom)

■ Number of spurs per shoot   ● % of fruiting spurs

FIGURE 9

Rootstocks affect tree size and, therefore, the tree density (trees per acre). Pruning time per acre was related to tree planting density, with trees planted at 500 to 900 trees per acre having the least pruning requirement.

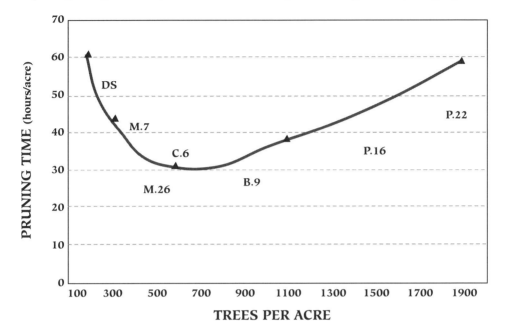

FIGURE 10

An integrative or holistic schematic model showing promotive and feedback interaction between the root system and the canopy due to hormone and/or assimilate concentrations. Aux = auxin; GA = gibberellin; Cyk = cytokinins; CHO = carbohydrates (after Saure, 1991).

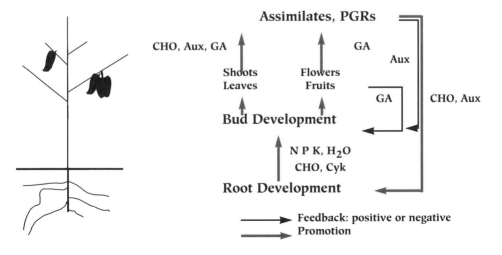

opment and continuing the cycle.

It is thought that size-controlling rootstocks would work by either preventing the downward movement of auxin into the roots, binding auxin in the root so that it is not metabolically active, or that the root meristems do not "recognize" the auxins or they are metabolized and do not stimulate

---

FIGURE 11

The effect of cultivar and growing habit on shoot and root growth during one season.

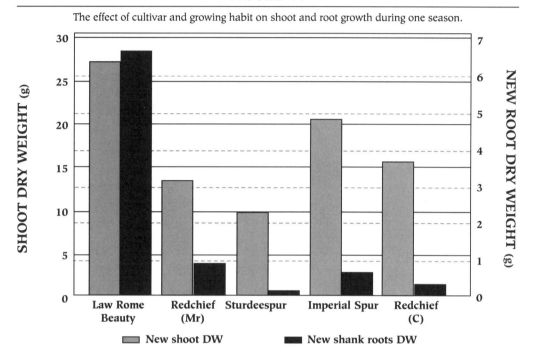

■ New shoot DW   ■ New shank roots DW

FIGURE 12

Scion cultivar growth habit affects the growth of both the scion and the rootstock; data represent means of Delicious, Golden Delicious, and Rome Beauty cultivars with spur and non-spur types of each.

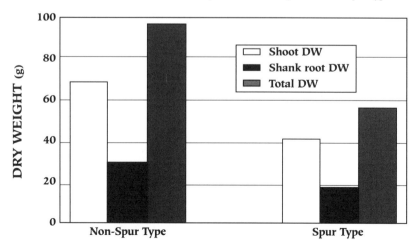

growth. Other theories suggest that dwarfing rootstocks do not produce high quantities of cytokinins to be translocated to the aerial portion of the tree and therefore do not increase shoot growth and canopy development. Although these are reasonable models and do explain some observations of growth, the evidence is conflicting, confounded and small.

Scion effects on rootstocks

Many of the rootstock effects on the scion are readily seen even by the casual observer. However, remembering that fruit trees are compound genetic systems (a combination of a scion and rootstock genotype which are different), there are also scion effects on the rootstock. Because the roots are underground, these effects are often forgotten.

Both apple and peach trees have different growth morphology types, ranging from spur-type trees with strong apical dominance to weeping, terminal bearing trees (*see Chapter 6*). Because of these characters and inherent differences in scion vigor and tree size, the scion has a profound effect on the root growth (*see Figure 11*). Several

studies have indicated that compact tree scions and spur-type scions reduce new root development and total weight and length of the roots (*see Figure 12*).

When these scion cultivars are propa-

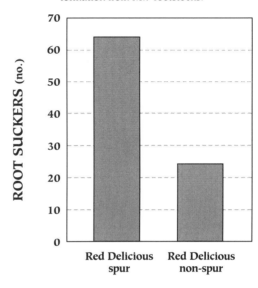

FIGURE 14

The effect of tree growth habit on root sucker formation from M.7 rootstocks.

FIGURE 13

The effect of cultivar on shank burr knot formation and shank rooting.
ns = non-spur type growth habit; s = spur type growth habit.

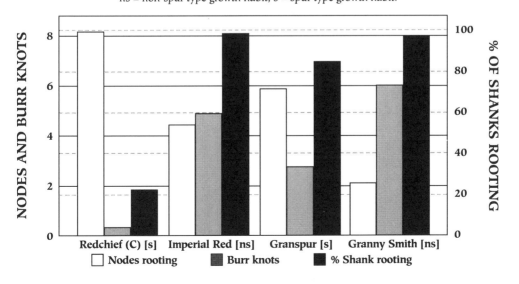

gated onto rootstocks which have weak root systems or limited root growth as a root characteristic, the effects become additive. In the orchard, this can be seen as trees that have poor anchorage and lean or fall. The scion cultivar also influences the burr knots which can form on the exposed shank of the rootstock *(see Figure 13)*. Rootstocks vary in their natural propensity to form root suckers. We have observed that spur-type scions tend to produce trees with a greater number of root suckers per tree than related scion cultivars which are non-spur types *(see Figure 14)*.

Other effects of the scion on the rootstock have not been as well studied or defined. It may be theorized that scion cultivars could differ in the ability to move water through their xylem (increased or decreased conductive resistance) or may differ in leaf transpiration (lose more or less water). This may have profound effects on root growth, as the root system either may not be able to take up sufficient water to meet the demands of the scion or the water moves so slowly through the system that root growth and development may subsequently be limited.

Some scion cultivars have genetic characteristics for calcium and/or magnesium metabolism problems. Thus, even though a rootstock may take up "sufficient" quantities of these ions, physiological disorders such as cork spot or leaf necrosis may occur regardless of the stock.

Orchard management and shoot-root interactions

It has been proposed that the aerial portion and root portion of a fruit tree grow in a *functional equilibrium* to each other. In other words, the growth of shoots and roots is proportional. The ratio of shoots to roots, either in dry weight or surface area (root to leaf area) is variable, depending upon the genetics of the scion and root cultivar. The precept of the equilibrium theory is that the growth of either shoots or roots is controlled by the growth of the other. Because of this interaction, affecting one component of the equilibrium will have a counterbalancing effect on the other *(see Figure 10)*.

Pruning the aerial portion of the tree reduces root growth. Numerous studies have indicated this point. Pruning during the dormant season tends to have less effect on root growth than pruning during the growing phase of the season. However, the response to pruning is apparent with the equilibrium concept. After pruning, root growth stops but there is a vegetative response—more shoot growth near the pruning cut—as the plant works to reestablish its equilibrium. After pruning, carbohydrates are allocated to new shoot growth and less to root growth.

Root pruning disrupts the root-shoot balance as well. After root pruning, shoot growth is reduced as root growth occurs, reestablishing the balance. Cropping is known to reduce the vegetative growth of the tree. Heavy crops can also reduce root growth. Other factors which affect growth of the top of the tree can minimize root growth. Damage to leaves by insects or disease reduces root growth and activity. Pest control of the aerial portion of the tree should be viewed holistically, as the effects of infections and infestations can be wider spread than visually apparent. Likewise, poor root growth conditions (e.g., compacted soils, flooded soils, droughts, lack of mineral nutrition, soil-borne pests, etc.) will also limit the growth and productive potential of the aerial portion of the tree.

In conclusion, roots are an important organ and structure of the tree. They provide anchorage and support, the uptake of nutrients and water, and affect the growth and productivity of the aerial portion of the tree. Roots have significant regulatory effects on the scion but conversely, the scion also affects regulation of root growth. The interaction of the roots and shoots should be viewed in a holistic sense when orchard management decisions are made.

Literature cited and additional reading

Andrews, P. and C.R. Rom, "Early performance of four apple cultivars, supported or free-standing on Mark rootstock," *Frt. Var. J.* 47 (1993): 4:198.

Fallahi, E., "Root physiology, development and mineral uptake," in: *Tree Fruit Nutrition, 19-30,* edited by B. Peterson and R. Stevens, Yakima, WA: Good Fruit Grower, 1994.

Faust, M., *Physiology of Temperate Zone Fruit Trees,* NY: John Wiley & Sons, 1989.

Ferree, D.C., S.C. Myers, C.R. Rom, and B.H. Taylor, "Physiological aspects of summer pruning," *Acta Hort.* 146 (1983): 243-252.

Flore, J., "Stone fruit," in: *Environmental Physiology of Fruit Crops,* edited by B. Schaffer and P.C. Anderson, 233-270, Boca Raton, FL: CRC Press, 1994.

Flore, J.A. and A.N. Lakso,, "Environmental and physiological regulation of photosynthesis in fruit crops," *Hort. Rev.* 11 (1989): 111.

Geisler, D. and D.C. Ferree, "Response of plants to root pruning," *Hort. Rev.* 6 (1984): 155-188.

Jones, H.G., *Plants and Microclimate.* Cambridge, MA: Cambridge Press, 1992.

Lakso, A.N. 1994. "Apple," *Environmental Physiology of Fruit Crops,* edited by B. Schaffer and P.C. Anderson, 3-42, Boca Raton, FL: CRC Press, 1994.

Lockhard, R.G. and G.W. Schnieder, "Stock and scion growth relationship and the dwarfing mechanisms in apple," *Hort. Rev.* 3 (1981): 315-375.

Muromtsev, I.A., "Active parts of roots systems of fruit plants," 1969, Moscow, Russia: Kolos Publishers, [translated from Russian, USDA, 1984].

NC-140 (9 authors in alphabetical order including C.R. Rom), "Abnormalities in 'Starkspur Supreme Delicious' on nine rootstocks in the 1980-81 NC-140 cooperative planting," *Frt. Var. Jrl.* 45(4) (1991): 213-219.

Rom, C.R., "Bud development and vigor in fruit trees, in: *Flowering and Pollination Shortcourse,* edited by B. Peterson, WSU Extension Publication, Pullman, WA, 1987.

Rom, C.R., "Pomology 101: Basics of fruit tree training," *Compact Fruit Tree* 26 (1993): 35-45.

Rom, C.R., "Fruit tree growth and development," *Tree Fruit Nutrition,* edited by B. Peterson and R. Stevens, 1-18, *Yakima, WA:* Good Fruit Grower, 1994.

Rom, C.R., "Balancing growth and cropping: Which comes first, the canopy of the crop," *Compact Fruit Tree* 27 (1994): 53-59.

Rom, C.R., R.A. Allen, and R.C. Rom, "Performance of the 1984 NC-140 apple rootstock trial in Arkansas: Aspects of tree nutrition," *Compact Fruit Tree* 28 (1995): 60-67.

Rom, C.R., R.C. Rom, W.R. Autio, D.C. Elfving, and R.A. Cline, "Foliar nutrient content of 'Starkspur Supreme Delicious' on nine clonal apple rootstocks," *Frt. Var. Jrl.* 45(4) (1991): 252-263.

Rom, C.R., R.C. Rom, W. Autio, D.C. Elfving, and R.A. Cline, "Rootstock effects on foliar nutrient content of 'Starkspur Supreme' in the NC-140 rootstock trial," *Compact Fruit Tree* 24 (1991).

Sauer, M., "Inferences of pruning with endogenous growth control," *Acta Hort.* 322 (1992): 241-248.

Swietlik, D. And M. Faust, "Foliar nutrition of fruit crops," *Hort Rev.* 4 (1984): 287-338.

Westwood, M.N., *Temperate Zone Pomology; Physiology and Culture* (3rd edition), Portland, OR: Timber Press, 1993.

6 Coordination of Vegetative and Reproductive Growth: Root Restriction, Branch Manipulation, and Pruning

Stephen C. Myers
Head, Department of Horticulture
University of Arkansas
Fayetteville, Arkansas

Amy T. Savelle
Department of Horticulture
University of Georgia
Athens, Georgia

In a fruiting plant, such as apple or peach, the final product represents a balance between the growth of a vegetative structure and associated fruiting. The production of fruit is tied to management practices which affect the way in which resources, such as carbohydrates, water, and hormones, are distributed throughout the plant. Economics force us to consider how and to what degree those resources need to be allocated toward vegetative or reproductive growth, both in the current season and in the long term.

The general objective of orchard management is to maximize fruit production while minimizing growth of unproductive wood. Within any scion/rootstock combination, there is a genetically-regulated balance between vegetative and reproductive growth. This balance is subject to modification by environmental conditions. In addition, anything which we do physically to alter the balance will affect the pattern of growth and development.

The goal for any orchard planting is to make a profit. Management practices promote early production of marketable fruit and must be designed to maximize production in a cost-effective manner throughout the life of the orchard. Regardless of cultural and management practices, there are certain basic principles of training and pruning that are common to any orchard planting (Myers, 1988; Rom, 1989; Tustin, 1991; Forshey et al., 1992), based on certain biological principles of growth and fruiting.

With a clear understanding of basic principles, the orchardist is in a better position to understand the reason for and ultimate result of a given training or pruning practice.

The purpose of this chapter is to review a number of methods used to manage resource allocation in the plant. However, it is only by understanding the basic physiological processes involved in growth and development that we can devise and refine cultural practices which effectively regulate the growth and development of roots and shoots.

Apical dominance and growth

Simply put, potential productivity of a tree is a function of the total number of buds that develop and percentage of those buds that develop flowers (Luckwill, 1978). In large part, this pattern of growth and flowering is regulated by a phenomenon called apical dominance. In effect, apical dominance controls the growth rate and length of the terminal shoot. Actively-growing apical or terminal regions of the shoot dominate growth and thereby influence development of lateral buds or shoots below the dominant regions. Apical dominance influences the number of shoot-forming lateral buds, the length of lateral shoots, and the angle at which shoots develop relative to the limb (Stebbins, 1980). Conditions of strong apical dominance favor vegetative growth at the expense of flower bud production. The intensity of apical dominance varies from one plant species to another, as well as between cultivars within a given species.

Shoot orientation effect on apical dominance

The orientation of a limb or shoot along the main branch has a major influence on apical dominance. The growth physiology of a limb is related to its natural orientation. Total shoot growth is greatest in the terminal section of limbs of apple and is greater in vertically-oriented limbs (Myers and Ferree, 1986) *(see Figure 1)*.

As limb orientation is shifted toward horizontal, the number of shoots which develop along that limb increases, while the average shoot length decreases (Myers and Ferree, 1983) *(see Figures 2 and 3)*. In vertical shoots, vigorous shoot growth occurs near the terminal bud, with fewer lateral shoots or spurs occurring with increasing distance from the apex. At orientations of

30 to 60 degrees from vertical, terminal and lateral growth near the apex is reduced, while number and length of laterals further from the apex is increased (Stebbins, 1980).

When limbs or shoots are bent to horizontal, below horizontal, or arched and bowed down, apical dominance is lost for a time. Lateral buds along the upper surface of the limb or highest part of the bow will develop, possibly becoming vigorous, upright watersprouts. As they develop, watersprouts re-establish strong apical dominance and vegetative growth typical of vertical shoots.

Balancing vegetative growth and flower bud production is the basis for limb spreading or positioning. Response varies with cultivar, rootstock, tree age, degree of spreading, and time of spreading. If both cultivar and rootstock are precocious, extreme limb spreading may result in excessive flower bud production and insufficient shoot growth, whereas, with more vigorous cultivars, wide limb spreading can result in severe loss of flowers due to production of watersprouts.

Time of spreading or positioning also affects response. Spreading in late season after growth has terminated will have little effect on vegetative growth during that season (Rom, 1989).

Conversely, extreme spreading in the dormant season before growth begins can

FIGURE 1

Natural limb orientation on shoot growth of Delicious/M.9 (Myers and Ferree, 1986).

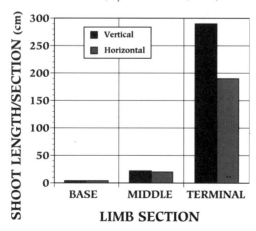

FIGURE 2

Orientation affects shoot number of young apple trees (Myers and Ferree, 1983).

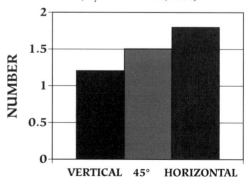

result in weak terminal shoot growth and excessive watersprout development. Cultivars vary in response to limb orientations. For example, spur-type Delicious is prone to watersprout development when scaffolds are oriented more than 60 degrees from vertical, whereas well-branched cultivars such as Golden Delicious are not.

Growth regulators

Apical dominance results from the interaction of a number of plant hormones, more correctly termed growth regulators. These growth regulators include auxin, cytokinin, gibberellic acid, and abscisic acid. Actively-growing shoots and newly-expanding leaves produce auxin, which moves downward in the shoot with gravity (toward the earth's center). Auxin may work by moving down the shoot and actively inhibiting development of lateral buds. It may direct nutrients, growth regulators, photosynthates, and other resources to the actively-growing shoot tip at the expense of other shoots and buds.

Cytokinins are produced in the roots and move in the opposite direction.

Abscisic acid is found primarily in inactive lateral buds and acts as a growth inhibitor. The complete role of growth regulators in apical dominance is not known. However, evidence suggests growth regula-

tors interact with environmental and physiological signals, forming various combinations which, in turn, direct a given pattern of apical dominance.

Apical dominance can also be modified by the application of growth regulators. For example, foliar application of benzyladenine, a cytokinin, to some apple cultivars during the spring when terminal shoots are approximately five centimeters in length will cause lateral buds to break and increase the total number of lateral shoots that develop (Myers, unpublished) *(see Figure 4)*.

In apple, the response is greatest in the one-year-old limb section. Application of benzyladenine and gibberellic acid caused a 40 to 60% increase in the number of laterals which developed in each limb section.

General response to pruning

Pruning is the most commonly used method to alter apical dominance, and there are a number of general responses. Pruning changes the balance between the above-ground part of the tree (shoots, buds, and leaves) and the below ground part (roots), as well as reducing the overall amount of dry matter accumulation (Myers and Ferree, 1983) *(see Figure 5)*.

When pruning shoots alters this propor-

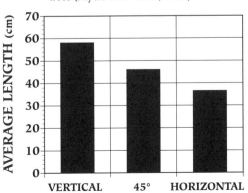

FIGURE 3

Orientation affects shoot length of young apple trees (Myers and Ferree, 1983).

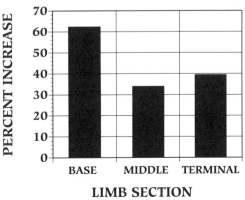

FIGURE 4

BA+GA$_{4+7}$ increases lateral growth of Delicious (percent increase over untreated limb) (Myers, unpublished).

tion, the tree responds with vegetative regrowth until the balance is re-established. Regrowth is stimulated in close proximity to the cuts. The amount of regrowth that follows pruning is in direct proportion to the severity of pruning (Forshey, 1986). Pruning removes the apical growing points which normally dominate growth and inhibit lower buds.

Cytokinins and other resources accumulate in these buds immediately below the pruning cut. One or two of the more apical shoots which develop re-establish apical dominance and control growth of lower shoots. With fewer growing points on the tree supported by the same root system, a greater relative supply of growth regulators, nutrients, and other resources is available to the remaining growing points.

Both number and length of lateral shoots which develop following pruning are relative to timing, severity, and age of wood pruned. If a current season's shoot of apple is pruned during the growing season, lateral shoots are stimulated, whereas normally a single, unbranched shoot would develop during a single season. On older wood, pruning decreases the number of lateral shoots but increases the average shoot length. As pruning severity increases, shoot number decreases and average shoot length increases, due to the decrease in the total number of growing points, the removal of apical buds which produce auxin, and the temporary loss of apical dominance (Barden et al., 1989) *(see Figure 6)*.

The tree's response to severe pruning favors strong vegetative growth at the expense of flower bud formation (Marshall, 1931) *(also see Figure 7)*. As pruning severity increases, flower bud production decreases proportionally. Pruning young trees will delay the onset and amount of early fruit production. Excessive pruning in bearing trees can result in excessive vegetative vigor, a reduction in spur and flower development, and a decrease in yield.

Although localized invigoration follows

FIGURE 5

Pruning decreases dry weight of young apple trees (Myers and Ferree, 1983).

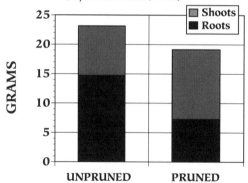

FIGURE 6

Pruning severity on growth of Delicious (Barden, DelValle, and Myers, 1989).

| Pruning severity | Shoot growth/limb | | |
	Shoot number	Average length (cm)	Total growth (cm)
0	20.4	19.6	402
1	16.0	23.6	361
2	14.9	24.8	362
3	8.4	29.6	244

FIGURE 7

Pruning severity on flower clusters of Delicious (Barden, DelValle, and Myers, 1989).

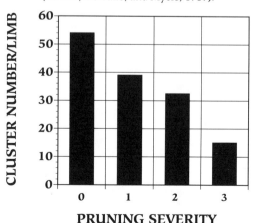

pruning, the net effect of pruning is that total growth is reduced (Forshey, 1986). Growth regulators, such as auxin, are normally moved from apical shoots to the root system to encourage root development. Pruning removes these apical shoots, and, as a result, decreases root development. With reduced root development, cytokinin production is decreased.

In addition, since total leaf area is reduced by pruning, fewer carbohydrates are produced during photosynthesis. These carbohydrates are moved to storage areas of the tree, such as the root system. With a reduction in carbohydrate production, root growth is reduced.

The vegetative growth which occurs following pruning creates a strong demand or "sink" for energy. Growth regulators, photosynthates, and other resources are diverted to shoot growth at the expense of other parts of the tree. As a result, the re-establishment of the balance within the tree results from an increase in shoot development and a slowdown in root development. Ultimately, pruning reduces the total dry matter production of the tree. As such, pruning remains one of the primary methods of tree size control in tree fruit production.

Types of pruning cuts

There are two basic types of pruning cuts: heading and thinning. Each results in different growth response and has specific uses.

Heading removes the terminal portion of shoots or limbs. By removing apical dominance, heading stimulates growth near the cut. Heading is the most invigorating type of pruning cut, and the shoot or shoots which develop immediately below the cut re-establish apical dominance.

Heading cuts are the most disruptive to the natural growth and form of trees, although they are useful to induce branching at specific points, such as in establishing scaffolds. In production systems where early fruit production is critical for economic return, use of heading cuts should be kept to a minimum (Barden et al., 1989; Rom, 1989).

Thinning, on the other hand, removes an entire shoot or limb to its point of origin from a main branch or limb. Thinning may also include the removal of a shoot back to a lateral shoot or spur. With thinning cuts, some terminal shoots are left intact, apical dominance remains, and the pruning stimulation is more evenly distributed among remaining shoots. New growth is dominated by the undisturbed shoot tips, while lateral bud development follows more natural patterns for that species or cultivar.

Thinning cuts are generally the least invigorating and provide a more natural growth form for trees. Important in maintenance pruning, thinning cuts are used to shorten limbs, improve light penetration into tree canopies, and direct the growth of shoots or limbs. Studies show that the use of heading cuts results in the development of high numbers of shoots and reduction in fruit number; whereas, use of thinning cuts increases fruit number and controls vegetative growth (Forshey, 1988) *(see Figure 8)*.

One misused and undesirable type of thinning cut is the bench cut, where an upright limb is pruned to a horizontal or flat limb (Myers, 1988). Watersprouts develop at the "bench" area, especially if the cut is large, since apical dominance is absent.

FIGURE 8

Pruning on shoot growth and fruiting of McIntosh/MM.106 (Forshey, 1988).

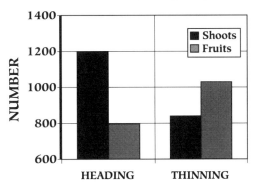

Bench cuts are structurally weak and subject to sunburn and winter injury. Ideally, scaffolds should be trained as closely as possible to the desired scaffold orientation for a given species or cultivar to minimize the need for severe cuts later.

Growth and fruiting habit

As a result of differences in apical dominance, there is a wide variation in both growth and fruiting habit between species and between cultivars within species. Growth habit refers to the characteristic growth pattern of the tree (Stebbins, 1980). Canopy shape is determined by how upright or spreading a given tree grows. Crotch angles are characterized as narrow to wide and limbs as poorly to heavily branched. Growth habit of apple cultivars can be characterized into one of four basic types (Lespinasse, 1981) *(see Figure 9)*.

Fruiting habit includes the overall pattern of fruiting, relationship of shoot length to flower production, age of shoots or spurs that fruit, and the location of the fruiting zone within the tree canopy (Stebbins, 1980). Peach fruit on one-year-old wood from flower buds formed the previous season. Thus, substantial new growth is required annually for good cropping.

Apple typically follow a different fruiting pattern. Shoots generally develop unbranched the first year. In the second year, some of the lateral buds along the previous season's terminal develop into spurs or shoots. These may remain vegetative or can initiate flower buds. Fruit are then typically borne in the third season, although there are exceptions to this pattern in apple.

Some cultivars will produce both lateral and terminal flowers on one-year-old shoots. Flowers on this type of wood are smaller, bloom later in the season, exhibit poor set, and develop smaller, poorer quali-

FIGURE 9

The four classes of growth habit of apple trees (Lespinasse, 1981).

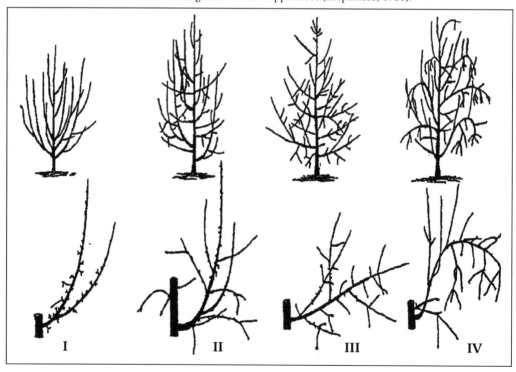

I   II   III   IV

ty fruit than flowers on two-year-old wood. The two-year-old limb section of apple is considered to be the most productive section because of lateral shoot and spur development which determine flower and fruit production (Feucht, 1968).

Generally, flower quality and quantity decrease as wood ages. This trend is most rapid in peach and slowest in sweet cherry.

Rootstock can have significant influence on apical dominance and, as a result, pattern of shoot growth and fruit production. For example, in apple, as size control of a rootstock increases, terminal shoot growth and total shoot growth tend to decrease. The decrease in growth with more size-controlling rootstocks occurs to the benefit of fruit production.

Root restriction and root pruning

The vast majority of research aimed at managing tree growth has focused on either genetic means or on cultural practices directed at the aboveground portions of the tree. However, managing the growth of the root system is also possible through various techniques (Ferree et al., 1992).

Root pruning and root restriction inhibit the normal development of a root system and cause a reduction in shoot growth, but are quite different in the manner the growth reductions are achieved. With root pruning, the root system will regenerate, forming a denser root system with many new root tips. Root restriction limits the root system to a confined space, also resulting in a denser system, but new root growth is limited.

Thus, root restriction defines the soil volume available to the root system for moisture and nutrient uptake, whereas a root-pruned tree can regenerate new roots out into an undefined volume of soil.

The effectiveness of root pruning is a function of timing. Studies on apple indicate root pruning at the late dormant (March) or full bloom stage gave maximum growth control, while root pruning at June

drop or preharvest (August) did not reduce shoot growth or increment increase in trunk area (Schupp and Ferree, 1987).

Experience from these studies and grower experiences indicate that meaningful growth control of apple trees can be achieved by root pruning on two sides at 60 to 100 centimeters from the trunk. The closer to the trunk the roots are pruned, the greater the degree of growth control. Time of root pruning of apple trees also influences root regeneration, with less regeneration occurring as time of pruning is delayed. The effect of root pruning on root distribution and other long-term effects on fruit trees is not known.

Other effects of root pruning include a significant reduction in pruning time as well as improved light penetration into the lower canopy (Schupp and Ferree, 1987), improving fruit color and quality. Yield of large-fruited apple cultivars generally has not been influenced by root pruning, although small-fruited apple cultivars may have reduced yields in some years. Fruit size generally has been reduced by root pruning, although fruit quality characteristics such as color, firmness, and soluble solids have been increased, and preharvest drop and cork spot reduced by root pruning (Schupp, 1988) *(see Figure 10)*.

The commercial use of root pruning has

FIGURE 10

Girdling (TG) and root pruning (RP) on yield and quality of Fuji/MM.106 (Hughes, 1995).

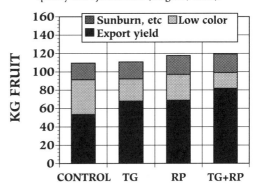

increased dramatically in recent years in apple production in the eastern United States with the development and sale of an inexpensive, tractor-mounted root pruner and the loss of the growth regulator, daminozide (Alar). Although fruit on root-pruned trees are redder, firmer, and stay on the tree longer, their maturity is not delayed sufficiently to improve long-term storage potential as occurred with daminozide.

Fabric containers that allow free exchange of moisture and penetration of small roots that will become constricted as they expand in diameter have been used for in-soil nursery production. Similar containers have been used successfully to control growth of apple and peach trees (Myers, 1992). Precocity and yield efficiency were increased dramatically in apple and peach. Root restriction reduced canopy volume in apple and peach, and within container treatments, growth control increased linearly with decreasing container volume.

During the third growing season, there was no treatment difference in fruit number per tree, total fruit weight per tree, or mean fruit size in peach. An average of 44% reduction in tree size resulted in an increase in yield efficiency in root-restricted peach trees. Fruit maturity period was concentrated and advanced in peach trees grown in fabric containers.

FIGURE 11

Allocation of resources varies with orchard age.

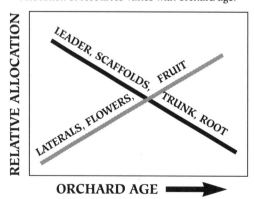

RELATIVE ALLOCATION

LEADER, SCAFFOLDS, FRUIT

LATERALS, FLOWERS, TRUNK, ROOT

ORCHARD AGE ➡

In the third season of growth, apple trees grown in fabric containers had a higher flower cluster number and percent fruit set than control trees. Within container treatments, flower cluster and fruit number per limb increased linearly with decreasing container volume.

Management objectives

It is with a proper understanding and manipulation of certain basic biological principles of growth and fruiting that we attempt to maximize our efforts in the orchard. However, it is clear that the end result comes from a complex interaction of factors. As such, we can only make generalizations about the effects of individual factors. Environmental factors, such as light, water, temperature, and soil, have not been covered but have important roles in growth and fruiting. True mastery of a given orchard system comes from combining these basic principles with sound management and judgment that comes from experience and keen observation.

The objective for any given orchard system is to fill the allotted space as quickly and inexpensively as possible with a canopy that provides early and sustainable yields of marketable fruit, thereby providing a competitive return on investment. This objective is accomplished by the allocation of resources within the tree from sources to sinks, which is controlled by both genetic and environmental factors. This allocation is the basis of orchard management, with management decisions based on orchard system and tree age *(see Figure 11)*.

Young nonbearing tree

In the young, nonbearing tree, the focus of management is development of tree structure with the objective of filling the allotted canopy space within the given orchard system. For many apple systems, this process may be initiated in the nursery, with the development of high quality, feathered trees. Once trees are planted, efforts focus on root system establishment and extension of vegetative growth.

Light pruning is more desirable than heavy pruning during this period, as heavily pruned trees exhibit smaller trunk diameter and root mass than trees which are lightly pruned (Savage et al., 1942) *(see Figure 12)*.

Pinching of developing laterals in apple results in a decrease in total shoot growth as severity of pruning increases (Tustin, 1991) *(see Figure 13)*. Although remaining shoots are significantly longer, shoot number is decreased.

Positioning of limbs influences the subsequent development of vegetative growth and lays the groundwork for the development of fruiting wood. Vertical limbs develop relatively few laterals with number of laterals increasing as orientation moves from vertical to horizontal. Although more shoots develop on horizontal limbs, average shoot length is reduced. Positioning limbs at moderate angles allows an increased number of laterals to develop while minimizing reduction in shoot length.

Young bearing trees

During this period, management of tree resources expands to include initial development of fruiting sites and the initial phase of flowering, as well as continued expansion of tree structure to fill allotted space.

Heavy pruning can delay the filling of the allotted canopy within the orchard by reducing total shoot number and total shoot growth (Barden et al., 1989).

In addition, pruning severity is directly related to flower cluster number, as flower cluster number decreases as pruning severity increases (Barden et al., 1989). Results indicate that pruning should be minimized in order to maximize the potential for early flowering and fruiting. In order to encourage branching, limbs may be positioned at desirable angles.

In addition, bagging of the central leader of apple is useful in some cultivars to encourage a higher number of shoots to develop (Schwalier, 1995) *(see Figure 14)*. The practice also increases the number of flower clusters and subsequent number of fruit.

FIGURE 13

Pinching severity on shoot length of first leaf apple trees (Tustin, 1991).

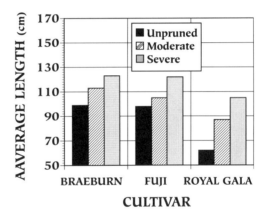

FIGURE 14

Bagging of leaders on shoot growth, flowering, and fruiting of Jonagold (Schwalier, 1995).

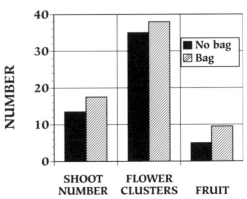

FIGURE 12

Pruning severity on growth of young peach trees (Savage, et al., 1942).

Pruning severity	Trunk circ. (cm)	Root dry wt. (kg)
Light	34.3	13.0
Heavy	30.5	9.7

Notching of buds also results in a higher number of lateral shoots per limb (Greene and Autio, 1992) *(see Figure 15)*. Notching is equally effective on all sections of the limb, with over 90% of notched buds developing into shoots. This effect has the highest impact in the basal and middle sections of the limb where natural lateral branching occurs less frequently.

The production of fruit has a tremendous impact on shoot growth and future fruit production. There is a limited supply of resources within the tree for growth. With the presence of fruit, there is a decrease in the supply of resources available for shoot and root growth (Forshey, 1986). As a result, shoot and root growth will decrease relative to the level of fruit production.

The presence of fruit modifies terminal shoot growth, total seasonal growth, and root growth, and promotes the onset of greater fruit production in a young, vigorous tree. Fruit often change the limb orientation, further influencing patterns of shoot growth and fruiting *(see Figure 16)*.

The regulation of fruiting in orchard systems is critical. In some situations, heavy fruit production too early in a tree's development can result in alternate bearing, inade-

---

FIGURE 16

Growth patterns of fruiting limbs of Type I (upper), III (middle), and IV (lower) tree forms.
(Tustin, 1991).

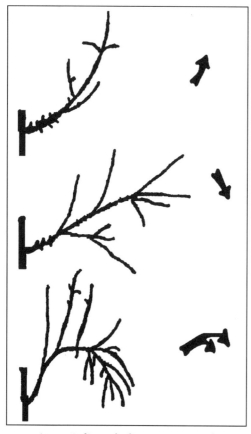

Arrows indicate the linear or rotational direction of branch development caused by growth and fruiting.

FIGURE 15

Notching and branch type on shoot growth of Spurcort/M.7 (Greene and Autio, 1992).

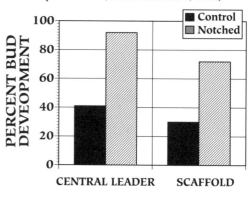

FIGURE 17

Pruning time on spur leaf area of Delicious/M.9 (Myers and Ferree, 1983).

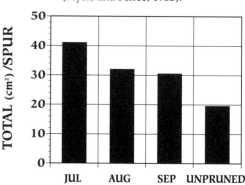

quate levels of shoot growth, failure to fill up allotted growing space, and a tree structure physically unable to support weight. Supplemental support is often required when trees are cropped early in their development (Myers, 1988). In other situations, such as with more vigorous cultivars, cropping should be promoted as early as possible to control vigor.

Mature bearing trees

After a tree's desired canopy has been attained, management begins to focus on the maintenance of fruiting sites to provide sustained flower and fruit production and the annual expansion of vegetative and reproductive components of the fruiting site. Maximizing productive allocation of resources can be accomplished with training system, scion/rootstock selection, and proper use of cultural techniques that can be used to modify allocation of resources.

Pruning and training will focus on maintaining tree size and productivity. Merging pruning and training techniques is necessary to maximize fruit quality and yield efficiency. Pruning cuts are used primarily to remove weak, unproductive wood, and training techniques are utilized to maximize development of fruiting wood within the tree canopy. Maintenance and renewal of fruiting sites is critical to sustained fruit quality as the tree ages (Rom, 1989). In addition, growth can be maximized with management of factors such as water, nutrients, and light.

Pruning affects the spur leaf area of apple, with summer pruning in July increasing spur leaf area significantly (Myers and Ferree, 1983) *(see Figure 17)*. Likewise, summer pruning of apple in July and August increases spur density, providing additional potential fruiting sites (Myers and Ferree, 1983) *(see Figure 18)*. Trunk girdling and root pruning are useful practices in controlling trunk growth while maintaining total yield (Hughes, 1995). In addition, these practices assist in changing fruit quality.

Additional management objectives focus on the prevention of allocation of resources to localized areas, resulting in excessive shoot growth. Removal of strong, upright watersprouts within the canopy of mature peach trees approximately four weeks prior to harvest increases fruit size, improves fruit quality, and increases flower bud formation in the following season (Myers, 1993) *(see Figure 19)*.

With careful attention and application of knowledge, resources can be managed within a tree to maximize growth and productivity over the life of the orchard.

FIGURE 18

Pruning time on spur density of Delicious/M.9 (Myers and Ferree, 1983).

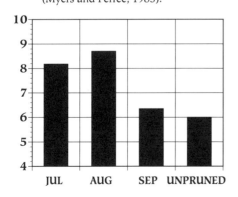

FIGURE 19

Preharvest watersprout removal (WSR) on packout of Redskin peach (Myers, 1993).

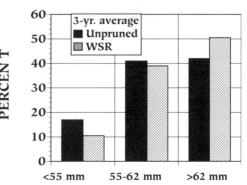

Literature cited

Barden, J.A., T.B.G. DelValle, and S.C. Myers, "Growth and fruiting of Delicious apple trees as affected by severity and season of pruning," *J. Amer. Hort. Soc.* 114(2) (1989): 184-186.

Ferree, D.C., J.R. Schupp, and S.C. Myers, "Root pruning and root restriction of fruit trees-current review,"*Acta Horticulturae* 322 (1992): 153-166.

Forshey, C.G., "Training and pruning apple trees," Cornell Univ. Info. Bull. No. 112, 1986.

Forshey, C.G., D.C. Elfving, and R.L. Stebbins, *Training and pruning apple and pear trees.* American Society for Horticultural Science: Alexandria, VA, 1992.

Feucht, W., "Fruitfulness in pome and stone fruit," Wash. St. Univ. Coop. Ext. Bull. No. 665. Translated from *Fruchtolz and Ertag der Olstbaume*, Verlag Eugen Ulmer, Stuttgart, West Germany, 1968.

Greene, D.W. and W.R. Autio, "Notching increases branching on apple trees," *Fruit Notes* 57(1) (1992): 9-15.

Hughes, J.G., "Fuji development-effects of trunk girdling and root pruning on fruit quality," HortResearch Commercial Report to NZAPMB. Client Report 95/126, 1995.

Lespinasse, J.M., "Apple tree management in float, vertical and palmette forms, by cultivar fruiting type," edited by L.D. Tukey, 103-130. In: Colloques Scientifiques No. 15, Colloque International: Montreal, 1981.

Luckwill, L.C., "The chemical induction of early cropping in fruit trees," *Acta Horticulturae* 65 (1978): 139-145.

Marshall, R.E., "The fruiting habit of the peach as influenced by pruning practice," Mich. Agric. Exp. Sta. Tech. Bull. No. 116, 1931.

Myers, S.C., "Basics in open center peach tree training," edited by N.F. Childers and W.B. Sherman. In: *The Peach*, Somerset, NJ: Somerset Press, Inc., 1988.

Myers, S.C., "Root restriction of apple and peach with in-ground fabric containers," *Acta Horticulturae* 322 (1992): 215-219.

Myers, S.C., "Preharvest watersprout removal influences canopy light relations, fruit quality, and flower bud formation of Redskin peach trees," *J. Amer Soc. Hort. Sci.* 118 (1993): 442-445.

Myers, S.C. and D.C. Ferree, "Influence of time of summer pruning and limb orientation on growth and flowering of vigorous Delicious apple trees," *J. Amer. Soc. Hort. Sci.* 108 (1983): 634-638.

Myers, S.C. and D.C. Ferree, "Influence of summer pruning on the growth pattern of vigorous Delicious apple limbs," *HortScience* 21 (1986): 252-253.

Rom, C.R., "Physiological aspects of pruning and training," edited by A.B. Peterson. In: *Intensive Orcharding*, Yakima, WA: Good Fruit Grower, 1989.

Savage E.F. and F.F. Cowart, "The effect of pruning upon the root distribution of peach trees," *Proc. Amer. Soc. Hort. Sci.* 41 (1942): 67-70.

Schupp, J.R., "Physiological responses of apple trees to root pruning," PhD Dissertation, Ohio State University, 1988.

Schupp, J.R. and D.C. Ferree, "Effect of root pruning at different growth stages on growth and fruiting of apple trees," *HortScience* 22 (1987): 387-390.

Schwalier, P., "Bags give more than just branches," *Fruit Notes* 60(4) (1995): 4-6.

Stebbins, R.L., "Training and pruning apple and pear trees," Pacific Northwest Extension Publication No. 156, 1980.

Tustin, S., "Basic physiology of tree training and pruning," Proc. Wash. St. Hort. Assoc. 87 (1991): 50-63.

Manipulating Vegetative and Reproductive Growth with Water and Nitrogen

R. Scott Johnson
University of California
Kearney Agricultural Center
Parlier, California

The ultimate goal in managing an orchard is to optimize fruit production and fruit quality with minimal inputs. Water and nitrogen are two powerful tools available to an orchard manager which allow him or her to manipulate the tree in various ways. Both these resources are critical to growth and development, and they affect many different processes within the plant. Having a sound understanding of the role of nitrogen and water on tree physiology allows us to better use these resources in beneficial ways.

Before discussing these two resources, it is important to establish a few basic principles. These principles apply particularly to perennial trees and are useful not only from a physiological perspective in helping us understand how the tree grows but are also useful from a management perspective.

1) Short- vs. long-term effects. A given manipulation may produce some immediate effect, but because of secondary and carryover effects on other processes, the long-term effect may be exactly opposite. For instance, heavy fertilization may stimulate growth and production one year, but because of shading out of fruiting wood, long-term production may be reduced.

2) Young vs. old trees. The pattern, intensity, and type of root and shoot growth can differ substantially from a young to a mature tree. Often, the goals in managing a young vs. a mature orchard are exactly opposite. This principle should also be kept in mind when adapting the results from one experiment to different aged orchards.

3) Critical periods. The organs on a tree follow different patterns of slow, fast, or no growth throughout the season. This implies that certain periods may be more critical in terms of imposing stress or manipulating growth in some way. In other words, if we can fine-tune our manipulations, we may be able to affect the growth of one organ but not the others.

4) Moderate vs. severe stress. Finally, it is important to keep in mind the extent of a manipulation or imposed stress. Severe stresses often yield negative results, but a more moderate stress may actually be beneficial in some way. This points out the importance of being able to measure and report the extent of the manipulation, so it can be applied to other situations.

Using water stress to manipulate growth

REGULATED DEFICIT IRRIGATION

Generally, studies on water stress have documented negative impacts on plant growth and development. However, there are some reports of beneficial effects, especially on fruit quality. Chalmers and Mitchell, working in Australia for a ten-year period, reported reduced vegetative growth and increased fruit growth in peaches and pears *(see Table 1)*.

Their approach with peach was to impose water stress during stage II or the lag phase of fruit growth and then relieve the stress during final fruit swell or stage III (Chalmers et al., 1981; Mitchell and Chalmers, 1982). With pear, there is no lag phase of fruit growth, but the timing of treatments was similar (Chalmers et al., 1986; Mitchell et al., 1984; 1989). The theory explaining why this approach produced beneficial effects can be summarized as follows.

Since the period of major shoot growth precedes and only slightly overlaps the period of major fruit growth, it creates a window or critical period during which stress might be imposed. Furthermore, since shoot growth is more sensitive to stress than fruit growth, a moderate stress would be expected to reduce vegetative growth without affecting fruit growth (Chalmers et al., 1984). Also, during this period of moderate stress, the fruit appear to osmoregulate, so that once the stress is relieved, they actually have a better water status (higher turgor potential) than normally irrigated fruit (Chalmers et al., 1986). Therefore, they grow at a faster rate for a

period of time and end up larger in size.

This irrigation strategy, which has been termed regulated deficit irrigation (RDI), has been attempted in many other locations around the world. Most other researchers have not had the same positive results that have been reported out of Australia *(see Table 2)*. There are probably several explanations for this.

First, the degree of stress may be quite critical; too little stress will have no effect, and too much will irreversibly reduce fruit growth. The conditions in Australia seem ideal for bringing the trees in and out of moderate stress. The soils used in these experiments are quite shallow, and the trees were planted close together, thus limiting the root zone. Other research has been conducted on deeper soils (Ebel et al., 1993; 1995; Girona, 1989), where it takes longer to both induce and relieve stress. This makes it much more challenging to create the right level of stress at the right time. Trees growing in pots (Behboudian and Lawes, 1994; Natali et al., 1985) have the potential of going into severe stress too rapidly.

A second explanation may have to do with the timing of stress. It has always been assumed that stage II is the best time to impose stress because fruit are growing at

TABLE 1

The results of regulated deficit irrigation experiments on peach and pear in Australia.

| Reference | Crop | % ET | | Year from initial treatment | Response (%) | |
		Stage I	Stage II		Yield	Fruit size
Chalmers	Peach	100	50	1	0	0
et al., 1981				3	+18 to +24	+5
		30	50	1	0	0
				2	negative	
				3	0	0
Mitchell &	Peach	100	12.5	1	+10 to +16	0
Chalmers, 1982						
Mitchell et al., 1984	Pear	46	46	1	+12	+10
Chalmers et al., 1986	Pear	0	23	1	+30	+14
				2	+11	-11
Mitchell et al., 1989	Pear	0	23	1-5	+15 to +20	-10 to +10

their slowest rate. However, Li et al. (1989) found a significant increase in yield and fruit size by imposing stress during stage I and no effect during stage II. To further support these findings, the later papers out of Australia (Chalmers et al., 1986; Mitchell et al., 1989) found that an initial period of withholding irrigation during early fruit growth seemed to enhance the effect of subsequent RDI. Therefore, the critical period to impose stress may be earlier than originally hypothesized.

Third, the effect of water stress on flowering also needs to be considered in these experiments. The Australian experiments reported increased flowering with RDI in both peach and pear, which helps explain increased yields in the experiments carried out for more than a year (Chalmers et al., 1981; Mitchell et al., 1989). However, others have reported decreased flowering due to water stress (Caspari et al., 1994; Kaufmann, 1972). Different species may respond to stress differently, and the level of stress may also be important. There is some evidence to suggest moderate stress increases flowering and severe stress decreases flowering in peach (Johnson et al., 1992; Proebsting and Middleton; 1980).

Finally, the effect of water stress on fruit drop needs to be taken into account. There is some indication that water stress decreases fruit drop in some varieties and explains some of the increased yield from the Australian experiments. Li et al. (1989) report substantial preharvest fruit drop which was reduced by two-thirds in RDI treatments. The peach varieties we have used in California have not shown substantial preharvest drop, nor has this changed with RDI treatments.

In conclusion, RDI appears to be a valid concept, but its practical implementation in the field is not simple. The timing and degree of stress are both critical and may be difficult to control as precisely as needed in many situations. The response of flowering and fruit drop would need to be known and may be important for successful implementation.

In California, our first attempt at RDI reduced fruit size, probably because the stress was imposed too late and too severely (Girona, 1989). Subsequent trials with less severe and earlier stress gave a slight indication of success. Over a five-year period, the RDI treatment had consistently larger fruit size and greater yields than the

TABLE 2

The results of regulated deficit irrigation experiments on various fruit crops in many countries other than Australia.

| Reference | Crop | % ET | | Year from initial treatment | Response (%) | |
		Stage I	Stage II		Yield	Fruit size
Natali et al., 1985	Peach	100	0	1		negative
Irving & Drost, 1987	Apple	100	20	1	0	0
Li et al., 1989	Peach	0	100	1&2	0 to +17	+7 to +10
		100	33	1&2	0	0
Ebel et al., 1993	Apple	100	25	1		-18
Girona et al., 1993	Peach	100	25	1-3	0	negative
Behboudian & Lawes, 1994	Pear	100	50	1		0
Caspari et al., 1994	Pear	100	50	1	0	0
Ebel et al., 1985	Apple	100	0	1		negative
Johnson et al., 1994	Peach	50	50	1-5	0	0

control, but the differences were small and never statistically significant (Johnson et al., 1994b).

POSTHARVEST WATER STRESS

We have conducted several research projects on the withholding of irrigation water after harvest of early maturing peach and plum cultivars (Johnson et al., 1992; 1994a; Larsen et al., 1988). The results generally have shown substantial savings of irrigation water with no detrimental effects on yield. There is some reduction in vegetative growth, but it is not large because the majority of shoot extension growth is complete by the time stress is imposed. Larsen et al., (1988) showed no decrease in shoot length but a slight decrease in girth. An increase in flowering has been observed in peach (Johnson et al., 1992) but not plum (Johnson et al., 1994a), and decreased flowering has been reported for apricots (Uriu, 1964). The main drawback to this practice has been an increase in fruit doubles and deep sutures induced by the stress

treatments. However, alleviating the stress in early August to early September by irrigation has been shown to greatly reduce this problem (Handley, 1991).

FUTURE RESEARCH

As orchard managers try to implement some of these controlled deficit irrigation strategies, it will be critical to have a method for assessing the degree of stress being imposed. Just measuring the amount of water applied or the amount in the soil will not give a true indication of what the tree is experiencing. Obviously, the best method will be to measure some parameter in the tree. We have experimented with different measurements, including crop water stress index, stomatal conductance, stem water flow, leaf potential, and stem water potential, and have concluded that stem water potential gives the lowest variability and the best consistency among species (Garnier and Berger, 1985; McCutchan and Shackel, 1992). It also seems to be a good integrator of the whole plant's water status.

FIGURE 1

The generalized response to nitrogen of peach vegetative and reproductive growth.

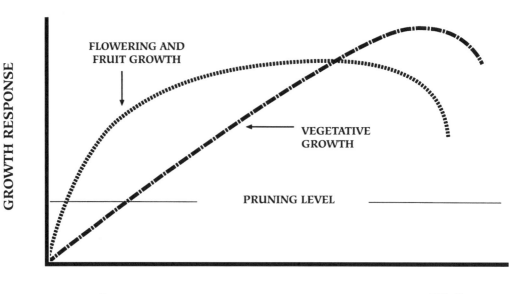

Using nitrogen to manipulate growth

Because of nitrogen recycling and reserves in the tree and soil, it is more difficult to rapidly affect growth with nitrogen fertilization than with water stress. (However, this could change as we better understand how to use foliar nutrient sprays.) Therefore, our goal is to maintain a certain level within the tree, a level that will stimulate enough vegetative growth for continued high production and promote maximum fruit size and quality. It is not always easy to keep the tree at just the right nutritional level. If it drops too low, fruit size and fruit wood renewal can be affected. With too much nitrogen, the resulting excess vigor can lead to poor fruit quality, shading out of lower fruiting wood, and a decrease in production.

After studying nitrogen fertilization rates in a Fantasia nectarine orchard over a 12-year period (Johnson et al., 1995), we concluded that there are more dangers from overfertilization than from underfertilization. We hypothesized that reproductive growth is less sensitive to nitrogen than vegetative growth *(see Figure 1)*. Therefore, lowering the nitrogen level will reduce vegetative growth without limiting yield or fruit size. Furthermore, high rates of nitrogen lead to poorer fruit color, dying out of lower fruiting wood, and greater susceptibility to diseases and insect pests (Daane et al., 1995).

Vegetative growth in the tops of the trees was excessive when the trees were young. As the trees matured, vegetative growth in trees fertilized with the highest nitrogen rate (325 lbs. N/acre) dropped off, probably due to a nutrient imbalance or greater wood rot.

The factors contributing to productivity were much less affected by nitrogen. Flower density showed no response to nitrogen rate even in the unfertilized treatment. Total yield and fruit size were decreased only by the unfertilized treatment. The lowest rate of nitrogen (100 lbs. N/acre) produced just as well as higher rates throughout the duration of the experiment. For this study, maintaining leaf nitrogen between 2.7 and 3.0% (on the lower range of what has been recommended in the past) is sufficient for good production, while avoiding some of the physiological, pathological, and environmental problems associated with higher nitrogen levels.

Literature cited

Behboudian, M. Hossein and G. Stephen Lawes, "Fruit quality in Nijisseiki asian pear under deficit irrigation: physical attributes, sugar and mineral content, and development of flesh spot decay," *NZ J. of Crop and Hort. Sci.* 22 (1994) 393-400.

Caspari, Horst W., M. Hossein Behboudian, and David J. Chalmers, "Water use, growth, and fruit yield of Hosui asian pears under deficit irrigation," *J. Amer. Soc. Hort. Sci.* 119 (3) (1994): 383-388.

Chalmers, D.J., G. Burge, P.H. Jerie, and P.D. Mitchell, "The mechanism of regulation of Bartlett pear fruit and vegetative growth by irrigation withholding and regulated deficit irrigation," *J. Amer. Soc. Hort. Sci.* 111(6) (1986) :904-907.

Chalmers, D.J., P.D. Mitchell, and P.H. Jerie, "The physiology of growth of peach and pear trees using reduced irrigation," *Acta Horticulturae* 146 (1984): 143-149.

Chalmers, D.J., P.D. Mitchell, and L. van Heek, "Control of peach tree growth and productivity by regulated water supply, tree density, and summer pruning," *J. Amer. Soc. Hort. Sci.* 106(3) (1981): 307-312.

Daane, Kent M., R. Scott Johnson, Themis J. Michailides, Carlos H. Crisosto, Jeff W. Dlott, Hugo T. Ramirez, Glenn Y. Yokota, and Dave P. Morgan, "Excess nitrogen raises nectarine susceptibility to disease and insects," *Calif. Agric.* 49(4) (1995): 13-18.

Ebel, Robert C., Edward L. Proebsting, and Robert G. Evans, "Deficit irrigation to control vegetative growth in apple and monitoring fruit growth to schedule irrigation," *HortScience* 30(6) (1995): 1229-1232.

Ebel, Robert C., Edward L. Proebsting, and Max E. Patterson, "Regulated deficit irrigation may alter apple maturity, quality, and storage life," *HortScience* 28(2) (1993): 141-143.

Garnier, E. and A. Berger, "Testing water potential in peach trees as an indicator of water stress," *J. Hort. Sci.* 60(1) (1985): 47-56.

Girona, J. "Physiological, growth, and production responses of late maturing peach (*Prunus persica* L. Batsch) to controlled deficit irrigation," MS Thesis. University of California, Davis. 1989.

Handley, D., "The formation of double fruit in peaches in response to postharvest deficit irrigation," MS Thesis. California State University, Fresno, 1991.

Irving, D.E. and J.H. Drost, "Effects of water deficit on vegetative growth, fruit growth, and fruit quality in Cox's Orange Pippin apple," *J. of Hort. Sci.* 62(4) (1987): 427-432.

Johnson, R. Scott, D.F. Handley, and K.R. Day, "Postharvest water stress of an early maturing plum," *J. Hort. Sci.* 69 (1994a):1035-1041.

Johnson, R. Scott, D.F. Handley, and T.M. DeJong, "Long-term response of early maturing peach trees to postharvest water deficits," *J. Amer. Soc. Hort. Sci.* 117(6) (1992): 881-886.

Johnson, R. Scott, F. Gordon Mitchell, and Carlos H. Crisosto, "Nitrogen fertilization of Fantasia nectarine, a 12-year study," *Kearney Tree Fruit Review.* Vol. 1, 1995.

Johnson, R. Scott, Claude Phene, Richard Mead, Bob Beede, Harry Andris, and Kevin Day, "Water use and water management of mid- to late-season stone fruit," CTFA Annual Report, 1994b

Kaufmann, Merrill R, "Water deficits and reproductive growth," edited by T.T. Kozlowski. In. *Water Deficits and Plant Growth*, Vol. III. New York: Academic Press, 1972.

Larson, K.D., T.M. DeJong, and R.S. Johnson, "Physiological and growth responses of mature peach trees to postharvest water stress," *J. Amer. Soc. Hort. Sci.* 113(3) (1988) : 296-300.

Li, S.H., J.G. Huguet, P.G. Schoch, and P. Orlando, "Response of peach tree growth and cropping to soil water deficit at various phenological stages of fruit development," *J. Hort. Sci.* 64(5) (1989): 541-552.

McCutchan, Harold and K.A. Shackel, "Stem water potential as a sensitive indicator of water stress in prune trees (*Prunus domestica* L. cv. French)," *J. Amer. Soc. Hort. Sci.* 117 (1992): 607-611.

Mitchell, P.D., B. van den Ende, P.H. Jerie, and D.J. Chalmers, "Responses of Bartlett pear to withholding irrigation, regulated deficit irrigation, and tree spacing," *J. Amer. Soc. Hort. Sci.* 114(1) (1989): 15-19.

Mitchell, P.D., D.J. Chalmers, P.H. Jerie, and G. Burge, "The use of initial withholding of irrigation and tree spacing to enhance the effect of regulated deficit irrigation on pear trees," *J. Amer. Soc. Hort. Sci.* 111(5) (1986): 858-861.

Mitchell, P.D. and D.J. Chalmers, "The effect of reduced water supply on peach tree growth and yields," *J. Amer. Soc. Hort. Sci.* 107(5) (1982): 853-856.

Mitchell, P.D., P.H. Jerie, and D.J. Chalmers, "The effects of regulated water deficits on pear tree growth, flowering, fruit growth, and yield," *J. Amer. Soc. Hort. Sci.* 109(5) (1984) :604-606.

Natali, S., C. Xiloyannis, and B. Pezzarossa, "Relationship between soil water content, leaf water potential, and fruit growth during different fruit growing phases of peach trees," *Acta Horticulturae* 171 (1985): 167-179.

Proebsting, E.L., Jr., and J.E. Middleton, "The behavior of peach and pear trees under extreme drought stress," *J. Amer. Soc. Hort. Sci.* 105(3) (1980): 380-385.

Uriu, K., "Effect of postharvest soil moisture depletion on subsequent yield of apricots," *Proc. Amer. Soc. Hort. Sci.* 84 (1964): 93-97.

Regulation of Reproductive Growth and Development

DR. DUANE W. GREENE
Department of Plant and Soil Sciences
Bowditch Hall
University of Massachusetts
Amherst, MA 01003
phone: 413-545-5219; fax: 413-545-0260

DR. FRANK DENNIS
Department of Horticulture
Michigan State University
East Lansing, MI 48824-1325
phone: 517-353-3251; fax: 517-353-0890

DR. JIM MATTHEIS
U.S. Department of Agriculture-Agricultural Research Service
1104 North Western Avenue
Wenatchee, WA 98801
phone: 509-664-2280; fax: 509-664-2287

8 Flower Development

Duane W. Greene
Department of Plant and Soil Sciences
University of Massachusetts
Amherst, Massachusetts

Flowering is the single most important physiological event to occur in tree fruit, since flowers are the first requirement to have fruit production. Flowering in many plants can be controlled quite precisely, because a single environmental event frequently triggers flower initiation. Flower bud formation in tree fruits is much more complex and less easily manipulated, since it is influenced by environmental factors, cultural and management techniques, and endogenous hormones.

Further, these factors interact to modify the flowering response. Flower bud formation spans two growing seasons and occurs over nearly a 12-month period. The purpose of this chapter is to review flower development, discuss factors that influence flower bud formation, indicate how these influence flowering, and where appropriate, suggest strategies to manipulate flowering.

Types and location of flower buds

The majority of flower buds on an apple tree occur terminally on short shoots called spurs. Flowers may form terminally on even longer shoots when terminal growth stops and a terminal bud forms. Cultivars such as Rome Beauty, Cortland, and, to a lesser extent, Granny Smith, initiate buds in a fairly high percentage on terminal shoots.

Flower buds may also develop in the axils of leaves on one-year-old wood. These flowers are generally considered undesirable, because they differentiate late in the season, open late, and fruit produced from these are generally small and frequently have poor finish.

Flower bud development

The inflorescence in a flowering spur contains flowers, bracts, true leaves, transition leaves, and budscales. Primordia for single flowers are found in the axils of the bracts, at the apex, and in the axils of the most proximal true leaves. Following dormancy in the spring, but before the time of flower formation, the apex of the vegetative bud (bourse bud) will initiate leaf-like primordia (appendages) then mature over the season to form budscales, transition leaves, and true leaves of a mature vegetative or reproductive bud (see Figure 1).

Budscales are initiated first, followed by the transition leaves, true leaves, and bracts. In general, the number for each bud ranges from 7 to 11 bud scales, 2 to 3 transition leaves, 3 to 6 true leaves, and 3 bracts (McLaughlin and Greene, 1991). The number of appendages (nodes) produced by a meristem before the formation of terminal flowers is tightly controlled and varies with variety (see Table 1).

The critical period appears to be after initiation of the last true leaf and before the initiation of the first bract. During that period, transition to the reproductive state occurs. It appears that the meristem must first reach the critical node number by a certain time in the season, and the meristem must then have the capacity to initiate flowers. Consequently, any environmental or plant factor that delays or limits cell division, and production of the critical node number, ultimately may prevent flower bud formation or result in weak or small flowers. Even if the proper number of nodes are produced and there is adequate time in the season for flower buds to form, flowering does not necessarily occur spontaneously. Other factors have a modifying influence and can determine whether a bud will remain vegetative or develop into a flower bud (Dennis, 1986).

Sequence of floral development

Flower bud formation is generally considered to proceed in three stages (Verheif, 1996).

Flower induction. This process is defined as the time when the meristem is committed to form a flower. This usually occurs early, during the initial period of active vegetative growth on the tree. There are no visible signs of flower formation in this stage. All changes are subcellular and biochemical.

Floral differentiation. This stage starts around the time terminal growth on a tree stops. It is during this stage that actual flowering structures appear and continue to develop. Before entering winter dormancy,

---

FIGURE 1

(A) Representative diagram of an apple spur late in the growing season when flowers have been initiated in the bourse bud.
(B) Cross section illustration through a bourse bud. From the outer to inner appendages: thick solid structures = budscales, flecked structures = transition leaves, unflecked structures = true leaves, and thin lines = bracts (Abbott, 1970). The small bud in the axil of the true leaf is vegetative, while all others are flower buds.
(C) Representative illustration of specific types of appendages (budscales, transition leaves, true leaves, and bracts), (after McLaughlin and Greene, 1991).

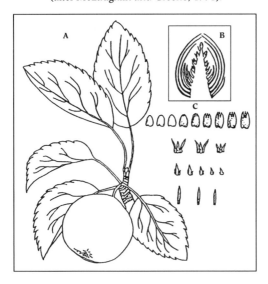

TABLE 1

Number and type of appendage initiated on spurs of several apple cultivars before formation of flower parts.[1]

| | No./spur | | | | |
	Bud scales	Transition leaves	True leaves	Bracts	Total
McIntosh	9	3	5	3	20
Delicious	9	3	5	3	20
Golden Delicious	9-10	2-3	3-4	3	19
Early McIntosh	10-11	2-3	5-6	3	22
Baldwin	7-8	2-3	5-6	3	18

[1]Data are a mean of 10 observations (after McLaughlin and Greene, 1991).

flower buds often have developed to 85% of their full size.

Anthesis (flower opening). In the spring of the following year, when temperature rises, growth and development of the flowers resume. Flowers open nearly a year after floral induction occurred.

Time of flower bud formation

Spur bloom. Determination of flowering in spurs usually occurs prior to any morphological change in the bud apex. Therefore, indirect methods such as defoliation, fruit removal, or gibberellin application must be used to establish the time of determination. Based upon results using these techniques, flowering on spurs may be established by 40 to 50 days after bloom. This emphasizes the importance of chemical thinning in regulating flowering.

There have been a number of reports, based primarily on hand thinning, that show flowering may be influenced as late as 120 days after bloom. When this happens, one or more of the following conditions exist. The variety in question is invariably one noted for being annual; growing conditions, especially light and water, were optimal; and warm sunny conditions conducive to growth persisted after normal harvest.

Terminal and lateral bloom. Flower formation on the ends of growing shoots occurs later than on spurs. Flower induction does not occur until terminal growth stops and a terminal bud forms. Lateral flower buds form in the axils of leaves even later, but the exact time has not been established. This varies depending on the conditions that influence terminal growth. Undoubtedly, there are several factors that influence when flowers do form in these axillary buds.

Factors influencing flower bud formation
TREE AGE

Following germination, all growing seedlings are incapable of forming flowers (*see Figure 2*). They are in the juvenile stage of their life. They must grow and mature to pass through this phase of life. The number of mitotic divisions in the apex apparently is the determining factor. Therefore, factors which promote growth, shorten the juvenile phase. Buds used in the vegetative propagation of fruit trees are obtained from tissue that is no longer juvenile, Even nursery trees have the ability to flower.

Even though these young trees may have attained the ability to reproduce, flower bud formation does not occur spontaneously. As a tree ages, it becomes less vegetative, and thus, it becomes progressively easier for a tree to initiate flower buds. The speed at which a tree matures through the vegetative or transition phase is ultimately determined by management decisions (*see Figure 2*).

Selection of a dwarfing rootstock, branch bending, ringing and scoring, and the use

---

FIGURE 2

Diagram illustrating the developmental phases in the life of an apple and the influence of management techniques on maturation through the vegetative (transition) phase (after Zimmerman, 1972).

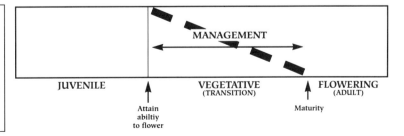

of ethephon are examples of management decisions that speed maturation through the transition phase and promote flower bud formation. Excess nitrogen fertilization, severe pruning, or the selection of a vigorous rootstock are examples of activities that discourage flower bud formation and delay maturation through the transition phase.

LIGHT INTENSITY

The amount of light, and presumably the energy made available from photosynthesis, are important factors in determining if flower buds form. Three zones of light have been identified in a tree. These are based primarily on the observations related to flower bud formation, fruit set, and fruit development. Zone 1 includes portions of the tree that receive between 60 to 100% full sun, zone 2 receives 30 to 60% full sun, and zone 3

receives between 0 and 30% full sun.

Cain (1971) was one of the first to recognize the importance of light levels in flower bud formation *(see Figure 3)*. He reported that all nonbearing spurs receiving above 60% full sun formed flower buds. In the portion of the tree receiving between 30 and 60% full sun, there was a very sharp decline in flower bud formation with declining light levels. No spurs formed flower buds in portions of the tree that received less than 30% full sun.

Jackson and Palmer (1977) later reported that flower buds will form on artificially shaded apple trees at lower light levels. However, the work of Cain may have more practical significance, since data generated in his investigation were under commercial orchard conditions where light levels could also influ-

---

FIGURE 3

Effect of light on return bloom of apple spurs
(after Cain, 1972).

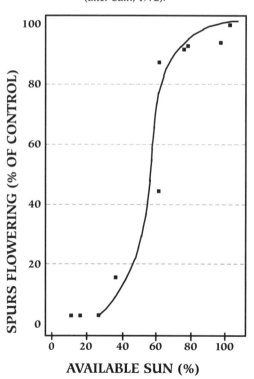

FIGURE 4

Effect of leaf area of Bartlett pear spurs on return bloom of fruiting and nonfruiting spurs
(after Huet, 1972).

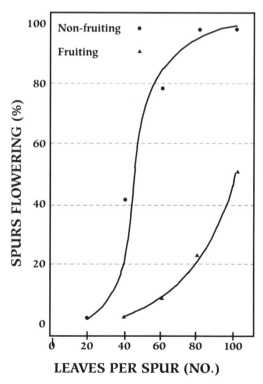

ence other factors affecting flower bud formation such as spur vigor and leaf area.

Spurs developing in inadequate light do not have the potential for maximum photosynthesis, and compensation from other portions of the tree does not occur because of the limited movement of carbohydrate within a tree (Rom, 1985).

SPUR LEAF AREA

Leaves are the structures that intercept the light and convert light to useful energy that is then used for flower bud formation. Several studies have established that there is a highly significant and direct relationship between flower bud formation and spur leaf area. Huet (1972) adjusted leaf number on nonfruiting Bartlett pear spurs to a range of leaf areas and then determined return bloom the following year (see Figure 4). He found that return bloom increased with increasing spur leaf area, up to about 90 cm^2 per spur. Above 90 cm^2 leaf area per spur (5-6 leaves), nearly all spurs formed flower buds.

TREE VIGOR

It has been known for many years that vigorous vegetative growth reduces flower bud formation. There are several ways that excessive tree vigor can inhibit flower bud formation.

Hormones. Shoot tips, including the apical meristem and young expanding leaves, are rich sources of gibberellins (Grauslund, 1972). It is well documented that gibberellins inhibit flower bud formation. Gibberellins produced in shoots are quite mobile and can move downward and retard flower bud development below. Treatments that retard growth or cause early cessation of growth, such as ethephon application, root pruning, or ringing and scoring, enhance flower bud formation. Presumably, part of this response is due to a direct reduction in the amount of gibberellins being produced by the shoot tip and being translocated down.

Shading and flower bud quality. Vigorous vegetative growth reduces light penetration into the interior portion of a tree. At moderate levels of reduced light, spurs become weak, flower bud size is reduced, fruit set is decreased, and fruit quality declines. Under high vigor conditions, it is likely that no flower buds will be formed in the interior, and spurs may actually die.

Apical dominance. The presence of a growing apical shoot inhibits the growth and development of buds below. This apical dominance phenomenon is accentuated on shoots that are rapidly growing. Auxin is produced in the shoot tip and young leaves, and moves downward in the shoot to prevent development of buds below. When a high concentration of auxin is moved down the stem for a large portion of the growing season, buds are preventing from growing and developing.

Under high vigor situations, buds either do not grow or grow so little, that buds may either die or be so underdeveloped and weak that, at best, they form weak spurs. When growth is maintained at a moderate level, axillary buds increase in size and ultimately develop into strong fruiting spurs.

The strength of apical dominance on lateral bud growth and development can be demonstrated by removing the tip from a rapidly growing shoot. Within a short period of time, buds will expand immediately behind the cut and grow, while those further away from the cut will increase in size without actually expanding. Keeping growth at a moderate rate is an important management strategy to assure that good healthy buds are coming along to form replacement wood for aging spurs.

CROP LOAD

Crop load has a more dramatic influence on flower bud formation than any other tree factor. It has long been recognized that the presence of fruit on a spur one year inhibits flower bud formation on that spur for the following year. Chemical thinning has become the major tool to combat biennial bearing by eliminating fruit from some spurs early enough to assure that these spurs will produce flower buds for the following year.

Chan and Cain (1967) did the classic work using Spencer Seedless apples to establish that it was the seeds rather than the carbohydrate demand imposed by growing fruit that ultimately determined whether a spur produced a flower cluster or remained vegetative *(see Table 2)*. Spencer Seedless is an apple that will set fruit without pollination.

If flowers are pollinated and seeded fruit develop, return bloom on those spurs was reduced to 13.1%. If pollination was prevented and a comparable load of seedless fruit was allowed to grow, nearly all of the fruiting spurs formed flower buds. If flowers were cut off at bloom and spurs carried no crop, repeat bloom was similar to that on spurs that carried seedless fruit.

John Neilson in his PhD research (personal communication) confirmed that seeds in the fruit on Spencer Seedless inhibited flower bud formation, but the inhibition was not as strong as reported by Chan and Cain. He further established that the further away potential flower buds were from the seeds, the less negative influence seeds had on flower formation. When the seeds were over 16 mm away from the fruit, regardless of seed number, seeds had a minimal effect on return bloom.

There is general agreement that it is the gibberellin component in the seeds that inhibit flower bud formation. Dennis and

---

TABLE 2

Effect of seeds and fruit on return bloom of Spencer Seedless apples.

Treatment	Flowering spurs (%)
Seeded fruit	13.1
Seedless fruit	95.3
No fruit	97.6

(after Chan and Cain, 1967)

FIGURE 5

Diagram illustrating the inhibitory effect of gibberellins present in the seed and the promotive effect of leaves on flower bud formation.

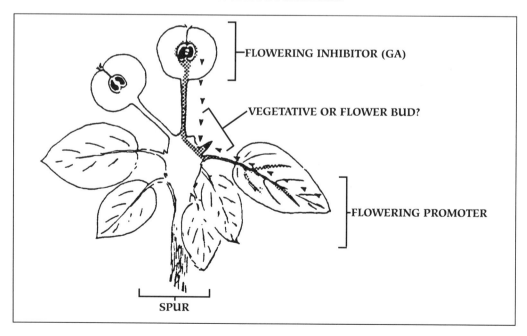

Nitch (1966) identified the primary gibberellins in apple seeds as GA_4 and GA_7. Later, Tromp (1982) determined that GA_7 was a strong inhibitor of flowering, while GA_4 was without effect.

Looney, et al (1985), provided evidence that GA4 in fact increased flowering. Greene (1993) applied GA4 to Golden Delicious trees in four separate years. Return bloom on GA4-treated trees was increased two years, one year it had no influence, and the fourth year it decreased return bloom. Clearly, the role of individual gibberellins in flower bud formation is complex.

Experience has shown that varieties differ dramatically in biennial bearing tendencies. The assumption has been that there are more gibberellins being produced in the biennial bearing varieties to inhibit flowering. This may not be the case.

Hoad (1978) determined the gibberellin content in the seeds of the biennial bearing variety Laxton's Superb and the annual bearing Cox's Orange Pippin over a 12-week period. Although gibberellin content changed over time, there was no difference in gibberellin content in the seeds of these two cultivars.

He also monitored the gibberellins migrating out of the fruits of these two varieties. Very little gibberellin moved out of the seeds of the annual bearing Cox's Orange Pippin. In contrast, substantial amounts moved out of the biennial bearing variety Laxton's Superb, starting soon after bloom.

The identity of the mobile gibberellin(s) was not determined. Consequently, the difference in flowering in biennial bearing cultivars appears to be attributed not to the gibberellin content in the seed but rather to the extent that gibberellins move out of the seed to the potential flowering bud.

FLOWERING PROMOTER

It is firmly established that leaves are important for flower bud formation because they provide energy required for flower bud formation to take place. The inhibitory effects of leaf removal on flower bud formation can be reversed by cytokinin application (Ramirez and Hoad, 1981). Leaves also contain substantial quantities of cytokinins (Greene, 1975). One can speculate that cytokinins act as flowering promoters and move out of the leaves and partially reverse the gibberellins migrating from the seeds (see Figure 5).

Supporting this suggestion is the data of Huet (see Figure 4). Increasing leaf area on fruiting Bartlett pear spurs had no influence on flower bud formation. As the number of leaves per spur increased above six to ten, there was a substantial increase in return bloom on these bearing spurs. One may speculate that about six leaves per spur are required to provide the energy for flower bud formation. Leaf area above six leaves per spur may provide the cytokinins that can partially reverse the inhibitory effect of seed on flowering. McLaughlin and Greene (1984) were able to partially overcome the inhibitory effect of gibberellins on Golden Delicious by an application of the cytokinin benzyladenine.

Conclusion

Flowering is a complex process that can be modified by many plant and environmental conditions. Cell division is important to assure enough nodes are formed so that flowers can form in the axils of the uppermost leaves and bracts. Energy is important. A threshold level of light and sufficient leaf area are required to assure flower bud formation. Vigor and vegetative growth must be controlled to provide physiological conditions for flowering. Hormones are involved. Gibberellins may inhibit or occasionally promote flowering, depending on the type present. Cytokinins may promote flower bud formation and partially reverse the inhibitory effects of gibberellins. Growers have ultimate control of flowering, since most of the factors that influence flowering are under direct management control.

Literature cited and suggested reading

Abbott, D.L., "The role of budscales in the morphogenesis of the apple fruit bud," edited by L.C. Luckwill and C.V. Cutting. In *Physiology of Tree Crops*, New York: Academic Press, 1970.

Cain, J.C., "Effect of mechanical pruning of apple hedgerows with a slotted saw on light penetration and fruiting," *J. Amer. Soc. Hort. Sci.* 96 (1971): 664-667.

Chan, B.G. and J.C. Cain, "The effect of seed formation on subsequent flowering in apple," *Proc. Amer. Soc. Hort. Sci.* 91 (1967): 63-68.

Dennis, F.G., "The physiology of flowering and fruit set in fruit trees," *Proc. Oregon Hort. Soc.* (1986) 77: 33-43.

Dennis, F.G. and J.P. Nitsch, "Identification of gibberellins A4 and A7 in immature apple seeds," *Nature* 211 (1966): 781-782.

Grausland, J., "Gibberellins in diffusates from shoots of apple trees," *Physiol. Plant.* 27 (1972): 65-70.

Greene, D.W., "Cytokinin activity in the xylem sap and extracts of MM 106 apple rootstocks, *HortScience* 10 (1975): 73-74.

Greene, D.W., "Effects of GA_4 and GA_7 on flower bud formation and russet development on apple," *J. Hort. Sci.* 68 (1993): 171-176.

Hoad, G.V., "The role of seed derived hormones in the control of flowering in apple," *Acta Hort.* 80 (1978): 93-103.

Huet, J., "Etude des effeis levieles et des fruits sur l'induction florale brachyblastes du poirier," *Physiol Vegetale* 10 (1972): 529-545.

Jackson, J.E. and J.W. Palmer, "Effect of shade on the growth and dropping of apple trees. II. Effects on components of yield," *J. Hort. Sci.* 52 (1977): 253-266.

Looney, N.E., R.P. Pharis and M. Noma, "Promotion of flowering in apple trees with gibberellins A4 and C-3 epi-gibberellin A4," *Planta* 165 (1985): 292-294.

McLaughlin, J.M. and D.W. Greene, "Effect of BA, GA4+7 and daminozide on fruit set, fruit quality, vegetative growth, flower initiation, and flower quality on Golden Delicious apple," *Amer. Soc. Hort. Sci.* 109 (1984): 34-39.

McLaughlin, J.M. and D.W. Greene, "Fruit and hormones influence flowering of apple. I. Effect of cultivar," *J. Amer. Soc. Hort. Sci.* 116 (1991): 446-449.

Ramirez, H. and G.V. Hoad, "Effect of growth substances on fruit-bud initiation in apple," *Acta Hort.* 120 (1981): 131-136.

Rom, C., "Bud development and vigor." In *Pollination and Fruit Set Shortcourse Proceedings*, 1-17. Yakima, WA: Good Fruit Grower, 1985.

Tromp, J., "Flower bud formation in apple as affected by various gibberellins," *J. Hort. Sci.* 57 (1992): 277-282.

Verheif, F.A., "Morphological and physiological aspects of the early phase of flower bud formation of apple," (Dissertation, Wageningen Agr. Univ. the Netherlands, 1996) 1-148.

Zimmerman, R.H., "Juvenility and flowering of fruit trees," *Acta Hort.* 34 (1973): 139-142.

9 Fruit Set

Frank G. Dennis, Jr.
Department of Horticulture
Michigan State University
East Lansing, Michigan

Flowering establishes the potential for cropload; fruit set and development determine how well that potential is realized. Fruit set can be defined several ways, the simplest is the growth of a flower into a fruit. However, horticulturalists often differentiate between initial set—the proportion of flowers that grow to form immature fruits—and final set—the proportion that actually reach maturity.

Fruit set is important because too much can lead to severe competition between fruits, leading to small and even unmarketable fruits, and too little will result in economic losses and/or poor quality fruit. The percentage of flowers that must set fruit in order to provide a full crop approximates 5 to 10 for apple, 10 to 15 for peach, and 25 to 30 for cherry. Much lower percentages are required for some fruits. In mango, for example, a single inflorescence may bear 5,000 flowers, and a heavy crop will result if 0.1% of them set fruit.

Is pollination necessary?

Most flowers require pollination in order for fruit set to occur (*see Table 1*).

Exceptions are parthenocarpic (virgin) fruits, such as banana and navel orange. These form fruits in the absence of pollination, and are seedless.

Bartlett pear will set parthenocarpically in some areas of California, but requires pollination elsewhere. Parthenocarpic cultivars of apple exist, but none is of commercial value. Some species or cultivars are self-fruitful—they will produce a commercial crop when the flowers are pollinated with pollen from the same tree or from a tree of the same cultivar.

Most peach and sour cherry cultivars are self-fruitful, and some apple cultivars (Golden Delicious, Wealthy) are at least partially self-fruitful. Other cultivars are "self-unfruitful"—a few fruits may set following self-pollination, but not enough for a commercial crop; this is the case for most apple and sweet cherry cultivars.

Other cultivars are "triploids" and produce little or no viable pollen. They cannot be relied upon for either self- or cross-pollination. Examples are Mutsu (Crispin) and Winesap apple.

An additional problem in providing for pollination is incompatibility between two cultivars—the cultivars produce viable pollen, but the pollen will not fertilize flowers of the other cultivar. Some examples are Bing, Lambert, Emperor Francis, and Napoleon sweet cherry (all combinations cross-incompatible), Bartlett x Seckel pear, and Cortland x Early McIntosh apple.

How is pollen transferred?

In most fruit species, pollen is transferred by insects, chiefly bees. Pollen of most of these species is heavy and sticky, and is not carried far by wind. Pollen of walnut, like that of pine, is light and dry, and can be carried long distances by wind; thus, walnuts are not dependent upon insects for pollination. In "the old days," when wild bees were more plentiful, growers could depend upon them for pollination.

Today, with large farms and few woodlots, hedgerows, etc., wild bees are not as plentiful, and growers often rent honeybees from a beekeeper or maintain colonies themselves.

Bumblebees are excellent for pollination, for they will work at lower temperatures than honeybees and visit more flowers, but they are much more difficult to maintain. Other means of pollination exist in nature (pineapples, for example, are pollinated by hummingbirds), but fruit growers depend upon insects, nut growers upon wind.

What happens after pollen transfer?

The pollen grain is deposited on the stigma—the tip of the style, which extends from the ovary (see Figure 1). Here it germinates, producing the pollen tube, which grows down the style to the ovary. An amazing "radar system" allows the pollen tube to find its way to the ovule, which will later become the seed. The tube penetrates the ovule, where it releases two nuclei; one of these unites with the egg cell, forming the zygote, the other joins the two "polar nuclei" to form the endosperm. The zygote undergoes cell division to form the embryo, and the endosperm cells enlarge and serve as a source of nutrients for the growing embryo; all are contained within the embryo sac, which is in turn surrounded by the nucellus (maternal tissue which also provides nutrients).

In commercial cultivars of most fruits, the presence of a fertilized ovule (seed) is a prerequisite for growth of the ovary. (Note exceptions above.) The act of fertilization and the subsequent development of the embryo apparently stimulates the production of hormones necessary for the ovary and attached tissues to begin growing. Thus, this process is an extremely important one. If pollen transfer is delayed by cold or rainy weather, bees will not fly, fertilization cannot occur, and the ovule will degenerate.

The "effective pollination period" (EPP, see Figure 2) is the interval of time during which fertilization can be effected. If ovules are viable for eight days, and two days are required for the pollen tube to reach the ovule, the effective pollination period is six (8 minus 2) days. If pollen is deposited on the stigma between days one and six, fertil-

---

TABLE 1

Terms used in describing pollination requirements, and selected examples.

Term	Definition and examples
Parthenocarpic	Requiring no pollination; seedless. Bartlett pear in the Sacramento Valley,California; Sultanina grape, banana, some cultivars of fig.
Self-fruitful	Capable of setting a commercial crop following self-pollination. Montmorency sour cherry, Stanley plum, most peach cultivars, Golden Delicious apple.
Self-unfruitful	Requiring cross-pollination for a commercial crop. Most sweet cherry, apple, and pear cultivars.
Triploid	Lacking viable pollen, therefore must be cross-pollinated. Mutsu, Winesap apple.
Incompatible	Having viable pollen, but incapable of setting fruit when cross-pollinated. Bing, Lambert, Napoleon, Emperor Francis sweet cherry; Bartlett x Seckel pear; Cortland x McIntosh apple; all strains of Delicious apple (reproductive structures are genetically identical).

ization can occur; deposition on day seven will be too late (7 days plus 2 for pollen tube growth = 9; by this time the ovule will have degenerated). Cool weather slows pollen tube growth, but prolongs ovule longevity, thus temperature plays a primary role in the race to beat the clock.

What limits fruit set?

everal factors other than weather limit set. In addition to being compatible, pollinizer cultivars must bloom at the same time as the cultivar being pollinated. This is less important in stone fruits than in pome fruits, as cultivars of the former tend to bloom almost simultaneously in the North Temperate Zone. In Delicious apple, especially, the "king" or center bloom is the first to open and produces the largest fruit. Therefore, for maximum fruit size, the pollinizer cultivar should be in bloom when the first Delicious flowers open. Winter Banana is recommended as a pollinizer for Delicious, based upon time of bloom *(see Figure 3)*.

FIGURE 1

Structures of the ovary, ovule, and pollen tube.

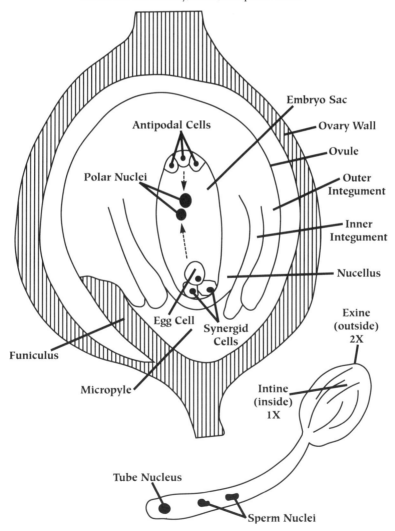

In addition to time of bloom, the cultivar should be "precocious," i.e., the tree should bloom at a young age. Golden Delicious is precocious; Northern Spy is notoriously late in coming into bloom. This has become less of a problem with increasing use of dwarfing rootstocks, for such trees usually bloom within two to four years. The pollinizer should be an annual bearer; Winter Banana is biennial (tends to bloom every other year). This can be controlled, however, by chemical thinning, or, if the trees are used only as pollinizers, by early removal of all fruits.

Placement of pollinizers

For maximum cross pollination, alternate rows are desirable. However, this is seldom convenient in commercial orchards. More commonly, two to four rows of a single cultivar are planted, alternating with two to four rows of another. If only a few pollinizers are required, these can be planted every third tree in every third row; this provides a pollinizer adjacent to each tree of the main

cultivar *(see Figure 4)*. The volume of pollinizer fruit produced can be further reduced by grafting a pollinizer limb on every tree. The pollinizer cultivar used should be clearly distinguishable from the cultivar to be pollinated to avoid mixing of cultivars at harvest. Crab apples are ideal for this purpose, given their small size.

As a temporary measure to provide pollen, flowering branches of pollinizer cultivars can be cut and the bases placed in barrels containing water. The cuttings should be taken just as the king flowers are opening to maximize the period of pollen availability. Placement recommended is the same as for pollinizer trees.

In recent years, solid blocks of single

FIGURE 2

Concept of the effective pollination period (EPP). In this example, the ovule is receptive for eight days following flower opening (anthesis). Pollen tube growth and fertilization require two days. Pollination at any time between zero and six days will result in fertilization; thereafter the ovule is not receptive when the pollen tube reaches it. Thus, EPP is six days (=8 minus 2).

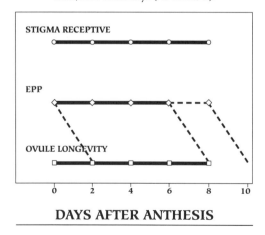

DAYS AFTER ANTHESIS

FIGURE 3

Flowering periods for commercial apple cultivars and for crab apples recommended as pollinizers.

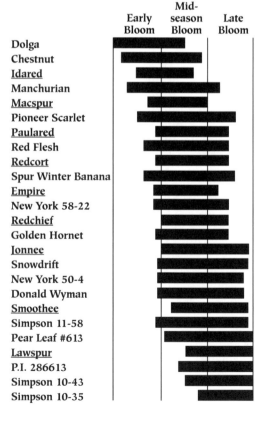

cultivars have become popular, using crab apples as pollinizers. The pollinizer trees are usually planted between the trees of the commercial cultivar in order to maximize production. In close plantings with dwarf rootstocks, recommendations call for one pollinizer every sixth tree in every second or third row; the pollinizer trees can be offset in the next row to minimize the distance (no more than 50 feet) between pollinizer tree and commercial cultivar. Several crab apple cultivars can be used to extend the period of bloom to assure adequate pollination, and data are available to indicate bloom periods relative to commercial cultivars *(see Figure 3)*.

Bees tend to work flowers of the same color; therefore, crab apples with white petals are preferable to those with red petals. The crab apples can be pruned heavily to reduce interference with the other trees.

Although apple flowers are attractive to bees, pear and plum flowers are less so. Competition with other sources of pollen may reduce bee visits. If dandelions are abundant on the orchard floor, for example, bees may work them instead of fruit blossoms, especially in cool or windy weather. Mowing or the use of herbicides can reduce such competition.

Bee rental is a good investment to assure adequate pollination. However, the bees should be well cared for prior to placement in the orchard, and each hive should have in it approximately six frames of brood (larvae) and contain about 30,000 bees. Two-story colonies are essential to allow sufficient space for this many bees. Because the brood is fed pollen, bees will be better pollen collectors if brood is abundant. The hives (2 per acre) should be placed in groups of four to six with 150 yards between groups, although 8 to 16 colonies at intervals of 200 to 300 yards can be used in large orchards. Each colony should be placed in a warm location with the entrance facing the sun, and grass and weeds should

not be allowed to grow up around the entrance, thereby interfering with bee flight.

Windbreaks are useful in sheltering from wind. Care should be taken in placing the bees in hedgerow plantings, as the insects tend not to cross rows; placement at the ends of the rows is therefore preferable to placement at the side of the planting. Insecticides should not be applied while the bees remain in the orchard.

Several methods are available for enhancing the effectiveness of bees and/or other pollinating insects. Containers of pollen ("pollen inserts") of selected cultivars can be purchased and placed at the entrance of the hive. Bees walk through the pollen on leaving the hive, and pick up pollen on their legs. Another method is a system whereby the bees are dusted with pollen as they walk through a device within the hive. Hand pollination can be used, but is expensive. The pollen can be diluted with *Lycopodium* spores (available at pharmacies) and applied to one flower in every four to five clusters, using a camel's hair brush or the index finger.

FIGURE 4

Planting plan for orchard with minimal number of pollinizer trees.

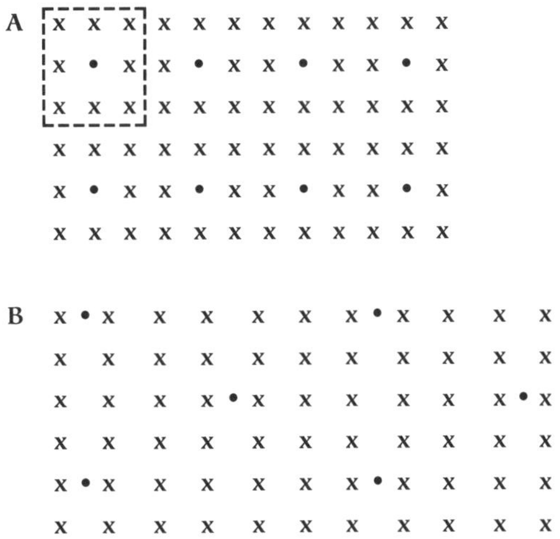

```
A  x  x  x   x  x  x  x  x  x  x  x  x
   x  •  x   x  •  x  x  •  x  x  •  x
   x  x  x   x  x  x  x  x  x  x  x  x
      x  x  x  x  x  x  x  x  x  x  x  x
      x  •  x  x  •  x  x  •  x  x  •  x
      x  x  x  x  x  x  x  x  x  x  x  x


B   x • x   x   x   x   x   x • x   x   x   x
    x   x   x   x   x   x   x   x   x   x   x
    x   x   x   x • x   x   x   x   x   x • x
    x   x   x   x   x   x   x   x   x   x   x
    x • x   x   x   x   x   x • x   x   x   x
    x   x   x   x   x   x   x   x   x   x   x
```

x = commercial cultivar
• = pollinizer

Flowers contain chemicals that are attractive to bees. Some of these have been identified and are available commercially for spraying on the trees to be pollinated. Results to date have been variable, some reports indicating considerable benefit, others little or none. More recently, a pher-

omone produced by the queen bee that attracts worker bees during swarming has been identified. This can also be sprayed on trees. Again, the results to date are not conclusive. Problems include cost and the volatility and water solubility of the chemical, which is easily washed off by rain.

FIGURE 5

Effect of shading on fruit set and fruit size of apple (Jackson, 1975).

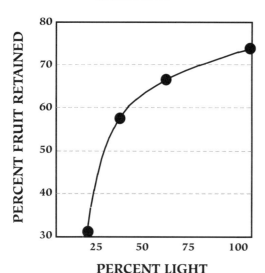

PERCENT LIGHT
TRANSMITTED BY SHADES

PERCENT LIGHT
TRANSMITTED BY SHADES

What other conditions affect set?

Weather conditions at times other than during bloom can affect flower quality, and therefore set. Observations in England indicate that temperatures from March through June (bloom occurs in April) are highly correlated with cropping of Cox's Orange Pippin apple.

Parallel results have been reported in New York State. The higher the temperature, the poorer the set, perhaps because the trees use carbohydrate reserves for respiration, leaving less for set.

What tree factors affect set?

A number of factors unrelated to pollen transfer affect set, including cultivar, bloom density, and tree age and vigor. Cultivars that are self-fruitful tend to set more heavily than those that are self-unfruitful; thus, Golden Delicious sets heavily, Delicious and McIntosh less so. As bloom density increases in apple, percentage fruit set declines as a result of competition among flowers. However, this is not the case in sour cherry or almond.

Young apple trees, especially on vigorous rootstocks, often set poorly, perhaps because of competition between vegetative growth and fruit set; fruit set on old trees may be excessive, even though fruit size is often small.

Set varies among rootstocks, trees on semi-dwarf and dwarfing stocks tending to set more fruit. Similarly, spur-type strains of apple cultivars usually set more heavily than standard strains, and therefore are in greater need of thinning.

What cultural practices affect set?

In addition to providing for adequate pollination, several cultural practices can influence set. Nutrition is a crucial factor, and growers apply nitrogen, in particular, either in the late fall or early spring, to assure that the tree has an adequate supply of this essential element. Pruning and training practices that improve penetration of sunlight, as well as control of diseases that reduce leaf surface, favor fruit set. Shading has a marked effect on fruit set, especially as the light level drops below 40% of full sun *(see Figure 5)*.

Ringing (removal of a section of bark around the trunk) or scoring (cutting the bark around the trunk) can improve set, although this affects fruit retention, rather than set per se *(see section on fruit development)*. Branch bending in apple can increase not only flower bud formation, but may favor fruit set as well. While not a practical method of improving set, data from several sources in Europe suggest that early harvest increases the quality of flowers and their ability to set fruit the following spring.

Summary

Fruit set is the second of the three main factors—flowering, fruit set, fruit development—in determining yield. Species differ considerably in the percentage of flowers that must produce fruits for a commercial crop to be obtained; among stone and pome fruits, the numbers range from 5 to 30. The primary factor in fruit set, aside from parthenocarpic species, is pollen transfer. Although weather is a crucial and often uncontrollable factor in determining the extent of pollen transfer, there are many ways by which the grower can assure that adequate pollination occurs, and that tree vigor is sufficient to set a good crop of fruit.

Literature cited and suggested reading

Dennis, F.G. Jr., "Factors affecting yield in apple with emphasis on Delicious," *Hort. Rev.* 1 (1979): 395-422.

Dennis, F.G., Jr., "Apple," 1-44, In: *Handbook of Fruit Set and Development*, edited by S.P. Monselise. Boca Raton, FL: CRC Press, 1986 (additional chapters on pear, peach, other fruits).

Free, J.B., *Insect Pollination of Crops*. 2nd ed. San Diego, CA: Acad. Press, 1993 (see esp. Ch. 57).

Jackson, J.E., "Effects of light intensity on growth, cropping, and fruit quality," 17-31, In: *Climate and The Orchard. Effects of Climatic Factors on Fruit Tree Growth and Cropping in South-eastern England*, Research Review No. 5, edited by H.C. Pereira, Commonwealth Bureau of Horticulture and Plantation Crops, E. Malling, Maidstone, Kent, England, 1975.

Jackson, J.E, and P.J.C. Hamer, "The causes of year-to-year variation in the average yield of Cox's Orange Pippin in England," *J. Hort. Sci.* 55 (1986): 149-156.

Johansen, C.A., ed, "Pollination and Fruit Set; Proceedings of the Shortcourse," March 1985. Yakima, WA: *Good Fruit Grower*, 1985.

Mayer, D.F., C.A. Johanson, and M. Burgett. Bee pollination of tree fruits. Pacific Northwest Coop. Ext. Publ. No. PNW 0282, 1986.

10 Fruit Development

Frank G. Dennis, Jr.
Department of Horticulture
Michigan State University
East Lansing, Michigan

Assuming sufficient flowers have been initiated and conditions have been conducive to fruit set, fruit growth is the next concern of the fruit grower. But let's first ask just what is a fruit? Botanists define a fruit as a ripened ovary plus closely associated parts.

Many plants—from corn to coconuts—produce fruits; however, some are considered pomological fruits, some are not. Pomological fruits are botanical fruits that are: a) edible, b) of economic importance, and c) produced by perennial plants. This definition rules out tung nuts (inedible), beech nuts (limited economic importance except for seed), and tomatoes (annual plant). Strawberry is considered a pomological fruit in the northern United States, where it is grown as a perennial, but not in Florida, where it is an annual crop. Thus do plant scientists distinguish between crops!

Fruit development

Economics dictate that growers must make a profit if they wish to remain in business. In some fruit crops, size is not a primary consideration. In sour cherries, for example, most of which are processed, no premium is paid for size within certain limits, although small fruits may be immature. Thus, fruit size is less important than in apple, where larger sizes fetch premium prices, and fruits less than a certain mini-mum diameter are consigned to the cider press. Aside from price, size is often related to quality; very large apple fruits often do not store well or are subject to disorders such as bitter pit.

Fruits differ in their morphology (see Figure 1). In temperate zone pomology, we deal primarily with berries, drupes, and pomes. In berries, such as grapes, the entire ovary wall is edible; there is no stone or core. In stone fruits (drupes), the inner ovary wall (endocarp) is hard and inedible; only the skin (exocarp) and flesh (mesocarp) are edible.

Pome fruits consist of more than an ovary wall; part of the stem (receptacle) encloses the flower and becomes a part of the fruit. Both the receptacle and the ovary wall are edible, with the exception of the endocarp, the parchment-like lining of the seed cavity that sticks in your teeth when you bite too deep.

Many other kinds of fruits exist, including true nuts (filbert; walnuts are actually drupes), achenes (strawberry), etc., but berries, drupes, and pomes are our major concern here.

Fruits differ in their rates and timing of growth. Both berries and drupes exhibit a "double sigmoid" growth curve: growth is rapid in the first and third stages of development, but slow in the second (see Figure 2). In drupes, the endocarp hardens during

---

FIGURE 1

In berries (tomato, grape), the entire ovary wall is fleshy. Drupes (cherry, peach, plum) have a hard inner ovary wall (endocarp). Pomes (apple, pear) contain both ovary and receptacle (stem) tissue and a "core."

BERRY (tomato)

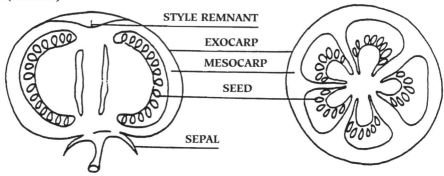

STYLE REMNANT
EXOCARP
MESOCARP
SEED
SEPAL

DRUPE (peach)

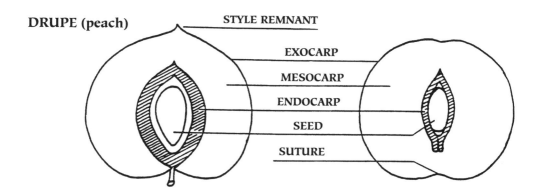

STYLE REMNANT
EXOCARP
MESOCARP
ENDOCARP
SEED
SUTURE

POME (apple)

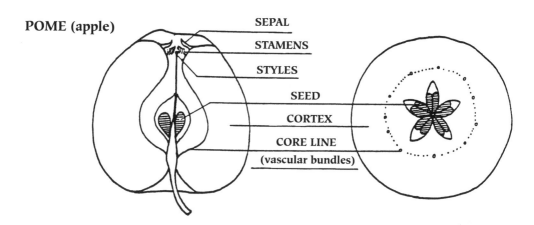

SEPAL
STAMENS
STYLES
SEED
CORTEX
CORE LINE
(vascular bundles)

THREE TYPES OF FRUITS

Stage II, and this has been interpreted as the reason for the slow growth of the fruit as a whole.

However, grapes have no endocarp, yet they, too, exhibit a slower development during Stage II. The seed tissues, too, develop rapidly during Stage II (see Figure 3), but slowing of growth of the fruit occurs even in seedless grapes.

In general, Stage II is shorter in early-ripening cultivars of cherry and peach than in later-ripening ones. Pomes (apple, pear, and quince) have a different growth curve (sigmoidal), with a relatively constant rate of growth (see Figure 2).

Fertilized seeds remain relatively small following fruit set; only after about four to five weeks does the embryo begin to grow rapidly (see Figure 3). During the next two to three weeks, it completely fills the seed; thereafter, it accumulates nutrients, but practically ceases to grow in size. In filbert, embryo growth is delayed even more; most of the growth occurs during the last three to four weeks on the tree.

WHY DO FRUITS GROW?

This question has been asked for thousands of years, but we know little more about the answer than did those who first asked the question. Most fruits require pollination and fertilization, with subsequent seed development, in order to grow. Exceptions include navel oranges and commercial cultivars of bananas, which lack seeds entirely. Some seedless grapes (e.g., Sultanina) are also "parthenocarpic," requiring no pollination; others (Thompson Seedless) require fertilization, but the embryos soon abort.

Seed tissues are rich in hormones, such as auxins, gibberellins, and cytokinins; furthermore, these compounds are capable of inducing fruit set in the absence of pollination, and/or stimulating fruit growth. These observations have led to the theory that hormones produced by seeds control fruit growth, at least in its early phases. Later stages of growth are apparently indepen-

dent of seed development; removal of seeds from Golden Delicious apple fruits in mid-July, for example, has little effect on subsequent development.

Despite hundreds of studies in laboratories around the world, little direct evidence

FIGURE 2

Growth of pome (A) versus stone (B) fruits
Top—cumulative growth;
bottom—rate of growth over time
(Dennis, 1984).

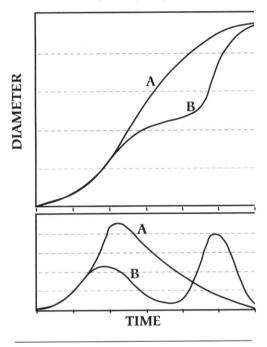

FIGURE 3

Growth in length of various parts of the apple fruit from bloom to maturity (Tukey and Young, 1942).

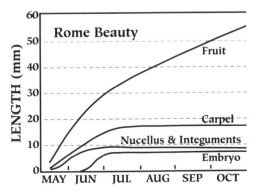

FIGURE 4

Contribution of cell enlargement and cell division to increase in diameter of the sour cherry fruit (adapted from Tukey, 1981).

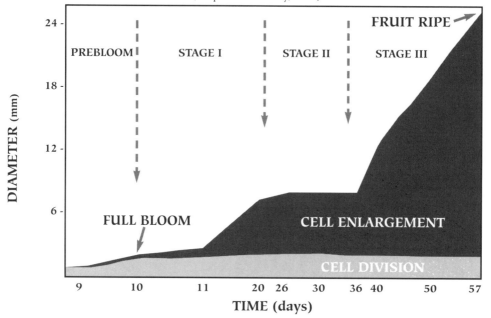

FIGURE 5

Relation between number of seeds per fruit and final fruit circumference of Delicious apples (Williams, 1979).

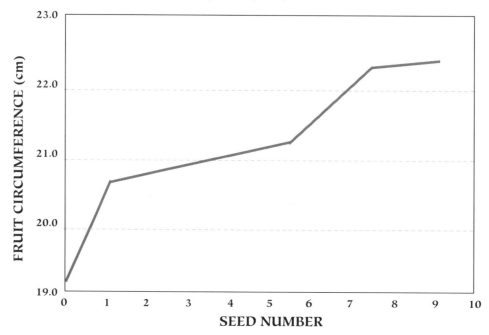

for the role of seed hormones in fruit development has been obtained. Their concentrations do not appear to be correlated with growth rate. This probably means that we do not yet know how to extract or measure these compounds, rather than that they do not control growth. New methods of study, especially molecular biology, may help solve the riddle.

Both cell division and cell enlargement occur in young fruits of most species. Cell division slows with time, and cell enlargement, together with increasing volume of intercellular spaces, is responsible for most of the subsequent increase in size *(see Figure 4)*. Division continues longer in pome fruits than in stone fruits; in avocado fruits, it persists as long as the fruit remains on the tree. Small fruits generally contain both fewer and smaller cells than large fruits, and early fruit thinning can increase both cell number and cell size.

WHAT DETERMINES FINAL FRUIT SIZE?

The most important factor controlling size is genetics; crab apples seldom exceed 1.5 inches (3.8 cm) in diameter, while Twenty Ounce and Wolf River apple fruits often reach 5 inches (12.5 cm) or more in diameter. Gala, Jonathan, and Empire are recognized as "medium-sized" apples in the eastern United States, and fruit thinning is generally necessary for adequate size. Within cultivars, however, many factors can influence size. Climate is one of the most important. Washington State, with its abundant sunshine and availability of water for irrigation, produces larger fruit than does Michigan, where skies are often cloudy and irrigation less common.

Seed number also can be important. This is well-established in grape and kiwifruit, in which fruit weight increases with seed number, but the same is often true for apple *(see Figure 5)* and pear. This relationship, together with the need for adequate pollination for fruit set, makes a good supply of bees imperative during bloom *(see Chapter 9)*.

Fruit density—the number of fruits per unit trunk or limb cross-sectional area—is a crucial factor in fruit size; as fruit density increases, the ratio of leaves to fruits decreases, resulting in less supply of photosynthate per fruit; fruit size therefore decreases *(see Figure 6)*.

Maximum returns are obtained when the leaf/fruit ratio is optimum; this optimum can only be established by experience, for orchards differ in carrying capacity under the influence of climate, cultivar, and management practices. In establishing leaf/fruit ratio, the effects upon flower initiation for the following year, as well as fruit size in the current year, must be considered *(see Chapter 8)*.

Fruit distribution and position on the tree also influence size. Only limited translocation of carbohydrates occurs between sections of a tree, therefore, heavily cropping limbs may bear small fruits even if the remainder of the tree crops lightly. Fruits in the top of the tree will be larger than those on limbs near the bottom because of shading of the latter, resulting in lower rates of photosynthesis. Thus, pruning and training are important for maximizing light penetration.

FIGURE 6

Effect of leaf/fruit ratio on size and yield of fruits (diagrammatic).

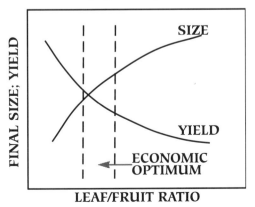

Fruit position on the cluster can affect fruit size. Apple inflorescences are "cymes;" the terminal flower is the earliest formed and largest, and therefore is capable of producing larger fruits than the lateral flowers *(see Figure 7)*. This is particularly noticeable in Delicious, whereas in cultivars such as McIntosh, the difference is less pronounced. In hand thinning, all but the

---

FIGURE 7

Relative sizes of fruits on a raceme (A) versus a cyme (B) (diagrammatic).

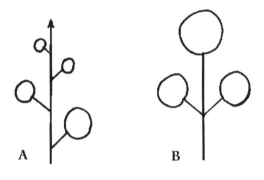

A   B

FIGURE 8

Change in length/diameter ratio over time in pear, peach, and apple (Westwood, 1993).

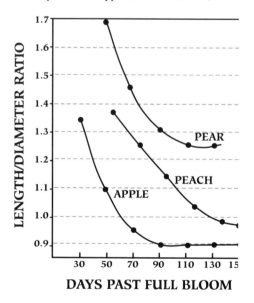

DAYS PAST FULL BLOOM

"king" fruit are often removed in order to maximize fruit size.

Pear and cherry inflorescences are racemes; the terminal flower is the last formed and therefore the smallest *(see Figure 7)*; thus, basal flowers tend to produce larger fruits than terminal ones. Again, species and cultivars differ as to the importance of this effect; in grape (raceme), terminal berries usually differ little from basal ones in size, whereas in tomatoes, the basal fruits are definitely larger.

Fruit size declines as trees age and become less vigorous; young trees can therefore support larger crops than old ones. This decline in fruit size, together with the ravages of disease, insects, and cold injury, dictates that orchards be replaced after 15 to 40 years, varying with species and other considerations.

The supply of nutrients and water also controls fruit size; commercial practices affecting these limitations will be discussed under cultural practices below. L.D. Tukey demonstrated that young fruits actually shrink during the morning and early afternoon as a result of moisture stress. Growth at night, when relative humidity is high, more than compensates for this shrinkage.

WHAT DETERMINES FRUIT SHAPE?
As is the case with fruit size, cultivar plays the most important role in establishing fruit shape. In apple, for example, Delicious is conical, whereas McIntosh is "oblate" (round, but flattened at the poles). Lobing of the calyx end of Delicious gives a more or less "typy" apple, but McIntosh exhibits no lobing. Similar differences occur among cultivars of other species.

Length/diameter (L/D) ratio declines rapidly as apple, pear, and peach fruits grow, then it stabilizes *(see Figure8)*. Length/diameter ratio in apple varies as a function of night temperature early in the season. Lobing of Delicious is essentially nil in South Carolina where nights are warm, intermediate in Michigan, and pronounced in the interior valleys of Washington State where nights are cool *(see Figure 9)*. Washington growers, in fact, use this "typiness" as a selling point. Probably the main reason such fruits are preferred by the customer, however, is that they are larger than "non-typy" fruits of the same diameter.

Students under my direction sorted Michigan-grown Delicious into several groups varying in shape and weight and used a vending machine to compare their sales. Customers preferred typy fruit only when the two choices were of the same diameter. No such preference was evident when fruits were of the same weight.

In apple, "king" fruits have lower L/D ratios than do lateral fruits. Rootstocks also affect L/D ratio, the ratio increasing with vigor of the stock. The L/D ratio also differs among apple strains, particularly in Delicious.

Seed number often affects fruit weight *(see above)*, and seed distribution can affect fruit shape. In some cultivars of apple, fruits are asymmetric when one side has no seeds. In stone fruits, which normally contain only one seed (one ovule aborts), the side of the fruit to which the seed is attached is larger than the opposite side *(see Figure 10)*. When both ovules develop into seeds, the sides are symmetrical.

In certain areas, including Egypt (peaches) and the Sacramento and southern San Joaquin valleys of California (sweet cherries), abnormalities may occur in the flowers of stone fruits, resulting in double or even triple fruits *(see Chapter 13)*. High summer temperatures during flower initiation were suggested as the cause of these problems in California, and evaporative cooling reduced, but did not eliminate the problem. Moisture stress may also play a role in this phenomenon.

WHAT CULTURAL PRACTICES CAN BE USED TO AFFECT FRUIT GROWTH?

Many cultural practices are employed to control fruit growth, based upon the known effects of the factors discussed above. Good pollination ensures sufficient seed development to promote fruit growth, therefore, growers encourage cross-pollination by providing pollinizer cultivars, renting bees, and/or buying pollen to supplement that available *(see Chapter 9)*.

Fruit size

Fertilizer, especially nitrogen, application is standard practice in the spring to assure an adequate supply for vigorous (but not overly vigorous) growth. Leaf nutrient content can be used as an index of whether too much or too little fertilizer is being applied before size is affected. Washington growers need no reminder of the importance of water in controlling fruit size. Irrigation is essential for sizing fruits in arid areas, such

---

FIGURE 9

Fruit shape of Delicious apples in South Carolina (A), Michigan (B), and Wenatchee, Washington (C) (diagrammatic).

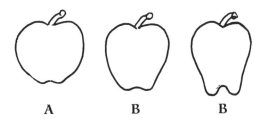

A   B   B

FIGURE 10

Effect of seed attachment on shape of plum fruits. Fruit on left contains one seed, fruit on right two (Dennis, 1984).

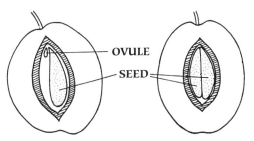

OVULE

SEED

as the Yakima Valley; in areas with higher rainfall, it may be beneficial only in some years or for some species. Peach is the most responsive among temperate zone tree fruits because of the tree's shallow root system. Some experimental data indicate that appropriate timing (regulated deficit irrigation, or RDI) can limit competition between shoot versus fruit growth and thereby improve fruit size and/or quality, particularly of peach *(see Chapter 13)*.

Weed control influences fruit growth by reducing competition for moisture and nutrients. Pruning has two major effects on fruit development; it reduces shading, thus increasing photosynthetic efficiency, and it reduces competition for photosynthates, stored carbohydrates, water, and nutrients among branches and fruits, thus increasing fruit size.

Ringing (cutting the bark around the circumference of the limb or trunk) and girdling (removal of a ring of bark), although seldom recommended, can have marked effects on flowering, fruit retention, and/or fruit growth in some species. Seedless grapes are girdled ("cinctured") to increase fruit set *(see Chapter 9)*, and apple and pear trees can be scored or ringed either to hasten flowering or increase fruit set. The prac-

tice has been recommended for peach in Alabama as a means of both increasing fruit size and hastening maturity. A spiral "S" girdle of scaffold branches proved most beneficial, and over 2,000 acres of trees were being girdled in the Southeast in the mid-1980s. Anyone contemplating this practice should check with farm advisors/extension personnel before proceeding, for detrimental side effects can occur.

Flower and fruit removal ("thinning") reduces competition among fruits, thereby increasing fruit size. The effect of this practice declines with time, the greatest response being obtained early, when flowers are thinned; little or no response can be expected late in the season *(see Figure 11)*. Flowers can be removed with caustic sprays, immature fruits either by hand or with growth regulator sprays.

Growth regulators have been used by orchardists for a number of effects for the last 50 years. One of the first compounds to be used commercially was NAA for fruit thinning—a chemical method to replace or supplement hand thinning. The effects are indirect; size is increased because some fruits are removed, thereby reducing competition among fruits.

The effects of other chemicals are direct. Succinamic acid dimethylhydrazide (better known by its trade name "Alar") reduces both fruit size and preharvest drop of apple and pear, while increasing firmness. The "Alar scare" some years ago forced the

---

FIGURE 11

Effect of time of thinning on final fruit size (diagrammatic).

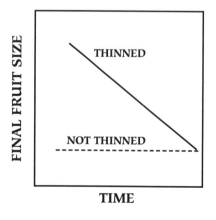

FIGURE 12

Response of Thompson Seedless grapes to application of GA$_3$. (A) control, not treated; (B) treated (after Weaver, 1972).

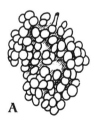 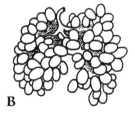

A   B

manufacturer to remove this compound from the market. Currently, experiments are in progress with aminoethoxyvinyl glycine (AVG), which shows promise in reducing preharvest drop of apples. This compound is also very effective in increasing fruit set in apple and pear, but registration for this purpose is not being pursued at this time.

Gibberellic acid (GA) is used commercially to increase size of Thompson Seedless and other seedless cultivars of grape *(see Figure 12)*, often in combination with cincturing. Gibberellic acid increases the length of the axis of the cluster (rachis), thereby "loosening" the cluster, and elongates individual berries.

Tim Facteau at Hood River, Oregon, pioneered the use of GA to delay maturation and increase fruit size, soluble solids, and firmness of sweet cherries. Many growers in the western United States now use GA for these purposes *(see Chapter 14)*. Sprays are applied about three weeks before normal harvest, as the fruit is changing color from green to yellow. However, effects on sour cherry have been disappointing.

The cytokinin 6-benzyladenine (BA) stimulates the growth of the apical portion of apple fruits, resulting in a greater L/D ratio. It is usually used in combination with $GA_{4/7}$ in the commercial product "Promalin" *(see Figure 13)*; Delicious and Golden Delicious are especially responsive, owing to their naturally conic shape. A different formulation of this combination (Accel),

with one-tenth the concentration of GAs, is effective as a thinning agent, and, under some conditions, increases fruit size over and above the thinning effect alone.

Summary

An understanding of the principles and practices involved in fruit development is essential in order for growers to optimize crop load, fruit size, and quality. Although much remains to be learned about why fruits grow, we know a great deal about how fruits grow and how their development can be controlled by cultural practices and chemical treatments.

Despite public concerns about the use of growth-regulating chemicals, I am confident that current research on the molecular aspects of the role of plant hormones will lead to better understanding—and control of—fruit development.

FIGURE 13

Effects of $GA_{4/7}$ plus benzyladenine on fruit shape of Delicious apple in South Carolina.
Left, treated; right, control (adapted from Stembridge and Morrell, 1973).

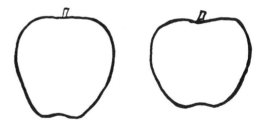

Literature cited

Dennis, F.G., Jr., "Fruit development," Ch. 10, 265-289, In: *Physiological Basis of Crop Growth and Development,* edited by M.B. Tesar, American Soc. of Agronomy/ Crop and Soil Science Society, Madison, WI, 1984.

Dennis, F.G., Jr., "Apple," In: *Handbook of Fruit Set and Development,* edited by S.P. Monselise, 1-44, Boca Raton, FL: CRC Press, 1986.

Monselise, S., *Handbook of Fruit Set and Development,* Boca Raton, FL: CRC Press, 1986.

Schaffer, and P. C. Andersen, eds. "Handbook of Environmental Physiology of Fruit Crops," Vol. I. *Temperate Crops,* Boca Raton, FL: CRC Press, 1994.

Stembridge, G.E., and G. Morrell, "Effect of gibberellins and 6-benzyladenine on the shape and fruit set of 'Delicious' apples," *J. Amer. Soc. Hort. Sci.* 97 (1972): 464-467.

Tukey, H.B., and J.O. Young, "Gross morphology and histology of the developing fruit of the apple," *Bot. Gaz.* 104 (1942): 1-25.

Tukey, L.D., "Periodicity in growth of fruits of apples, peaches, and sour cherries with some factors influencing this development," Bull. 661, Pennsylvania State University, University Park, PA, 1959.

Tukey, L.D., "Growth and development in tree fruits," edited by R.B. Tukey and M.U. Williams, In: *Tree Fruit Growth Regulators and Chemical Thinning,* 1-45, Washington State University, Pullman, WA, 1981.

Weaver, R.J., *Plant Growth Substances in Agriculture,* San Francisco, CA: W. H. Freeman and Co., 1972.

Westwood, M.N., "Temperate Zone Pomology." *Physiology and Culture,* 3rd ed., Portland, OR: Timber Press, Inc., 1993.

Williams, M.W., "Chemical thinning of apples," *Hort. Reviews* 1 (1979): 270-300.

11 Fruit Maturity and Ripening

Jim Mattheis
U.S. Department of Agriculture
Agricultural Research Service
Wenatchee, Washington

The processes of fruit development culminate in maturation and ripening. Like the growth phase of fruit development, ripening is closely controlled at the genetic level but is also influenced by environmental and cultural factors.

Characteristics of fruit respiration at the onset of ripening separate fruits into two groups *(see Figure 1)*. Fruits with a relatively rapid increase in respiration rate are known as climacteric fruits, and the rapid increase in respiration is referred to as the climacteric. Conversely, nonclimacteric fruits do not exhibit an increase in respiration rate when ripening begins. Apple, apricot, avocado, banana, kiwi, peach, pear, plum, and tomato are examples of climacteric fruits. Some nonclimacteric fruits are blueberry, cherry, grape, citrus, pineapple, and strawberry.

Many processes of ripening, such as softening, de-greening, wax accumulation, and aroma production, accelerate after the climacteric occurs. Because fruit storage compounds (organic acids, lipid, starch, sugars) are utilized at an increased rate after the increase in respiration rate begins, optimum harvest time for maximizing fruit storage life corresponds to this point in development for climacteric fruits.

Ethylene

A colorless, odorless gas, ethylene is an essential component regulating the ripening process of climacteric fruits. Ethylene is also produced by plant tissue in response to many types of stress. Typically, the amounts produced are very low, a characteristic of plant hormones. The onset of the climacteric can be advanced by exposure of pre-climacteric fruits to ethylene. Fruits produced by plants that have been genetically modified to prevent ethylene synthesis only ripen after exposure to ethylene. Ripening of nonclimacteric fruits can also be stimulated by exposure to ethylene, however, these fruits resume their normal ripening patterns if ethylene is removed from their environment.

Ethylene is synthesized *(see Figure 2)* via a series of steps elucidated by S.F. Yang and colleagues. The initial portion of the pathway cycles via the amino acid methionine through several intermediates, including S-adenosyl methionine (SAM). SAM is converted to aminocyclopropane-carboxylic acid (ACC) by the enzyme ACC synthase. This is the rate-limiting step in the pathway, as ACC is readily converted to ethylene by the enzyme ACC oxidase. ACC oxidase develops first during the maturation process followed later by ACC synthase, meaning ethylene synthesis can be controlled by the presence or absence of enzymes necessary for synthesis. This mechanism operates at the level of gene expression and is one means by which plant growth and development is controlled.

A number of compounds act to inhibit the synthesis of ethylene. The adenosylation of methionine is prevented by 2-aminoethoxy-4-hexanoic acid (AHA). Conversion of SAM to ACC is prevented by aminoethoxyvinylglycine (AVG) and aminooxyacetic acid (AOA). The final synthesis step, conversion of ACC to ethylene, is inhibited by high temperature, several transition metals (Co, Ag, Ni, Cu), low oxygen (O_2) and/or high carbon dioxide (CO_2) concentrations.

Insertion of antisense copies of the gene coding for ACC oxidase into the plant genome is a new method to inhibit ethylene synthesis. Ethylene synthesis can be stimulated at the step converting SAM to ACC by auxin as well as wounding. The final step in the pathway can be stimulated by low temperatures, while O_2 and low concentrations of CO_2 are required for this reaction.

Ethylene action or response is dependent on development of a multi-component response pathway. In the absence of complete development of this pathway, plant tissues do not respond to ethylene. This can also be a means of developmental regulation in that development of the capacity for ethylene synthesis prior to development of the response pathway would result in ethylene production without a response. The components and regulation of the response pathway are current subjects of considerable research.

Norbornadiene and diazocyclopentadi-

FIGURE 1

Respiration during climacteric and nonclimacteric fruit development (Biale, 1964).

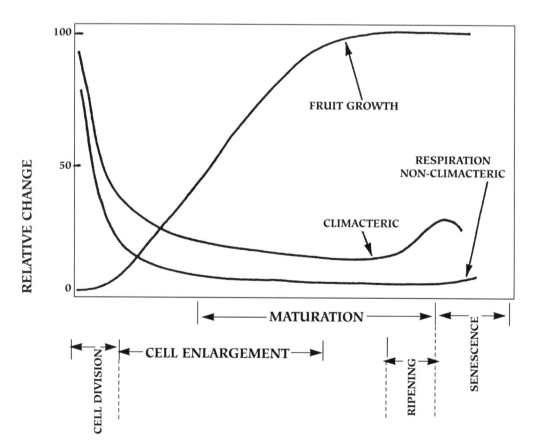

ene (DACP) are two compounds that interfere with ethylene action by preventing ethylene binding to its receptor(s). When these compounds are present, ethylene synthesis increases, but ethylene-mediated responses are inhibited. For example, apples treated with norbornadiene have a reduced rate of softening, but starch breakdown continues unchanged. This means softening requires ethylene action, while starch hydrolysis does not (Blankenship and Sisler, 1989).

Ethylene sensitivity increases as fruit maturation nears completion. The amount of ethylene necessary to accelerate ripening decreases as maturation progresses (Knee et al., 1987). This can be observed by treating pre-climacteric fruits with ethylene at various concentrations while measuring fruit respiration (oxygen absorption). As fruit development progresses, oxygen absorption increases at lower exogenous ethylene concentrations, indicating ethylene sensitivity has increased *(see Figure 3)*. Ethylene sensitivity of carnation flowers can be enhanced by treatment with short chain (C8-10) fatty acids (Whitehead, 1989).

Reduced ethylene sensitivity may be the cause of the residual effects of controlled atmosphere (CA) storage (Bangerth, 1984). Apples previously stored in CA exhibit reduced rates of respiration, softening, and volatile production upon return to ambient atmosphere conditions, compared to ripening of fruits after regular atmosphere (RA) storage (Smock, 1979).

Ethylene measurements can be a useful index for estimating optimum apple harvest dates for long-term CA storage. Pre-climacteric fruits ripen slower and maintain quality for longer periods than post-climacteric fruits. However, fruit picked too early does not develop its full potential because flavor development is impaired. Patterns of ethylene production differ between apple cultivars *(see Figure 4)* making the use of an absolute value of ethylene for determination of harvest more difficult. From a practical perspective, ethylene analysis along with other maturity indices (starch, firmness, titratable acidity, color changes, or soluble solids content) provides a more comprehensive estimate of fruit develop-

---

FIGURE 3

Oxygen absorption of pre-climacteric fruit in response to ethylene treatments (Wills et al., 1981).

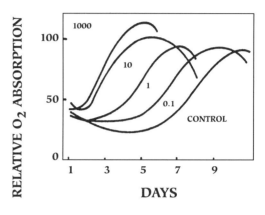

FIGURE 2

Pathway of ethylene synthesis with sites of inhibitors and promoters.

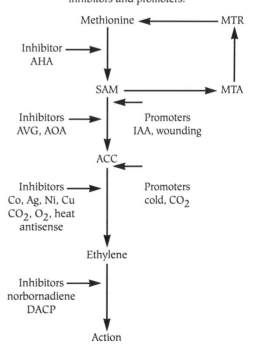

mental stage and serves as an additional tool to estimate fruit storage potential.

Ethylene production by d'Anjou pear fruits is not detectable at commercial maturity. The capacity to produce ethylene develops during storage, and fruits removed from storage too early do not produce ethylene in significant quantities. Quality changes associated with ripening occur at slow rates for pears not producing ethylene (Blankenship and Richardson, 1985). Softening, color changes, and aroma development during d'Anjou pear ripening are all mediated by ethylene.

Starch

Apple starch is composed of two glucose polymers, amylose and amylopectin. All the glucose residues comprising amylose are connected via the same bonding pattern,

FIGURE 4

Internal ethylene concentration during Gala, Delicious, and Fuji maturation. Arrows indicate optimum harvest date for long-term CA.

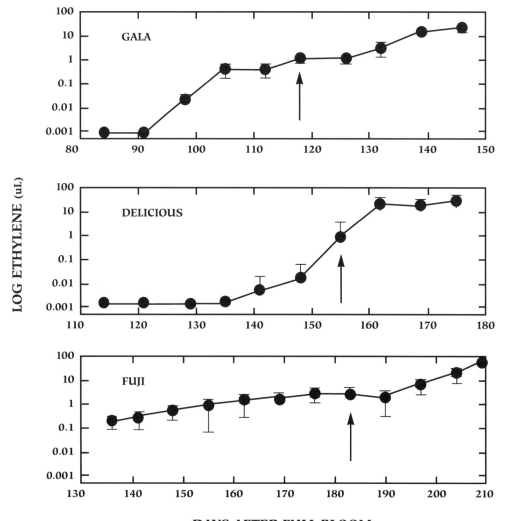

DAYS AFTER FULL BLOOM

resulting in a molecule with a straight chain structure. Amylopectin has two types of bonds linking the glucose components, resulting in a branched chain structure. The potassium iodide-iodine (KI-I_2) solution used to visualize starch is bound much more efficiently by amylose than amylopectin. When apple tissue containing starch is drenched with an KI-I_2 solution, the black color observed is primarily due to absorption by amylose.

Differences in amylose to amylopectin ratios exist between different apple varieties, and the ratio can change during ripening (Fan et al., 1995). For Fuji apples, amylose degradation accelerates relative to amylopectin loss during the final stage of fruit maturation, resulting in an increased rate of change in the starch rating. The relationship between total starch content determined analytically and the starch index determined using a KI-I_2 solution is not linear for Fuji apples. The initial period of starch breakdown results in a loss of greater than 70% of the total starch, while the starch index ratings change approximately 40% during the same period.

In spite of the poor correlation between starch content and the starch-iodine test, use of the starch index is a valuable maturity indicator for apple varieties in the Pacific Northwest, less subject to seasonal variation when plotted against days from full bloom compared to ethylene production. The pattern visualized by the KI-I_2 solution of starch breakdown during maturation is unique for each apple cultivar, as is the relationship between starch loss and ethylene production. Starch breakdown can be accelerated by ethylene treatment of pre-climacteric fruit.

As starch breakdown progresses, the accumulation of sugars released from the glucose polymer chains results in increased fruit soluble solids concentration (SSC). Varieties harvested with low starch scores (such as Delicious) exhibit higher SSC values after storage because the starch remaining at harvest continues to be degraded to sugar. A smaller increase in SSC during storage occurs in varieties picked with little starch remaining at harvest, such as Fuji.

Sugars released during starch breakdown are utilized for respiratory metabolism, as is malic acid, the organic acid present in largest amounts in apples, pears, and sweet cherries. Although the sugar concentration greatly exceeds malic acid in all three of these fruits, malic acid is consumed at a faster rate during ripening. This results in an increase in the sugar-to-acid ratio, a change that has consequences for fruit flavor. The flavor change can be positive or negative, depending on consumer preferences and varietal characteristics.

Color changes

Color changes during apple maturation and ripening are largely the result of chlorophyll breakdown, increased carotenoid concentration, and increased anthocyanin concentration in red varieties. The loss of chlorophyll results in decreased green color. This process can occur via several routes, one of which is catalyzed by a family of enzymes called chlorophyllases. Activity of these enzymes is stimulated by ethylene and increases during the climacteric rise in respiration (Looney and Patterson, 1967).

Several products of chlorophyll breakdown are possible, with only chlorins and purins being colorless compounds. Pheophorbide is a brown compound that can be formed during chlorophyll breakdown; however, little is known regarding its formation in apple fruit. The loss of chlorophyll and increase in carotenoids is most noticeable in apple varieties where yellowing of the peel occurs. The rate of carotenoid synthesis increases during the early stages of ripening in apples, but this process can lag behind chlorophyll loss (Knee, 1972).

Differences in regulation of chlorophyll loss and carotenoid synthesis between varieties leads to variety-specific patterns of background color development. A whitish background color stage is evident in apples where chlorophyll loss occurs at a greater rate than carotenoid synthesis. Seasonal temperature variation may also affect this process. Tree nutritional status can also affect color changes during ripening.

High nitrogen availability and uptake delay the maturation process (Benson et al., 1957), as well as the synthesis of anthocyanin. Light is required for anthocyanin accumulation in most apple cultivars (Beacon is an exception), and no relationship between red color development and climacteric ethylene production has been demonstrated. Regulation of anthocyanin synthesis varies between cultivars and strains. Low temperature exposure is an important factor regulating anthocyanin synthesis in many, but not all, red apple cultivars and strains.

Cuticle development

Many different compounds compose the fruit cuticle, the waxy, hydrophobic material deposited on the fruit surface. The cuticle slows fruit water loss, and its composition is regulated by developmental and environmental factors. During apple development, the cuticle is composed primarily of high molecular weight, high melting point hydrocarbons, fatty acids, alcohols, and ursolic acid, a large, 30-carbon triterpene. During ripening, cuticle composition changes, with a large accumulation of fatty acids having one or more double bonds in their carbon chains. These fatty acids have a lower melting point due to the double bonds; therefore, their accumulation results in a change in the physical properties of the cuticle. This change is quite noticeable in some varieties, Granny Smith and Jonagold for example, because it results in development of a slippery, greasy character of the peel as fruit ripening progresses.

The tendency for greasiness to develop in storage is closely linked to maturity at harvest, with late-harvest fruit more likely to become greasy in storage (Leake et al.,

1987). Cold temperatures result in increased production of unsaturated lipids by plant tissues in general. The increase in fatty acid accumulation during apple ripening can be slowed by low oxygen CA storage.

Nonethylene volatiles

Many compounds produced throughout fruit development are volatile within the temperature range experienced by fruits on the plant or in storage. Apple fruits produce numerous volatiles; in excess of 300 different volatile compounds have been identified from various apple varieties (Dimick and Hoskin, 1982). The types of compounds produced typically belong to one of several groups, primarily esters, aldehydes, alcohols, or ketones, with other compounds present in smaller amounts. In pre-climacteric apples, aldehydes and alcohols are the largest quantitative groups of volatiles produced.

After apple ripening begins, ester production increases and becomes the largest quantitative group in many cultivars. Esters have fruity, sweet odors, and these compounds are responsible in part for the development of characteristic flavor of many apple cultivars. The increase in ester production in Delicious and Fuji apples is related to the onset of the climacteric; however, seasonal variation can result in relatively large quantities of esters being produced by immature fruit. Not only does the total quantity of esters produced increase during ripening, so does the number of individual esters produced.

Although the mixture of esters produced by ripening apples is similar between varieties, quantities of individual esters produced is characteristic of each variety. For example, 2-methyl butylacetate is the largest quantitative ester produced by ripening Delicious apples, while butyl acetate is the largest produced by Gala apples. Of the volatiles emitted by Granny Smith apples, 2-methyl 1-butanol, an alcohol, is the largest quantitative component. This is indicative of the fact that Granny Smith apples are not efficient ester producers.

The change in production of volatile compounds by apple fruit is closely linked to ethylene. Fruits treated with ethylene synthesis inhibitors, AVG for example, produce esters at a lower rate compared to nontreated fruits (Halder-Doll and Bangerth, 1987). The effects of AVG can be overcome by exposing treated fruits to ethylene. DACP, an ethylene action inhibitor, also inhibits production of apple volatiles (X. Fan, unpublished). Therefore, ethylene is required for volatile synthesis to operate efficiently, and this also explains why fruit maturity is critical for development of flavor during storage.

Ethylene production and respiration rates of apples harvested immature lag those of mature fruit during storage. While immature fruit remain viable in storage for longer periods, the increase in volatile synthesis also lags that of mature fruit. This can contribute to the lack of development of varietal flavor during storage (Dirink et al., 1989).

Ethylene is an essential component of the fruit ripening process, mediating many processes of fruit ripening and senescence. Although the pathway and much of the regulation of the ethylene synthesis pathway is known, the developmental progression of the response pathway has not been characterized. This is an active area of current research in plant senescence, and progress will likely increase the understanding of the role of ethylene in regulating fruit ripening and maturation.

Literature cited

Bangerth, F., "Changes in sensitivity for ethylene during storage of apple and banana fruits under hypobaric conditions," *Sci. Hortic.* 24 (1984): 151-163.

Benson, N.R., R.M. Bullock, I.C. Chmelir, and E.S. Degmank, "Effects of levels of nitrogen and pruning on Starking and Golden Delicious apples," *Proc. Amer. Soc. Hort. Sci.* 70 (1957): 27-39.

Biale, J.B., "Growth, maturation, and senescence in fruits," *Science* 146 (1964): 880-888.

Blankenship, S.M., E.C. Sisler, "2,5-norbornadiene retards apple softening," *HortScience* 24 (1989): 313-314.

Blankenship, S.M. and D.G. Richardson, "Development of ethylene biosynthesis and ethylene-induced ripening in d'Anjou pears during the cold requirement for ripening," *J. Amer. Soc. Hort. Sci.* 110 (1985): 520-523.

Dimick, P.S. and J.C. Hoskin, "Review of apple flavor-state of the art," *CRC Critical Reviews Food Sci.* 18 (1982): 387-409.

Dirinck, P., H. De Pooter, and N. Schamp "Aroma development in ripening fruits." In *Flavor Chemistry, Trends and Developments,* edited by R. Teranishi, R.G. Buttery, and F. Shahidi. American Chemical Society, Washington, DC, 1989.

Fan, X., J.P. Mattheis, J.K. Fellman, and M.E Patterson, "Changes in amylose and starch content in Fuji apples during maturation," *HortScience* 30 (1995): 104-105.

Halder-Doll, H. and Bangerth, F., "Inhibition of autocatalytic C_2H_4-biosynthesis by AVG applications and consequences on the physiological behavior and quality of apple fruits in cool storage," *Sci. Hort.* 33 (1987): 87-96".

Knee, M., S.G.S. Hatfield, W.J. Bramlage, "Response of developing apple fruits to ethylene treatment," *J. Exp. Botany* 38 (1987): 972-979.

Knee, M., "Anthocyanin, carotenoid, and chlorophyll changes in the peel of Cox's Orange Pippin apples during ripening on and off the tree," *J. Exp. Bot.* 74 (1972): 184-196.

Leake, A.L., S.M. Hoggett, and C.B. Watkins, "Solving the greasiness problem in Granny Smiths," *The Orchardist,* May, 1989.

Looney, N., M.E Patterson, "Chlorophyllase activity in apples and bananas during the climacteric phase," *Nature* 214 (1967): 1245-1246.

Smock, R.C., "Controlled atmosphere storage of fruits," *HortReviews* 1 (1979): 301-336.

Whitehead, C.S. and A.H. Halevy, "Ethylene sensitivity: the role of short-chain saturated fatty acids in pollination-induced senescence of Petunia hybrida flowers," *Plant Growth Reg.* 8 (1989): 41-54.

Wills, R.H.H., T.H. Lee, D. Graham, W.B. McGlasson, and E.G. Hall, "Postharvest, an introduction to the physiology and handling of fruit and vegetables," AVI, Westport, CN 1981.

part IV Regulation of Fruit Quality

DR. JOHN FELLMAN

Department of Horticulture and
Landscape Architecture
Washington State University
Pullman, WA 99164-6414
phone: 509-335-3454; fax: 509-335-8690

DR. SCOTT JOHNSON

University of California
Kearney Agricultural Center
9240 South Riverbend Avenue
Parlier, CA 93648
phone: 209-891-2500; fax: 209-891-2593
sjohnson@uckac.edu

DR. NORM LOONEY

Agriculture and Agri-Food Canada
Pacific Agri-Food Research Centre
Summerland, B.C. V0H 1Z0, Canada
phone: 250-494-6361; fax: 250-494-0755
looneyn@em.agr.ca

DR. DUANE W. GREENE

Department of Plant and Soil Sciences
Bowditch Hall
University of Massachusetts
Amherst, MA 01003
phone: 413-545-5219; fax: 413-545-0260

Pome Fruit Quality in Relation to Environmental Stresses

John K. Fellman
Department of Horticulture & Landscape Architecture
Washington State University
Pullman, Washington

An important concept to examine is seasonal growth, as growth during the early season (after pollination and set) influences subsequent growth rates and ultimate size of the fruit. It is important to examine limiting factors to understand the interaction of fertilizers, pruning, growth regulators, thinning programs, and the like on the quality of the product.

Growth and development

The periods for cell division are: apple, four to five weeks; pear, seven to nine weeks post-anthesis. This is the major period that determines the final cell number for tree fruits. All growth after the cell division period is largely expansion of the cells laid down after bloom anthesis. Obviously, in all fruits, some cell division in the epidermal area continues for a much longer period.

Sometime during the cell division period, cell enlargement begins at a rapid rate. As the cells enlarge, in apple, for example, the development of intracellular air spaces takes place and remains constant for the rest of the growing season. Eventually, vacuoles comprise the majority of the cell's volume. The combined growth resultant from cell division, enlargement, and air space formation results in a sigmoid-shaped growth curve.

CELL SIZE AND NUMBER

There have been research studies done on cell numbers and the factors affecting them, especially in apples, because cell number influences size and postharvest storage behavior to some extent. Some generalities were discovered as a result of a pioneering study by U.S. Department of Agriculture scientists in Wenatchee, Washington:

1) Large fruit usually has more cells than small ones from the same tree.

2) Early thinning usually stimulates cell division and sometimes cell enlargement; this phenomenon is usually more pronounced on heavy-setting cultivars.

Cell size and number combine to give various fruit sizes with different storage characteristics. There are a variety of factors that can act simultaneously on the fruit, including those identified as being associated with increases in cell size: few cells/fruit, light bloom/set, adequate soil moisture, strong fruiting spurs, king-bloom fruits, excess nitrogen nutrition, high leaf-to-fruit ratio, late-season thinning, healthy leaves, and excessive chemical or hand-thinning.

The converse of these tend to decrease cell size. A general axiom: "Grow fruit with relatively many cells of medium size rather than with fewer cells of large size."

SHAPE OF POME FRUITS

The shape of fruits ("typiness") is economically important. Pears have an expected shape in the marketplace, as does the "Washington Red Delicious." Delicious apples have different shapes depending on growing conditions. The warm days and cool nights characteristic of the inland Pacific Northwest give the characteristic type that consumers use to identify the Washington State apple.

Other factors influencing typiness include invigorating rootstocks, heavy thinning/light bloom, king bloom, use of growth hormone sprays containing gibberellins and cytokinins. One of the most important factors influencing shape is effective pollination of each ovary in the fruit. If pollination is sporadic, there will be a higher proportion of odd-shaped, atypical fruit at the packout.

RESPIRATORY PATTERNS

As growth continues, respiratory characteristics of the fruit change, with a constant decrease throughout the growing season until just before the onset of ripening. When pome fruits are ready to ripen, they exhibit a burst of respiratory activity termed the climacteric. Harvesting fruits at the proper respiratory state, the minimum before the climacteric, ensures a long, healthy storage and marketing life.

The assessment of proper harvest maturity is a very important aspect of successful pome fruit marketing, and the Washington industry has adopted a maturity assessment program that helps growers make the important decision: "When do I harvest my crop?" The next section discusses disorders that result from improper harvesting decisions.

Classes of disorders
GROWTH-RELATED DISORDERS

There are a number of growth-related problems that are related to environmental conditions under which fruit is grown. The major problems can be categorized into those that affect immature fruits and those

that affect overmature fruits, once again underscoring the importance of selecting fruit of the proper harvest maturity for the ultimate end use.

In the Pacific Northwest, apples and pears are harvested for several end uses, largely due to the great volumes of fruit grown and the storage and marketing requirements of the industry. Apples and pears need to be harvested at different maturities, depending on the plans for length of storage. Storage for longer-term marketing requires fruit that are less mature than those destined for immediate marketing.

Immature fruits. In this category, there is a growth-related disorder called russeting, a condition where cork tissue (phellogen) appears on the surface of the apple or pear. The disorder may be of a slight nature, or the russeting may cover the entire fruit surface. In some pear cultivars (Bosc), this is a desirable condition. The disorder can be initiated early in the fruits' growth, often 11 to 30 days after petal fall, when cells are actively dividing.

Cracking, thin cuticles, surface wax deposition, and irregular cell division are involved in russet development. Factors that influence russet development include high night temperatures coupled with high humidity, conditions rarely found in most inland Pacific Northwest growing districts.

As apples elongate and the epidermal cells are exposed to water (either on the surface or in the atmosphere), excessive turgor pressure causes them to rupture, which activates neighboring cells to form corky tissue as a defense response. Apples that have large amounts of epidermal wax do not russet as readily as those apples with little wax, such as Golden Delicious. Accordingly, sprays of gibberellin, a growth stimulant, help prevent russet. Other causes of fruit russeting are frost, certain spray chemicals and surfactants, and powdery mildew infections.

Scald is a physiological disorder of apples that has caused quality and marketing problems as long as apples have been stored and commercially marketed. Until 1957, when DPA (diphenylamine) was discovered to control scald, it was the most important storage disorder of apples. Scald is manifested by occurrence of brown/black patches on the surface of the fruit, rendering it unmarketable. Scald is the result of damage and subsequent death of epidermal and hypodermal cells. Damage occurs in storage and the longer the affected fruits are held in storage, the more severe the symptoms become.

Time and again, research studies have shown that scald is the most severe when fruit is harvested before the onset of ripening. Many green-life studies ("green-life" is the period of time between fruit detachment and the onset of ripening) show that the shorter the green-life period, the less scald susceptibility in storage. Any treatment that advances fruit maturity, such as ethephon sprays, will decrease the incidence of scald.

Some research leads one to believe that preharvest temperatures seem to help predict the onset of scald in storage. Generally, it is thought that warm temperatures before harvest aggravate the incidence of scald. Studies of preharvest temperatures also can be interpreted as determining the ultimate onset of maturity and ripening, with cooler preharvest temperatures hastening the advance of ripening. There are a number of packing house treatments that are effective in scald control, most notably the use of DPA as a postharvest drench.

There are data to suggest that storage environments influence scald as well. Temperature, oxygen, and carbon dioxide concentration all influence the severity and incidence of scald in storage. Aside from the use of chemicals, it may be possible to minimize apple scald incidence by harvest of fruit at the proper maturity, followed by prompt storage at the minimum temperature without damage, in the lowest oxygen and highest carbon dioxide levels tolerated by that particular cultivar.

Core flush, as the name implies, is a yellow/pinkish/brown color of apple core tissue. Depending on where the fruit is grown and where the research was conducted, fruit picked too early or too late can develop the disorder. In this context, core flush may be considered as the "picked too early" symptom, and core browning (see below) the "picked too late" symptom. The symptoms are nearly identical, with core flush symptoms less severe than those associated with core browning.

Core flush is associated with other growth-related factors, including high nitrogen, large size, shaded on the tree, and extended periods of excessively wet and cloudy weather before harvest. Generally, apples decrease in their susceptibility to core flush with advancing maturity.

Overmature fruits. Contrary to the maladies associated with immature fruit, there are disorders that result from storing fruit that has been harvested too late for the intended use. A prominent disorder that affects some apples and pears is **watercore.** Watercore is usually not detectable in intact fruit, and requires cutting open the fruit to view typical symptoms.

Symptoms of watercore are a water-soaked appearance of tissue, usually around the ten main vascular bundles in slight cases, more soaked in severe cases. Water-soaking occurs as a result of cellular leakage into the air-filled spaces prevalent in mature apple flesh tissue. Watercored fruit can command a premium price in some markets, but it is hard to separate the affected fruit during the normal packing process.

Watercored fruit does not store well. Depending upon the severity of the symptoms, there will be a proportional amount of tissue death and subsequent browning in cold storage. Since the tissue is waterlogged, gas exchange is restricted, making watercored fruit poor candidates for controlled-atmosphere storage. Fruit with mild symptoms will usually cure themselves in cold storage.

Causes of this disorder have been investigated since the turn of the century, and it is thought that several factors interact to cause watercore development. Factors that increase susceptibility include inadequate calcium nutrition, high leaf-to-fruit ratio, and cold temperatures before harvest. Once again, this points to the maturity of the fruit as an overriding influence.

There are also genetic factors, as some varieties like Golden Delicious never show watercore symptoms, but Starkrimson Delicious suffers this disorder frequently. The easiest way to minimize the problem is to harvest at the proper maturity. Any steps taken to promote the onset of ripening should be viewed with caution if the fruit is known to be a watercore-susceptible variety.

Senescent breakdown, as the name implies, is associated with old age. Symptoms include a browning of tissue usually beginning under the skin, often near the calyx end. When fruit is removed from cold storage and ripened, it is not unusual for the entire fruit tissue to turn brown and become mealy. In some apples, this can occur on the tree, as in the case of Lodi and Yellow Transparent. The skin of red apples becomes dark, and the skin of green or yellow apples becomes brown.

Breakdown, although associated with old age, can occur early in storage if fruits are harvested in an overmature condition. There has been an extensive amount of research into causal factors, of which light crops, large fruit size, and inadequate calcium nutrition have been implicated.

Brown heart (also known as **brown core)** is another disorder associated with overmature fruit, with the symptoms being like those of core flush (above) but much more severe. If fruit are picked too late and placed in controlled-atmosphere storage with carbon dioxide levels greater than 1%, the chances of brown core development are high. It is associated with restricted movement of gases into and out of fruit flesh.

In cultivars such as Fuji, late harvested fruit are known to develop the disorder, as the flesh tissue density is higher than most apples. Symptoms are also aggravated by prolonged low-temperature storage. Tests with pears have shown that fruit harvested beyond the optimum maturity window are much more susceptible to the brown heart disorder.

TEMPERATURE-RELATED DISORDERS

Temperature-related disorders have a dual nature; they can be caused by temperature events early in the growing season, or occur relatively late in the development of the fruit.

Frost russeting during the cell division period of the fruit is an example of an early growing season event. The russet phenomenon is identical to that described in the previous section, but the manifestation of the symptom is different. Mild frost usually leaves a ring of corky tissue around the end of the fruit distal to the stem.

Frost damage has different symptoms depending on the stage of fruit development and the severity of the freezing incident. If the frost event occurs soon after pollination during early fruit development, the fruitlet usually dies and falls off the tree. If the fruitlet does not fall off, it usually grows to be a misshapen cull.

Sunburn is a symptom that occurs late in the growing season, and is manifested as a bronzing of the sunny side of an apple, which subsequently turns brown in storage. This disorder is more prevalent with the introduction of new orchard systems that use dwarfed trees and are managed for early cropping. Usually, red-skinned apples that grow and develop in full sunshine do not have sunburn problems. Apples that develop within the canopy are especially susceptible when the fruit weight bends the limb into a more exposed position. Severe cases of sunburn show darkened areas within the bronzing, and are easily culled during harvest.

A more insidious form of sunburn is called **delayed sunscald,** where initial symptoms are minimal and not easily recognized. After storage, the sunscalded areas senesce and turn brown, rendering fruit unsalable (except for juice!). Red cultivars usually have little or no problem with delayed sunscald.

Watercore is another disorder that can be heat induced. In contrast to maturity-related watercore, heat-induced watercore occurs as a glassy appearance due to the flooded intercellular spaces caused by heat damage to cell membranes, usually near the surface of the fruit. It is possible to induce this type of watercore with a heat lamp in the laboratory.

Another late-season event is **freezing,** where cold temperatures at harvest time actually freeze the fruit. This is especially troublesome with late-harvested cultivars such as Granny Smith and Fuji. Even if temperatures are not damaging, sometimes a long, high-speed ride to the packing house causes the wind chill factor to freeze the fruit atop the bins.

Damage can range from slight to extremely severe. The symptoms of a slight freezing event usually involve some degree of skin browning. More severe freezing usually results in internal damage involving flesh browning to complete water soaking of the tissue that disintegrates upon thawing.

Fruit that have been frozen, even if no symptoms are apparent, always have a shortened storage life. Apples become mealy, and pears fail to ripen properly. Apples can withstand freezing on the tree better than when detached. Fruit nearer the desired harvest maturity will be more susceptible to damage. If apples and pears are frozen, or under suspicion of having been frozen, do not move them at all until they have warmed up, otherwise severe bruise damage will result. Freeze-damaged fruit should be marketed as soon as practical.

CLIMATIC EFFECTS

It should be obvious that seasonal weather differences have major effects on storage quality of pome fruits. Fortunately, the Pacific Northwest is blessed with a near-ideal climate for growing fruits of the highest storage quality. Fruits generally have higher sugar, soluble solids, and acids level when grown in climates that have warm days and cool nights. It is known that fruits keep best when they are grown in a high-sunlight environment without any moisture stress. **Cracking** is a problem associated with late-season water stress.

Cool, wet summers may predispose pome fruits to higher incidences of core flush, russeting, low temperature injury, and increased incidence of storage rots. Hot, dry summers can minimize the aforementioned disorders, while creating a new set of worries such as scald, heat-induced watercore, regular watercore, and fruit cracking.

According to some opinions, most climatic effects can be attributed to the subsequent influence on fruit maturity. If fruit are not as mature due to colder conditions, the grower will see more disorders related to fruit immaturity, and vice versa for warmer conditions. A complicating factor is the fact that not all cultivars behave the same way at different sites in different years, so readers are cautioned to assess these matters for themselves and use this information as general guidelines for their own particular situation.

13 Environmental Stresses and Stone Fruit Quality

R. Scott Johnson
University of California
Kearney Agricultural Center
Parlier, California

Stone fruit seem to be particularly susceptible to various fruit disorders. Every year, tons of fruit are thrown away due to such problems as skin cracks, bumps, discoloration, scars, russet, depressions, split pits, doubles, deep sutures, and pit browning. This report will focus on those disorders that are related to environmental conditions and will emphasize problems that can be influenced somewhat by cultural practices. Defects caused by insects and diseases will not be included.

Fruit cracking

Fruit cracking is a particular problem for cherries (Callan, 1986; Glenn and Poovaiah, 1989) but has also been reported for plums, prunes (Uriu et al., 1962) and nectarines (Fogle and Faust, 1976). In general, two different types of cracks have been identified: those associated with water (irrigation or rain) and those that have been termed growth cracks.

In prunes, cracks that occur on the stylar end of the fruit have been associated with irrigation practices (Uriu et al., 1962). Allowing the soil to dry down and then re-irrigating causes this disorder.

Side cracks, however, are unrelated to irrigation, and their cause is unknown. They are probably similar to the type of cracking observed in many nectarine cultivars (Fogle and Faust, 1976). These cracks often appear after an increase in the growth rate, such as the transition from the lag phase (stage II) to the final fruit swell phase (stage III) of growth. However, a comparison of 41 different cultivars showed no correlation between growth rate and propensity to crack. Calcium levels in the fruit did not correlate with cracking either. Probably these growth cracks are caused by a combination of factors, including growth rate, cell wall strength, water relations, nutrient levels, etc.

Cracking in cherries has been clearly associated with rain. However, fruit soluble solids content and water relations, including the turgor potential, are not the direct cause of this disorder (Anderson and Richardson, 1982). Instead, structural factors such as cell wall strength seem to be more closely related. Therefore, sprays of calcium (Callan, 1986; Glenn and Poovaiah, 1989) have been effective at reducing cracking in cherries. The calcium probably acts by strengthening cell walls.

Nectarine pox

Nectarine pox is a skin disorder that can be a serious problem in some years and some orchards in California and the eastern United States (Baugher and Miller, 1991a). It can be quite transitory in nature, appearing extensively in an orchard one year and not at all the next. The disorder is characterized by bumpy outgrowths on the fruit that sometimes have scabs. The tissue below these bumps appears normal.

In California, numerous attempts have been made to identify a causal agent and to control this disorder. Suggestions have been put forth regarding fungal and viral pathogens and copper and boron deficiencies, but all results have been negative or inconclusive. In West Virginia, root pruning significantly reduced the amount of nectarine pox (Baugher and Miller, 1991b). Fruit nitrogen also correlated positively with percent pox, suggesting vigor to be a contributing factor to the problem. Observations in California indicate that factors other than vigor are much more important in the development of nectarine pox.

Pit browning and russet scab

Pit browning occurs in some varieties of plum such as Casselman and appears to be heat related. It starts in the flesh near the center of the fruit and progresses outward. It can be particularly severe after periods of very hot temperatures, especially if preceded by cool temperatures. There are no practical approaches to eliminating this problem.

Russet scab is a problem of French prune which develops on the stylar end of the fruit (Michailides, 1991). In some ways, it seems similar to russeting on pears and apples because it is particularly severe when rain occurs within one week after full bloom. No causal agent has been isolated from the scab area, but standard fungicide treatments applied at full bloom are still effective at reducing the severity of russeting.

Fruit doubles and deep sutures

We have had extensive experience with the cause and prevention of fruit doubles and deep sutures in several peach cultivars. Fruit doubling is a disorder where two fruits are fused together and can be quite extensive in some years. It is generally not considered a serious problem because the fruit can be easily identified and removed at thinning time.

Deep sutures, however, are not easily identified early on and can therefore be a more serious problem. This disorder is characterized by a deep cleft in the suture, starting at the stem end of the fruit and extending one-third to two-thirds of the distance to the stylar end. According to U.S. Department of Agriculture quality standards, this fruit is unmarketable. Our research has shown these two disorders to be related to each other.

Research studies reducing irrigations after harvest in a June-maturing peach orchard clearly demonstrated the impact of water stress on double fruit formation (Johnson et al., 1992). Trees left unirrigated after harvest produced 10 to 35% doubles in the following year. The year-to-year variation also suggested some interaction with climatic conditions. Although data was only collected for three years, the degree of doubling correlated well with maximum temperatures during late August and early September of the previous year. This period corresponds to the time of carpel differentiation within the flower bud.

Additional research work concentrated on relieving stress during the critical carpel differentiation period (Handley, 1991). A single flood irrigation in early August or low-volume irrigation for about a month starting in mid-August were both effective at greatly reducing the percent of double fruits and deep sutures. Thus, very substantial savings in irrigation water could be achieved without hurting yield, fruit size, or fruit quality in early-maturing varieties.

Other species respond differently to water stress. Similar studies of postharvest water stress on plums showed very low levels of fruit doubling even on trees that had defoliated extensively due to stress (Johnson et al., 1994). Cherries can produce many double and deep-sutured fruit when grown in hot climates. However, the effect appears to be more related to direct heat and is not alleviated by optimum irrigation. Overtree sprinklers to reduce canopy temperatures are effective at reducing the occurrence of abnormal fruit (Southwick et al., 1991).

Split pits

Some varieties of peaches and nectarines have a strong tendency to produce many split pits. This defect is caused by the pit splitting open at about the time of pit hardening. If the flesh or mesocarp of the fruit does not split open (internal split), the fruit can still be marketed as a fresh product. However, often the flesh splits apart near the stem (external split) making an entry for disease organisms. Such fruit are unmarketable. For canning peaches, even internal splits are a problem because pit fragments can end up in the canned product. Therefore, much of the research on this disorder has been conducted on some old canning varieties that tended to produce abundant split pits.

Researchers early on noted that split pits occurred more frequently in larger fruit (Davis, 1933), leading to the conclusion that the disorder was related to growth rate. By experimenting with different cultural factors that affect fruit growth, Claypool et al. (1972) further substantiated this conclusion. High nitrogen, high soil moisture content during pit hardening, and low crop loads all tended to increase percent split pits. However, the correlations were not great, only accounting for 15 to 20% of the total variability. The conclusion was that cultural practices may have some influence on the occurrence of split pits, but will not completely control the problem.

Nutrients in the fruit have also been shown to correlate with the occurrence of split pits. For instance, calcium is generally lower in fruit with the disorder compared to normal fruit (Evert et al., 1988). However, calcium applied to the foliage (Evert et al., 1988) or to the nutrient solution (Woodbridge, 1978) did not decrease the incidence of split pits, even though tissue calcium levels were increased.

Finally, temperatures during fruit devel-opment, and especially around the time of pit hardening, have been shown to influence split pits. Using growth chambers, Monet and Bastard (1979) demonstrated that cool temperatures during fruit development induced less lignification in the pits and caused more split pits compared to warm temperatures.

However, the highest incidence of split pits occurred when trees were transferred from the cool chamber to the warm chamber during pit hardening. Therefore, the change in temperature may be more important than the absolute temperature. In trying to explain the year-to-year variability in split pits for canning peaches in California, we found the best correlation with temperatures during pit hardening (positive relationship).

In general, anything that promotes more rapid growth appears to increase the occurrence of split pits.

Skin discoloration

In California, we have had a serious problem recently with skin discoloration or inking, especially on more highly colored peaches and nectarines (Crisosto et al., 1994). This disorder has been reported in the eastern United States (Denny et al., 1986), as well as other countries around the world. Skin discoloration is caused by minor abrasion injury and contamination from some causal agent. Iron, copper, and aluminum ions have been shown to be particularly deleterious contaminants (Crisosto et al., 1994).

Dipping the fruit in a solution with chelate has been shown to reduce skin discoloration (Phillips, 1988), presumably by tying up the heavy metal contaminants. Crisosto et al. (1994) have shown high levels of heavy metal contaminants in many standard fungicide, insecticide, and foliar nutrient sprays. When these are applied near harvest, skin discoloration can be particularly severe. One practical solution is to make sure these materials are not applied too close to harvest.

Literature cited

Anderson, P.C. and D.G. Richardson, "A rapid method to estimate fruit water status with special reference to rain cracking of sweet cherries," *J. Amer. Soc. Hort. Sci.* 107(3) (1982): 441-444.

Baugher, Tara Auxt and Stephen S. Miller, "Nectarine pox: A disorder of nectarine fruit," *HortScience* 26(3) (1991a): 310.

Baugher, Tara Auxt and Stephen S. Miller, "Growth suppression as a control for nectarine pox," *HortScience* 26(10) (1991b): 1268-1270.

Callan, Nancy W., "Calcium hydroxide reduces splitting of Lambert sweet cherry," *J. Amer. Soc. Hort. Sci.* 112(2) (1986): 173-175.

Claypool, L.L., K. Uriu and P.F. Lasker, "Split-pit of Dixon cling peaches in relation to cultural factors," *J. Amer. Soc. Hort. Sci.* 97(2) (1972): 181-185.

Crisosto, Carlos H., Kevin Day, Themis Michailides, David Garner, and Katrina Simpson, "Peach and nectarine skin discoloration," *California Tree Fruit Agreement Report*, 1994.

Davis, L.D., "Size and growth relations of fruit in splitting of peach pits," *Proc. Amer. Soc. Hort. Sci.* 30 (1933): 195-200.

Denny, E.G., D.C. Coston, and R.E. Ballard, "Peach skin discoloration," *J. Amer. Soc. Hort. Sci.* 111(4) (1986): 549-553.

Evert, D.R., T.P. Gaines, and B.G. Mullinix, Jr., "Effects of split-pit on elemental concentrations of peach fruit during pit hardening," *Scientia Horticulturae* 34 (1988): 55-65.

Fogle, Harold W. And Miklos Faust, "Fruit growth and cracking in nectarines," *J. Amer. Soc. Hort. Sci.* 101(4) (1976): 434-439.

Glenn, Gregory M. And B.W. Poovaiah, "Cuticular properties and postharvest calcium applications influence cracking of sweet cherries," *J. Amer. Soc. Hort. Sci.* 114(5) (1989): 781-788.

Handley, Dale, "The formation of double fruit in peaches in response to postharvest deficit irrigation," M.S. Thesis. California State University, Fresno, 1991.

Johnson, R. Scott., D.F. Handley, and K. R. Day, "Postharvest water stress of an early maturing plum" *J. Hort. Sci.* 69(6) (1994): 1035-1041.

Johnson, R.S., D.F. Handley, and T.M. DeJong, "Long-term response of early maturing peach trees to postharvest water deficits," *J. Amer. Soc. Hort. Sci.* 117(6) (1992): 881-886.

Michailides, Themis J., "Russeting and russet scab of prune, an environmentally induced fruit disorder: symptomatology, induction, and control," *Plant Dis.* 75 (1991): 1114-1123.

Monet, R. and Y. Bastard, "Split pit of peaches. Effect of temperature," *Ann. Amélior. Plantes* 29(5) (1979): 535-543.

Phillips, D.J., "Reduction of transit injury-associated black discoloration of fresh peaches with EDTA treatments," *Plant Disease* 72(2) (1988): 118-120.

Southwick, Stephen M., Kenneth A. Shackel, James T. Yeager, Wesley K. Asai, and Matt Katacich, Jr., "Overtree sprinkling reduces abnormal shapes in Bing sweet cherries," *Cal. Ag.* 45(4) (1991): 24-26.

Uriu, K., C.J. Hansen, and J.J. Smith, "The cracking of prunes in relation to irrigation," *Proc. Amer. Soc. Hort. Sci.* 80 (1962): 211-219.

Woodbridge, C.G., "Split-pit in peaches and nutrient levels," *J. Amer. Soc. Hort. Sci.* 103(2) (1978): 278-280.

14 Effects of Gibberellin-based Plant Bioregulators on Fruit Quality

N. E. Looney
Agriculture and Agri-Food Canada
Pacific Agri-Food Research Centre
Summerland, B.C., Canada

Several gibberellin-based plant bioregulators (PBRs) are proving to be very useful tools to improve important aspects of fresh fruit quality. While the bulk of this usage is with table grapes and citrus, several technologies applicable to deciduous tree fruits are now well established and others are emerging. Looney (1983a, 1983b) and Miller (1988) have reviewed this topic with specific reference to deciduous fruit trees and crops.

This chapter will deal with the theory and practice of improving apple fruit finish with gibberellin-based PBRs; improving apple fruit size and shape with a proprietary cytokinin/gibberellin combination (Promalin); and improving sweet cherry size, firmness, and appearance with gibberellic acid.

Finally, since fruit quality, in the eyes of some, is enhanced by reduced insecticide and fungicide usage, I will introduce the concept of using PBRs within the framework of "integrated fruit production" (IFP), where the philosophy is to reduce the use of pest control chemicals and other costly and/or intrusive inputs to the greatest extent possible.

Reducing apple fruit russeting

Many apple cultivars are prone to developing fruit surface russet (see Figure 1). Russet appears when cracks in the cuticle of young fruit (usually during the first month following bloom) are "repaired" by suberization (the production of phellogen by subepidermal cells).

Russet is often more severe in humid growing areas, but even under the relatively

FIGURE 1

A severe case of surface russet on a Golden Delicious apple growing in a maritime climate.

dry conditions found in the interior valleys of the Pacific Northwest, fruit surface russet is frequently observed on Golden Delicious. It can also be a concern for Fuji, Jonagold, and a few other sensitive cultivars. When the severity of russet or the proportion of the fruit surface affected exceeds a specified tolerance, economic returns can be substantially reduced.

The earliest reports that gibberellin sprays could be employed to reduce climate-related surface russet came from Australia (Taylor, 1975), but much of the subsequent research on this subject has been done in Europe (e.g., Eccher, 1978; Eccher and Boffelli, 1981; Wertheim, 1982; Taylor and Knight, 1986) and North America (Elfving and Allen, 1987; Looney et al., 1992).

A mixture of gibberellins A_4 and A_7 (GA_{4+7}), both known to be native to apple, is more effective than the standard gibberellic acid (GA_3) product more widely used in horticulture. Multiple sprays commencing at petal fall are more effective than single sprays, and rates as low as 10 parts per million (ppm) active ingredient in each spray are often as effective as higher rates.

Gibberellin sprays applied to reduce russet do not adversely affect fruit sizing and may actually increase average fruit weight at harvest (Looney et al., 1992).

The mechanism of gibberellin action in reducing russet relates to a more "regular" or "controlled" enlargement of epidermal cells leading to an epidermis less prone to cracking (Eccher, 1978). Taylor and Knight (1986) also examined the effect of GA_{4+7} treatment on apple cuticle. They observed a substantial increase in the average size of epidermal cells, and when the cuticle was stretched, it exhibited 25% greater plasticity.

Eccher (1978) suggested that cytokinins are likely to have the opposite effect on russet development because epidermal cells are encouraged to proliferate, leading to a greater potential for cracking. This could explain why Promalin, which contains a cytokinin (6-benzyladenine) as well as GA_{4+7}, has proven unreliable for reducing russet or cracking of apple (Eccher and Maffi, 1986; Visai et al., 1989).

Finally, Wertheim (1982), Looney (1983), and Looney et al. (1992) have suggested that GA_4 is more effective than GA_7 for russet control and also less likely to have residual effects on return flowering.

The extent to which these findings are reflected in the formulation of commercial russet control agents is still unknown.

PRODUCT AND PRACTICE

The product available to apple producers in North America is ProVide (Abbott Laboratories, North Chicago, Illinois). ProVide contains 2% GA_{4+7} in a liquid concentrate. The relative amount of each gibberellin is not specified.

The label recommendation is to apply two to four sprays, commencing at petal fall, during the first 30 days of postbloom fruit development. From 6.5 to 13 ounces of this product per acre and per spray (10 to 20 ppm when applied with 100 U.S. gallons) has resulted in substantial reductions in the incidence of surface and stem-bowl russeting of Golden Delicious apples. Since some wetting agents are in themselves likely to cause russeting, it is not recommended that a wetting agent be added to the ProVide spray solution.

For those interested in preparing smaller quantities of spray solutions with the chemical concentration indicated precisely in parts per million, ProVide contains 21 grams of active ingredient per litre (9.93 g per U.S. pint). Ten ml of product (0.21 g a.i.) in 10.5 litres of water gives a spray concentration of 20 ppm.

The label limit on total amount of product that can be applied per acre per year (40 ounces) reflects the possibility that flower bud formation can be suppressed by gibberellins applied early in the growing season. This is seldom a serious concern in the Pacific Northwest with standard strains of Golden Delicious. However, some spur-type strains of this variety are more prone to biennial cropping, and flower and fruitlet thinning practices must be aggressively pursued to minimize this problem.

In mature semi-dwarf trees with a fully developed canopy, low cropping is often a problem in the poorly illuminated regions of the canopy. Unfortunately, this is also the location where fruit russeting is likely to be the most severe. This creates something of a dilemma for growers wishing to control russet with ProVide. Over-spraying the interior of the tree may further reduce the likelihood of shaded spurs developing flower buds.

Obviously, this problem is less severe with trees on fully dwarfing rootstocks, assuming that tree and row spacing is appropriate. With larger trees, interior light conditions can be improved by branch positioning and by judicious dormant season pruning.

Improving apple fruit size and shape

Delicious apples grown in the northwestern states and British Columbia are often preferred to those grown in warmer climates. This is due, at least in part, to their characteristic angular shape and prominent calyx lobes (see Figure 2). They are said to exhibit superior "type."

However, even within this geographic region, there are microclimates where fruit shape (typiness) is considered problematic and where a PBR tool to address this deficiency has been welcomed by producers. Furthermore, since some other PBR treatments can cause apples to be less elongated (Alar [daminozide] in the past; perhaps other shoot growth retardants in the future), it is important to know that fruit elongation can be encouraged with a specific PBR-based product.

It was observed in the 1960s (Westwood and Bjornstad, 1968) that gibberellic acid treatment can enhance fruit elongation in apple. At about the same time, Letham (1963), conducting experiments in New Zealand with several cytokinins known to enhance cell division, found that apple fruit cell division, especially at the calyx end, was stimulated by some of these chemicals.

Williams and Stahly (1969), working in New Zealand and Wenatchee, combined GA_{4+7} with 6-benzyladenine (BA) and found that fruit shape was very dramatically influenced. Using this mixture, Delicious apples grown in warmer climates could be made to look like those found normally in Washington State (Unrath, 1974).

The BA component causes the calyx lobes to develop, whereas the gibberellins promote overall fruit elongation. The result

---

FIGURE 2

Red Delicious apple fruit treated with Promalin during the bloom period and photographed in mid-season. Note the prominent calyx lobes and angular shape of this fruit.

is an apple with somewhat greater fresh weight at harvest and a length-to-diameter ratio often greater than one.

Since the aim is to promote cell division as well as cell elongation, it is not surprising that application during the normal period of cell division has been shown to be important. In fact, experience has demonstrated that applications made even before full bloom effectively promote fruit elongation.

However, since much subsequent work has demonstrated that at least one component of this mixture, BA, can act as a fruitlet "thinner" (now available as Accel), there has been much discussion about parallel effects on crop reduction (Miller, 1988) and on the possibility of using spray timing to address this concern.

Unfortunately, there is still no clear resolution of this issue, but fruitlet thinning effects are likely to be more important in regions where the blossom period is extended and more than one spray is recommended. This is not often the case in the Pacific Northwest.

A related question exists as to whether or not the fruit weight increase often observed is simply due to the thinning of competing fruits early in the growing season. McLaughlin and Greene (1984) were among the first to note that BA causes apple fruit enlargement that is independent of crop reduction. Subsequent work with even more powerful cytokinins has now established that this is probably true (Ogata et al., 1989).

PRODUCT AND PRACTICE

The commercial product registered for improving "typiness" of Delicious apple is Promalin (Abbott Laboratories). Promalin is a liquid concentrate containing 1.8% (w/w) N-(phenylmethyl)-1H-purin-6-amine (also known as 6-benzyladenine) and 1.8% GA_{4+7}. One U.S. pint contains 9.48 grams of each of these two active ingredients.

The effective uptake of Promalin from a whole-tree spray is via the calyx and the fruit receptacle. Thus, an ideal application technology would target these tissues. Nonetheless, whole tree sprays applied early

in the bloom period are usually very effective. This may be due, at least in part, to the fact that total leaf area is still quite low.

The recommended spray concentration is 25 ppm of the active ingredients of Promalin (1 pint/100 U.S. gallons) and an application rate of one to two pints of product per acre is suggested, depending on tree age and spacing. The volume of water and the spray application equipment must be such that there is very good coverage of the flower parts, including the fruit receptacle. As indicated above, spraying early in the bloom period permits better coverage of the receptacle tissues.

Gibberellins to improve stone fruit quality

As pointed out in an earlier chapter, gibberellins have many different kinds of effects on plants. Among the most interesting to commercial fruit growers is their ability to delay certain manifestations of fruit ripening and senescence and at the same time improve fruit quality. With peach and nectarine growers, the suppression of flower formation is proving to be of commercial interest.

TABLE 1

Effects of gibberellic acid treatment on the incidence of bruising and pitting of Van sweet cherries, apparent after 21 days of cold storage (after Looney and Lidster, 1980).

Treatment	Harvest number[1]	Bruised fruit(%)	Pitted fruit(%)	Fruit with other marks(%)
1977				
No spray	1	13.1[2]	55.1[2]	16.8[2]
20 ppm GA_3		11.4	38.1	19.8
No spray	2	43.1	11.9	27.6
20 ppm GA_3		28.1	9.6	27.9
1978				
No spray	1	6.8	70.8	13.3
30 ppm GA_3		8.5	28.3	15.5
No spray	2	14.0	22.5	12.3
30 ppm GA_3		8.5	7.5	7.5

[1] First harvest at color comparator #3 (red); second harvest at dark mahogany.

[2] Highly significant effects of GA_3 and harvest time on pitting in 1977 and 1978; highly significant effect of harvest time on bruising in 1977; significant effect of harvest date on other surface marks in 1977.

SWEET CHERRIES

Proebsting (1972) was the first to point out the potential benefits of extending the harvest season of sweet cherries with a preharvest gibberellic acid spray. He noted the potential for larger, firmer fruit and reported that fruit coloring was delayed by several days.

Looney and Lidster (1980) showed that GA_3-treated cherries were much less likely to develop bruise-related pitting during storage and handling and further demonstrated that harvest maturity influences the relative severity of bruising and pitting. Fruit harvested early in the harvest period is more bruise-resistant but more susceptible to developing pitting. GA_3 treatment reduced the incidence of pitting in fruit harvested either at the red or dark mahogany stages of fruit ripening (see Table 1).

Since part of the pitting symptom is a darkening of the damaged tissues (Porritt et al., 1971), this effect of GA_3 may be similar to its effect on white cherries, where browning during and after canning is greatly suppressed (Proebsting et al., 1973).

Today, gibberellic acid is widely used in the Pacific Northwest to improve sweet cherry quality and give flexibility to producers during the harvest period. For an up-to-date coverage of PBR usage on sweet and sour cherries the reader is referred to Looney (1995).

PRUNES AND PLUMS

Early Italian prunes produced in the Pacific Northwest and shipped across North America for fresh consumption often develop an internal browning disorder that seriously detracts from their value in the marketplace. The potential benefits of a preharvest gibberellic acid treatment were first reported by Proebsting and Mills (1966).

Subsequent work has shown that in addition to reduced internal browning, GA_3-treated prunes are firmer and, probably because harvest can be delayed a few days, develop larger fruit size.

In a series of experiments conducted by Proebsting between 1964 and 1974, the average increase in fruit weight was nearly 5% when the standard 50-ppm treatment was applied.

Proebsting and Mills (1969) also tested combinations of GA_3 (50 ppm) and ethephon (40 ppm) and observed very good results in some experiments. Skin coloration was substantially advanced, and

TABLE 2

Location of 1994 flowers on one-year shoots and average time required to hand thin peach trees treated with GA_3 in 1993.[1]

	Cultivar					
	Harbrite		Redhaven		Harbrite	Redhaven
Location on shoot:	Mid 1/3	Bottom 1/3	Mid 1/3	Bottom 1/3		
GA_3 (ppm)	—% of nodes with flowers—				—Thinning time (min/tree)—	
0	90.2	67.6	96.4	77.3	33.1	29.8
38	75.6	27.1	74.9	15.0	22.2	15.9
75	62.6	6.7	25.1	0.5	13.0	12.6
150	8.1	0.0	12.1	0.0	9.7	6.4
Analysis						
GA_3 vs. control	**[2]	**	**	**	**	**
GA_3 linear effect	**	**	**	**	**	*

[1] GA_3 applied June 10, 1993 when average shoot length was 20 cm.
[2] Highly significant (P=0.01).

soluble solids levels increased, even though both fruit size and flesh firmness were improved compared to the unsprayed control trees. Internal browning following harvest was also suppressed by this combination treatment.

It is notable, however, that this GA_3 and GA_3 + ethephon technology has seen relatively little uptake, even though the benefits can be substantial. This may relate to the cost of the 50-ppm GA_3 treatment and the relatively poor prices for prunes!

Japanese plums *(Prunus salicina)* are also amenable to treatment with gibberellins to improve fruit firmness and reduce flower bud formation. This technology is described more fully in the next section.

PEACHES AND OTHER STONE FRUITS

Peaches, nectarines, plums, and apricots respond to GA_3 treatment with reduced flower bud formation (which can mean reduced hand thinning costs the following year) and, in the season of application, greater fruit flesh firmness and delayed fruit ripening. This technology is being actively developed for the California fruit industry. See Southwick and Fritts (1995) for a recent review.

In work at Summerland, GA_3 was applied to Redhaven and Harbrite peaches at the pit hardening stage or somewhat later in 1993, 1994, and 1995. We used rates ranging from 0 to 150 ppm and observed a very clear and concentration-dependent effect on flowering in the following season *(see Table 2)*.

Flower suppression was always greatest in the bottom one-third to one-half of one-year shoots. This localization of the effect permits the use of dormant season pruning (following the forcing of flowering of cut branches) to adjust the potential crop. Rates of 50 to 75 ppm gave good flowering suppression, substantially reduced hand-thinning time the year after treatment *(see Table 2)*, and improved fruit firmness in the

year of application *(see Table 3)*. A small delay in fruit maturation was observed in the 1993 experiment but the effect on fruit firmness was independent of this delay.

Only the highest rate of GA_3 (150 ppm) resulted in reduced per tree yield the year following treatment. Lower rates resulted in tree yields comparable to the control, and fruit size and juice soluble solids were improved *(see Table 4)*.

Another very consistent effect noted in the Summerland experiments was enhanced shoot elongation in the year of treatment *(see Table 3)*.

PRODUCTS

The gibberellic acid products registered for use on sweet cherries in North America are: a) ProGibb 2X Liquid Concentrate (Abbott Laboratories) which contains 20.0% GA_3; ProGibb 4% which contains approximately 1 gram GA_3 per fluid ounce of product; and Activol (Zeneca Agro, Stoney Creek, Ontario) which contains approximately 1 gram GA_3 in each quick-dissolve tablet.

All of these products are used on sweet cherries and would be suitable for application to Early Italian prune. However, a perusal of recent labels suggests that this latter usage is not presently supported by the manufacturers.

For peaches and some other stone fruits, Abbott Laboratories has obtained a California label for Release LC, a 4% gibberellins product especially designed for use on stone fruits other than cherries. While the specific gibberellins in Release LC are not identified, it can probably be assumed that GA_3 is the primary active ingredient.

PRACTICES

To extend the harvest period and improve fruit quality of sweet cherry, 20 ppm gibberellic acid (Activol or Pro-Gibb) is applied to full foliage wetness about three weeks before expected harvest. Fruit color should be straw yellow, coinciding with the end of the "lag phase" of cherry fruit enlargement (note that most of the weight of the mature fruit is accumulated during the last 3 weeks of development).

GA$_3$-treated sweet cherries of all cultivars with black skin color at full maturity are harvested when the skin color is of the desired degree of redness. This will occur two to four days later in GA$_3$-treated fruit. The normal situation is for cherries to darken evenly as they ripen, making the decision about harvest date relatively straightforward. However, on occasion, the stylar end of GA$_3$-treated fruit remains light red throughout the desired harvest period. In such cases, B.C. producers are advised to proceed with harvest using shoulder color as the guide. Uneven coloring of this nature is not seen as a serious problem for the fresh market, but it may be problematic for cherry processors.

Label advice for the use of Release LC to improve firmness of peaches and other stone fruits in California is to apply a single spray of 16 to 48 grams of actual gibberellins per acre one to four weeks before harvest. Experience to date suggests that for improving fruit firmness, application rates of 16 or 24 grams per acre have been about as effective as the highest rates tested (48 g/acre).

To reduce flower bud formation the application time for Release LC may be somewhat different since the treatment must be applied during the period of flower bud initiation. For very early maturing cultivars, a postharvest application may be advised. For most cultivars, however, a single spray time will achieve both aims.

The use of gibberellins to regulate cropping (reduce thinning costs) and improve aspects of stone fruit quality in the season

FIGURE 3

High density sweet cherry plantation facilitated by training system (Tatura trellis), Promalin paint to promote lateral branching, and Cultar (Zeneca Agro International, U.K.) sprays to control shoot elongation. Blenheim, New Zealand.

of application is an exciting new area and appears to have great potential. However, we still must refine our practices to optimize application rates and timing. There may also be long-term tree growth and development effects that will require adjustments to other orchard management practices.

PBR usage in "integrated fruit production"

While there are many definitions and components of integrated fruit production (IFP), reducing or eliminating the use of insecticides and fungicides is a common aim. The general goal is to minimize or eliminate inputs in a manner consistent with good husbandry, economic sustainability, and an awareness of the greater environment.

There can be no doubt that many consumers believe that fruit produced without insecticides or fungicides applied to the fruit is more "wholesome" and thus of higher quality. I would therefore like to briefly introduce the concept that plant bioregulators, as a class of "soft" or "biorational" agricultural chemicals, can play an important role in moving us forward toward a more widespread adoption of IFP principles.

Admittedly, we do not start from the strongest position, since we have largely failed to explain to the public at large the important differences between plant bioregulators and the group of chemicals legitimately called "pesticides."

TABLE 3

"In-season" effects of GA_3 applied to peach trees in 1993 (Summerland, B.C.): enhanced fruit firmness and shoot elongation (end of season shoot length).[1]

	Cultivar			
GA_3 (ppm)	Harbrite	Redhaven	Harbrite	Redhaven
	——Firmness (Newtons)——		——Mean shoot length (cm)——	
0	19.5	37.7	45.8	50.6
38	27.6	43.6	55.8	61.4
75	33.9	45.7	62.5	66.6
150	35.1	49.8	65.2	70.9
GA_3 vs. Control	**[2]	**	**	**
GA_3 Conc. Linear	**	ns	**	**

[1] GA_3 applied June 10, 1993 when average shoot length was 20 cm.
[2] Highly significant (P=0.01).

TABLE 4

Effect of 1993 GA_3 treatments on average yield per tree, average fruit weight and juice soluble solids in 1994. Summerland, B.C.

	Cultivar				
Treatment	Harbrite	Redhaven	Harbrite	Redhaven	Harbrite
(ppm GA_3)	Yield (kg)		Mean fruit wt (g)		Sol. solids (%)
0	59.5	51.6	164.7	154.5	10.7
37.5	48.7	76.6	156.4	211.6	11.3
75	46.2	47.5	186.3	228.4	11.6
150	23.4	37.4	186.9	222.3	12.4
Analysis					
1993 GA3 effect[1]	*	*	*	*	*

[1] Significant at P:0.05

Nonetheless, there are many examples of how some past and present PBR products/practices have reduced pesticide usage and otherwise improved the "sustainability" of specific fruit production systems. The examples given below are representative of the great potential that exists in this area.

Reducing tree size or improving canopy architecture to accommodate advances in spray technology. It can be argued that the necessity to use powerful air-blast sprayers to deal with orchard insects and diseases has contributed to a public image of excessive, even irresponsible, pesticide usage by fruit producers. We know that smaller trees require less pesticide and can even be adapted to using sprayers specifically designed to avoid chemical wastage.

For those crops lacking vigor-controlling rootstocks, GA biosynthesis inhibitors that control shoot elongation can be extremely valuable tools.

For example, in several countries where it is registered for use, very small quantities of paclobutrazol, while having little or no adverse effect on fruit quality, dramatically reduce tree size. Sweet cherry producers in New Zealand use paclobutrazol alone or in combination with other growth regulators to confine closely spaced trees to an area fully protected from birds and rain and to a size amenable to efficient harvesting and spraying (see Figure 3).

Use of PBR technology to avoid insect or disease problems. Sweet cherry growers in parts of British Columbia have used early cultivars and daminozide treatment to advance harvest and thus avoid damage from the cherry fruit fly emerging a few days after harvest. Another example is the use of gibberellic acid by Florida grapefruit producers to retain rind chlorophyll levels. This treatment profoundly reduces fruit susceptibility to attack by the Caribbean fruit fly (Greany et al., 1987).

Using PBRs to achieve orchard sanitation objectives. Orchard sanitation is a key ingredient for success in all no- or low-pesticide production systems. British Columbia cherry growers have used ethephon to remove the fruit remaining after hand harvest is completed. This reduces the incidence of brown rot and eliminates the need for a late-season cherry fruit fly spray. Conversely, preventing fruit drop of apple with daminozide was a key ingredient of the low pesticide management strategy for McIntosh apples developed for Massachusetts growers (Prokopy, 1988).

Since apple maggot will not emerge from fruit attached to the tree, delaying fruit drop into early winter reduces future populations of this pest. Coincidentally, daminozide treatment also controlled fruit drop in orchards heavily infested with leafminers. Without daminozide treatment, these pests caused serious fruit drop, requiring a late-season insecticide spray.

Some other very specific uses of PBRs to reduce pesticide usage include the use of GA_3 to "thin" or elongate grape clusters to reduce the incidence of bunch rot (Weaver et al., 1962) and the use of ethephon to initiate flowering of tropical crops such as mango, so that crop development coincides with the dry season where pest and disease pressures are lowest (T.L. Davenport, University of Florida, personal communication).

Note that the gibberellins are involved in several of the above examples. They may be particularly valuable in the implementation of various IFP strategies because, as natural plant products, they should be more readily accepted by registration agencies for such uses. However, I believe that many other presently known PBRs meet all reasonable criteria for integrated fruit production and that we will see a wider recognition of this potential in the future.

Literature cited

Eccher, T., "Russeting of Golden Delicious apples as related to endogenous and exogenous gibberellins," *Acta Hortic.* 80 (1978): 381-385.

Eccher, T. and G. Boffelli, "Effects of dose and time of GA_{4+7} on russeting, fruit set and shape of Golden Delicious apples," *Scientia Hortic.* 14 (1981): 307-314.

Eccher, T. and A. Maffi, "Treatments for prevention of Golden Delicious russeting," *Acta Hortic.* 179 (1986): 821-822.

Elfving, D.C. and O.B. Allen, "Effects of gibberellin A_{4+7} applications on Golden Delicious fruit russet," *Crop Research* 27 (1987): 11-18.

Greany, P.D., R.E. McDonald, P.E. Shaw, W.J. Schroeder, D.F. Howard, T.T. Hatton, P.L. Davis, and G.K. Rasmussen, "Use of gibberellic acid to reduce grapefruit susceptibility to attack by the Caribbean fruit fly *Anasttrepha suspensa* (Diptera: Tephritidae). *Trop. Sci.* 27 (1987): 261-270.

Letham, D.S., "Regulators of cell division in plant tissues. I. Inhibitors and stimulants of cell division in developing fruits: Their properties and activity in relation to the cell division period." New Zealand *J. Bot.* 1 (1963): 336-350.

Looney, N.E., "Growth regulator usage in apple and pear production." In: *Plant Growth Regulating Chemicals,* edited by L.G. Nickell. Boca Raton: CRC Press, Vol. 1 (1983): 1-26.

Looney, N.E., "Growth regulator use in the production of Prunus species fruits." In: *Plant Growth Regulating Chemicals,* edited by L.G. Nickell. Boca Raton: CRC Press, Vol 1 (1983): 27-39.

Looney, N.E. and P.D. Lidster, "Some growth regulator effects on fruit quality, mesocarp composition, and susceptibility to postharvest surface marking of sweet cherries," *J. Amer. Soc. Hort. Sci.* 105 (1980): 130-134.

Looney, N.E., R.L. Granger, C.L. Chu, S.L. McArtney, L.N. Mander, and R.P. Pharis, "Influences of gibberellins A_4, A_{4+7}, and A_4 + iso-A_7 on apple fruit quality and tree productivity. I. Effects on fruit russet and tree yield components," *J. Hortic. Sci.* 67 (1992): 613-618.

Looney. N.E., "Principles and practice of plant bioregulator usage in cherry production," 279-295. In: *Cherries: Crop Physiology, Production and Uses,* A.D. Webster and N.E. Looney, editors. CAB International, Wallingford, UK. (1995)

McLaughlin, J.M. and D.W. Greene, "Effects of BA, GA_{4+7}, and daminozide on fruit set, fruit quality, vegetative growth, flower initiation, and flower quality of Golden Delicious apples," *J. Amer. Soc. Hort. Sci.* 109 (1984): 34-39.

Miller, S.S., "Plant bioregulators in apple and pear culture," *Horticultural Reviews* 10 (1988): 309-402.

Ogata, R., T. Saito, and K. Oshima, "Effect of N-phenyl-N'-(4-pyridil) urea (4-PU) on fruit size of apple, Japanese pear, grapevine, and kiwifruit. *Acta Hortic.* 239 (1989): 395-398.

Porritt, S.W., L.E. Lopatecki, and M. Meheriuk, "Surface pitting—a storage disorder of sweet cherries," *Can J. Plant Sci.* 51 (1971): 409-414.

Prokopy, R.J., "Benefits of Alar to apple IPM programs. Mass. Fruit Notes 53(2) (1988): 7-8.

Proebsting, E.L., "Chemical sprays to extend sweet cherry harvest," Wash. State Univ. Extension Multilith 3520. 1972.

Proebsting, E.L., Jr. and H.H. Mills, "Effect of gibberellic acid and other growth regulators on quality of Early Italian prunes (*Prunus domestica* L.)," *Proc. Amer. Soc. Hort. Sci.* 89 (1966): 135-139.

Proebsting, E.L., Jr., G.H. Carter, and H.H. Mills "Quality improvement in canned Rainier cherries (P. avium L.) with gibberellic acid," *J. Amer. Soc. Hort. Sci.* 98 (1973):334-336.

Southwick, S.M. R. and Fritts, Jr., "Commercial chemical thinning of stone fruit in California by gibberellins to reduce flowering," *Acta Hortic.* 394 (1995): 135-147.

Taylor, B.K., "Effects of gibberellin sprays on fruit russet and tree performance of Golden Delicious apple," *J. Hortic. Sci.* 53 (1978): 167-169.

Taylor, D.R. and J.N. Knight, "Russeting and cracking of apple fruit and their control with plant growth regulators," *Acta Hortic.* 179 (1986): 819-820.

Unrath, C.R., "The commercial implications of gibberellin A_4A_7 plus benzyladenine for improving shape and yield of Delicious apples," *J. Amer. Soc. Hort. Sci.* 99 (1974): 381-384.

Visai, C., O. Failla, and T. Eccher, "Effects of Promalin and paclobutrazol on cracking and quality of Neipling Stayman apples," *Acta Hortic.* 239 (1989): 451-454.

Weaver, R.J., A.N. Kasimatis, and S.B. McCune, "Studies with gibberellin on wine grapes to decrease bunch rot," *Amer. J. Enol. Vitic.* 13 (1962): 78-82.

Westwood, M.N. and H.O. Bjornstad, "Effects of gibberellin A_3 on fruit shape and subsequent seed dormancy of apple," *HortScience* 3 (1968): 19-20.

Williams, M.W. and E.A. Stahly, "Effect of cytokinins and gibberellins on shape of Delicious apple fruits," *J. Amer. Soc. Hort. Sci.* 94 (1969):17-19.

15 Ethylene-based Preharvest Growth Regulators

Duane W. Greene
Department of Plant and Soil Sciences
University of Massachusetts
Amherst, Massachusetts

The growth-regulating properties of ethylene have been known for many years. Its involvement in hormonal regulation of plant growth and development was not immediately recognized by the scientific community for two reasons. First, there were no good bioassays to determine accurately and conveniently endogenous levels of ethylene. Second, it was difficult to accept major regulatory activity of a simple two-carbon compound that readily moved both inside and outside the plant.

In the 1960s, the gas chromatograph was adopted widely as a precise method to determine ethylene. It was only then that the growth-regulating properties were fully recognized and ethylene gained stature as a legitimate and important plant hormone.

There are two ethylene-related plant growth regulators that are or will become important in fruit production. The first is 2-chloroethylphosphonic acid, commonly referred to as ethephon. It is an ethylene-generating compound. The second, aminoethoxyvinylglycine (AVG), is an inhibitor of ethylene biosynthesis.

Ethephon

Ethephon was the first ethylene-based plant growth regulator to be introduced on the market. It was introduced in 1971 to stimulate latex production in rubber trees. Since that time, it has been registered for use on over 20 crops, including fruit crops such as apple, cherry, pineapple, and grapes.

Ethephon is an extremely convenient ethylene-dispensing compound. The problems associated with administering ethylene in its gaseous form to a plant are immense. Ethephon simplifies this. It is a compound that is quite stable in aqueous solutions at low pH levels, but at high pH levels, it becomes unstable.

Ethephon is applied to tree fruit in an aqueous spray, where it is absorbed and moves into the cytoplasm that has pH level slightly below neutrality (pH 7). Ethephon is unstable in this pH range and breaks down to liberate ethylene gas in the cell. The ethylene liberated from the breakdown of ethephon frequently stimulates the plant to produce even more endogenous ethylene.

Uses of ethephon in tree fruit

Ethephon can influence many aspects of growth and development in tree fruit. However, its commercial use generally has been restricted to three broad areas: thinning, vegetative growth control, and to advance ripening and increase red color of fruit.

CHEMICAL THINNING

Ethephon is a very effective abscission agent and it is used extensively in some areas of the United States, Australia, and in other areas as a bloom and a postbloom thinner. The thinning response to ethephon can be quite variable due to weather, thus limiting its general use as a thinner in many areas with unpredictable weather.

GROWTH CONTROL

Ethephon is an effective growth retardant. It has also been used to promote flower bud formation, especially on trees that have been propagated on vigorous rootstocks. Its use has been generally restricted to application shortly after bloom on nonbearing trees because of the likelihood of extensive thinning. Many of the apple trees being planted in commercial orchards are now propagated on dwarfing rootstock. Since these trees come into production early, there is a some-

what limited use of ethephon to control growth and enhance flowering.

Occasionally, the crop on blocks of bearing trees is lost due to frost. Under these conditions, excessive vegetative growth is likely, and application of ethephon would be useful on a full range of tree sizes. In larger trees, vegetative growth can be reduced and the resulting dormant pruning can be reduced. There is a delicate balance between vegetative growth and fruiting in high intensity orchards. High vigor caused by crop loss may tip the balance so far in favor of vegetative growth that it may be difficult to bring the planting back into an appropriate balance between vegetative growth and fruiting. Ethephon may be useful in retarding growth and preventing growth and fruiting from getting too far out of balance.

FIGURE 1

Cumulative drop from 15-year-old Gardiner Delicious/MM.106 trees after various growth-controlling treatments were applied eight days after petal fall (after Autio and Greene, 1994).

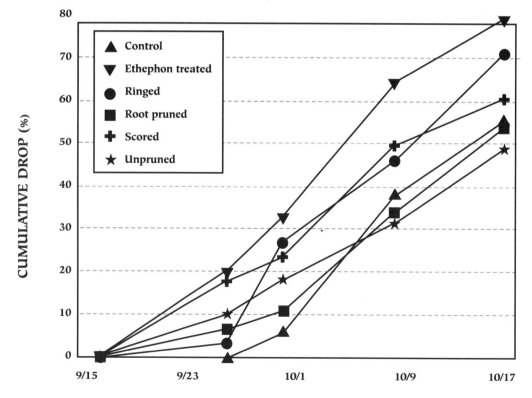

Ethephon can be used on bearing trees, but thinning is likely. In general, thinning is undesirable under conditions where growth control is appropriate. Crop load is an important component in modification of vegetative growth. Three approaches have been used to control growth and promote flowering on bearing trees.

Postbloom application on nonbearing trees. The normal time to apply a growth retardant or make treatments that control growth is about seven to ten days after bloom when terminal shoot growth is three to five inches long. Maximum growth control is achieved when ethephon is applied at this time and at a concentration that will assure growth control to midsummer. Generally, 250 to 500 parts per million (ppm) is applied. Growth control is more difficult on nonspur varieties and on trees budded on vigorous rootstocks. Increased flower bud formation can be expected the year following application.

Postbloom application on bearing trees. Occasionally, orchardists incorrectly match the rootstock-scion combination with site. The result is that trees are too vigorous for the allotted space. Ethephon or other growth control treatments can be used to retard vegetative growth to help

alleviate this problem. Fruit ripening may be advanced. When 500 ppm ethephon was applied to Gardnier Delicious/MM.106 eight days after petal fall, preharvest drop was initiated early *(see Figure 1)* and fruit ripening was advanced, based on starch rating and a rise in internal fruit ethylene (Autio and Greene, 1994).

Apply after June drop. A strategy to avoid thinning on bearing trees is to wait until the end of June drop to apply ethephon. Using this approach, growth control will be less, little or no thinning will occur, some increase in bloom will occur, but treatments can and frequently do advance ripening (Greene et al., 1977).

Make multiple small applications. Multiple doses of 100 or 200 ppm ethephon applied at 12 weekly or 6 biweekly times did not cause any fruit thinning of Starkrimson Delicious, but fruit ripening was advanced as determined by starch rating (Byers, 1993). Effective growth control was achieved.

All early applications of ethephon at moderate concentration can cause fruit thinning. Thinning can be avoided if application of higher rates is delayed until after June drop, or multiple low-concentration sprays are applied. However, regardless of

TABLE 1

Effect of (AVG) and (NAA) applied to Ace Delicious apple trees on fruit characteristics at harvest, Belchertown, Massachusetts.

Treatment (ppm)	Fruit firmness[1] (lb)	Soluble solids (%)	Starch rating[2]	Watercore rating[3] (%)
Control (0 AVG)	14.8	2.9	6.5	4.0
AVG 100	15.5	12.6	4.9	2.8
AVG 200	15.7	12.6	4.4	2.9
NAA 10	14.6	12.7	6.2	4.2
Significance[4]				
AVG	***	NS	***	***
AVG vs. NAA	***	NS	***	***

[1] *Harvested October 22, 1992.*

[2] *1-3 immature, 4-6 mature, and 7-9 over-mature*

[3] *1 none, 2-3 slight, 4-5 moderate, and 6-7 severe*

[4] ****, NS Significance at P=0.001 or nonsignificant*

the time of application, there is the potential to increase preharvest drop and to advance ripening regardless of time of application.

ADVANCE RIPENING

Application of ethephon to advance ripening can be a benefit to both consumers and growers (Looney, 1984). The advantage to consumers is that they will be able to purchase high quality apples earlier in the season, whereas growers will be able to start the marketing season early. However, the use of ethephon should be considered a tool, and, as with all tools, it should be used properly.

Ethephon-treated fruit should be treated differently for several reasons. The storage life and the shelf life may be reduced. In some years, there may be no effect, while in others, the effect may be dramatic. Factors influencing storage life of ethephon-treated fruit include the concentration of ethephon used, the time interval between application and harvest, the temperature during the time the fruit are on the tree, and the time from harvest until the internal fruit temperature is reduced to near 32°F in storage.

Fruit yield will be reduced because fruit will be harvested 10 to 15 days early. Fruit increase in size 1% per day that they remain on the tree, thus harvesting fruit 15 days early would translate into a 15% reduction in yield.

Ethephon should be applied two to three weeks before normal harvest at concentrations ranging from 1/2 to 1 pint per 100 gallons of water (based upon a dilute application). Increased red color will be noted within five to seven days. Fruit color will continue to increase at a faster rate than on nonsprayed trees. This response is accompanied by fruit flesh softening. Treated fruit should be monitored daily, once notable ripening starts, to reduce the risk of fruit becoming overripe on the tree.

A preharvest drop control strategy is necessary if ethephon is used. Ten to 20 ppm naphthaleneacetic acid (NAA) is required, and it should be applied with or

---

FIGURE 2

Changes in the internal ethylene concentration in the core of Lodi apples (after Walsh, 1977).

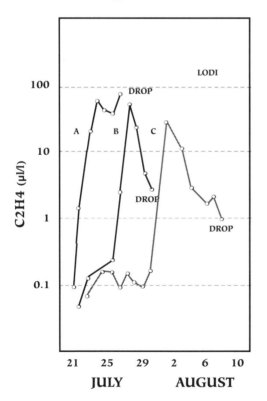

TABLE 2

Effect of (AVG) and (NAA) applied to Marshall McIntosh apple trees on red color of fruit at harvest, Belchertown, Massachusetts.

Treatment (ppm)	Red color[1] (%)
Control (0 AVG)	92
AVG 30	91
AVG 60	89
AVG 90	86
AVG 120	87
NAA 10	93
Significance[2]	
AVG	***
AVG vs. NAA	***

[1] Harvested September 22, 1995.

[2] Significance at P=0.001 or nonsignificant

shortly following ethephon application. A second application of NAA may be necessary. In some years, NAA inadequately controls preharvest drop. Unrath (1996) has reported that preloading with four 5 ppm applications of NAA at weekly intervals is an effective way to control preharvest drop on Delicious. Treatments should begin a month before anticipated harvest.

Over the past few years, preloading with NAA has been a much better way to control drop on Delicious than the traditional application of 10 to 20 ppm made when the first sound fruit start to drop. If ethephon is used to advance ripening, neither NAA preloading nor 50 gai/acre AVG (aminoethoxy-vinylglycine) will adequately control drop. The addition of NAA at the time of ethep-

FIGURE 3

Cumulative drop on Ace Delicious apple trees treated with AVG as a dilute spray on August 27, 1991.

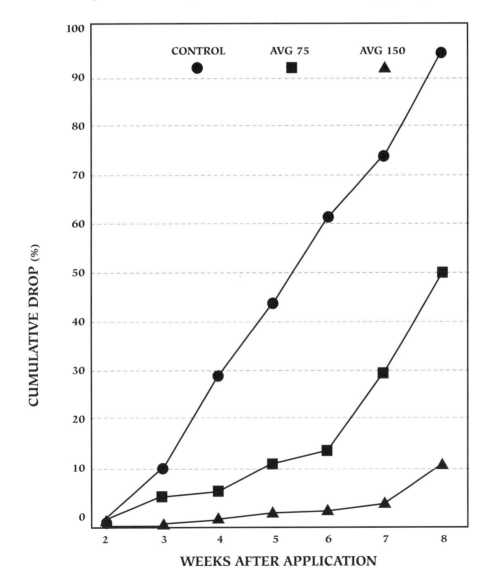

WEEKS AFTER APPLICATION

hon application is necessary, in addition to the use of NAA preload or AVG application.

INCREASE RED COLOR

Nearly all red coloring varieties benefit from additional color. Further, the development of suitable red color is the factor that frequently determines when a grower starts to pick a block of fruit. Ethephon application of 1/4 to 1/2 pint per 100 gallons (based upon a dilute application) made seven to ten days before anticipated harvest may increase red color.

The use of ethephon to increase red

FIGURE 4

Flesh firmness of Marshall McIntosh apples at harvest and at four-week intervals in air storage at 32°F. AVG and NAA were applied on August 25 and September 8, respectively, and fruit were harvested on September 18, 1992.

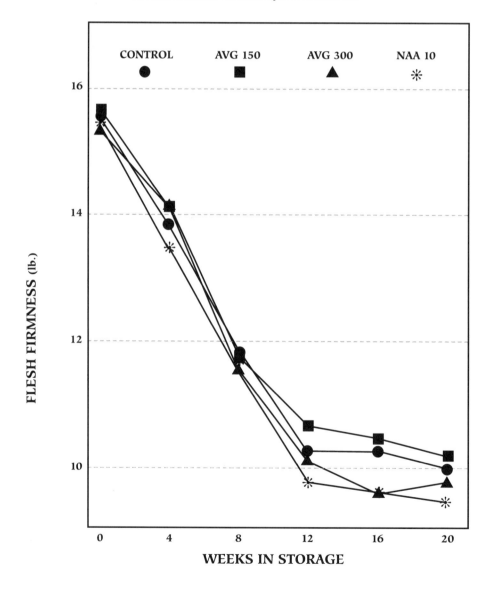

color comes with some risks, because there is also the potential to reduce storage life. Ethephon will not completely overcome conditions unfavorable for development of red color. At elevated temperatures, fruit ripen at an accelerated rate, while red color may increase little. It is important to harvest fruit before fruit condition is lost, and to cool fruit immediately.

Good light exposure is an important component when using ethephon. Experience has shown that ethephon works best on young, well-pruned trees. Ethephon should not be used on large, dense trees or poorly pruned trees. Fruit may ripen excessively before adequate color develops.

FIGURE 5

Flesh firmness of Marshall McIntosh apples at harvest and following storage at room temperature in a well-ventilated room. AVG and NAA were applied on August 25 and September 8, respectively, and fruit were harvested on September 18, 1992.

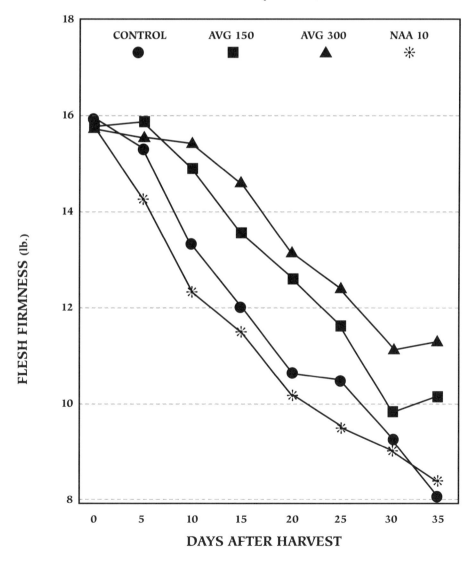

CARRYOVER EFFECTS

There can be carryover effects following ethephon application. If applied at reasonably high concentrations late in the season, fruit set and terminal growth may be reduced the following year. Ketchie and Williams (1970) applied ethephon at concentrations between 250 and 500 ppm during the last two weeks in September and observed reduced fruit set and a retardation of vegetative growth in some instances on Delicious and Golden Delicious the following year.

Williams (1975) also showed that a 300 to 450 ppm spray application of ethephon to Delicious on either August 29 or September 10 reduced the fruit L/D ratio from 0.96 to 0.92 the following year. Warm weather following ethephon application favors a reduction of carryover effects. Conversely, uncommonly cool weather following application intensifies the carryover effects.

Aminoethoxyvinylglycine
(AVG)

AVG is a naturally occurring plant growth regulator that was first discovered in the early 1970s by scientists at Hoffman LaRoche. Its primary mode of action is to inhibit ethylene biosynthesis. It blocks the enzyme ACC synthase, a key enzyme in the ethylene biosynthetic pathway. Thus, the effect of AVG on apples is primarily due to the marked reduction in the amount of ethylene produced by the fruit and the tree.

AVG elicits many responses in a tree. These responses include increasing fruit set, increasing vegetative growth, stimulating branching, increasing fruit L/D ratio, and increasing flesh firmness of fruit. Efforts to register this product in the early 1980s were not pursued because of the perceived high cost of producing this compound.

Abbott Laboratories was able to apply expertise used in the production of pharmaceuticals to produce a 15% (wt/wt) formulation of AVG (trade name ReTain) economically by fermentation (Clarke, et al., 1996,

Shafer, et al., 1995, 1996). Development of AVG for use on apples has been going on for several years. In 1995, Abbott received an experimental use permit for AVG to retard preharvest drop and to influence fruit quality at harvest and following storage. An expanded EUP is anticipated in 1996, and a full registration is targeted for 1997.

PREHARVEST DROP

As fruit mature and approach the appropriate time for harvest, there is a rise in carbon dioxide and ethylene. This is called the climacteric, and it is a definitive signal that the fruit is ripe. Generally, 0.5 to 1 ppm internal ethylene is considered the time a fruit enters the climacteric. Soon, the fruit is producing large amounts of ethylene, which then move through the intracellular space to the abscission zone in the fruit.

High amounts of ethylene trigger the production of enzymes in the abscission zone of the fruit that ultimately result in breakdown of the cell walls and the dissolving of the pectin that holds the cells together. When the abscission zone is sufficiently weakened, the fruit fall off.

Walsh (1977) followed internal ethylene in several apple varieties. He found that fruit drop followed the rapid rise in internal ethylene in Lodi *(see Figure 2)* and McIntosh. The length of time between fruit drop and the rise in ethylene increased as the temperature went down. This supports the observation that the rate of fruit drop slows later in the season as overall temperatures become lower.

CONCENTRATION AND TIME OF APPLICATION

AVG (ReTain) has been effective when applied between two and eight weeks before anticipated harvest. Over a wide range of climatic conditions, application at about four weeks before anticipated harvest yields the most satisfactory results. This is the time that is specified on the present label. It should be emphasized that the suggested time of application is before anticipated harvest rather than normal harvest. Therefore, if certain blocks are designated to be harvested late, then the AVG should be applied to correspond with the later harvest date.

AVG is a very water soluble compound. It is known that the effectiveness of AVG will be diminished if rain comes within 24 hours of application. If a block of trees is under overhead irrigation, it should not be watered for at least 24 hours after AVG application.

According to the EUP label for ReTain, the amount of AVG applied is restricted to 50 gai per acre. On a tree row volume (TRV) basis, this is equivalent to 33 to 265 ppm in blocks with a TRV ranging from 400 down to 50 gallons per acre, respectively. It appears that it is not necessary to apply AVG in a dilute application, but it is important to apply AVG in a large enough volume of water to get good coverage and get the spray to the top of the trees. However, it is useful to make the TRV calculation, because response to AVG is linear and it will give a grower an idea of the intensity of response. Drop control, harvest delay, and fruit effects are greater at 132 ppm than they are at 33 ppm.

PREHARVEST DROP CONTROL

AVG can control drop at concentrations as low as 30 ppm (Greene, 1996). However, drop control is more effective and lasts longer when a larger amount of AVG is applied. Significant drop control was achieved on Ace Delicious with both 75 and 150 ppm AVG (see Figure 3). At the beginning of normal harvest on October 4, 30% of the fruit on untreated trees had already dropped. At this same time, 7% and 1% of the fruit abscised from trees treated with 75 and 150 ppm AVG, respectively. Even on October 25, nearly three weeks after normal harvest, there was less than 4% drop on trees treated with 150 ppm AVG.

NAA is the only drop control material currently registered for used to retard preharvest drop of apples. Frequently, NAA is ineffective when applied according to label directions (Unrath, 1996). ReTain is the most effective drop control material that has been tested or has been used in the past 25 years.

TIME OF RIPENING

AVG can retard ripening significantly as determined by starch chart rating (see Table 1). The degree of retardation is dependent upon the time of harvest, the amount of AVG applied, and the weather. When applied one month before anticipated harvest, there is a small but noticeable effect. If harvest is delayed, the difference between treated and untreated fruit usually gets larger. The higher the concentration of AVG used, the greater delay of ripening that is observed. AVG delays the time of the onset of the ethylene climacteric, and it also initially reduces the amount of ethylene given off by the fruit.

FRUIT QUALITY AT HARVEST

AVG delays the loss of flesh firmness of fruit (see Table 1). The response is linear, and the difference in firmness between treated and untreated fruit usually varies between 0.5 and 1.0 pound. NAA-treated fruit are usually softer than control fruit, and the difference between AVG-treated fruit is even greater.

Occasionally, soluble solids are reduced on AVG-treated fruit. Invariably, this is due to delayed ripening and retarded degradation of starch. With time, differences diminish, and ultimately they disappear.

AVG has no direct effect on fruit size. In no instance over several years and in a number of experiments, has there ever been a reduction in fruit size attributable to AVG. However, AVG-treated fruit are usually larger. The reason is that AVG reduces preharvest drop. Consequently, these fruit are harvested later in the season. Fruit size increases 1% for each additional day a fruit remains on the tree.

In some years, watercore can be a serious problem that shortens the postharvest life of fruit. AVG delays watercore development, and in some years, the difference between control fruit and AVG-treated fruit can be large *(see Table 1)*. In years when watercore is severe, AVG could have a large impact on improving fruit quality out of storage, in large part by reducing the amount of watercore that develops in harvested fruit.

AVG delays ripening and sharply reduces ethylene production. As a consequence, red color development is delayed *(see Table 2)*. High rates of AVG, above 100 ppm, invariably reduce red color, and concentrations below that may lower red color. If one were to compare red color development of treated and untreated fruit at a comparable starch rating, usually there is no difference between AVG-treated fruit and control fruit. Therefore, the reduction in red color appears to be more of a function of delayed ripening than a direct inhibitory effect of AVG.

STORAGE POTENTIAL

Fruit treated with AVG have been evaluated following storage in air at 32°F and following CA storage (Bramlage, et al., 1980). Results have been mixed. In one study, Marshall McIntosh apples were treated with either 150 or 300 ppm AVG or 10 ppm NAA, and then at the normal harvest, fruit were placed in air storage at 32°F. Flesh firmness dropped at a comparable rate in all fruit *(see Figure 4)*.

At the end of 20 weeks in storage, NAA-treated fruit were softer, and there was no difference between firmness of AVG-treated and control fruit. While AVG is a potent inhibitor of ethylene biosynthesis, it does not make treated fruit immune to the ethylene produced by nontreated fruit in the storage. It appears that the firmness loss was caused by ethylene evolved from the surrounding nontreated fruit in the storage. In the future, strategies to slow flesh firmness loss in storage should include segregating treated and nontreated fruit.

If fruit harvested from the above-treated trees are allowed to remain at room temperature, and flesh firmness determined at five-day intervals, a different result is noted *(see Figure 5)*. AVG-treated fruit soften at a much slower rate than control fruit. In this situation, AVG-treated fruit are not surrounded by ethylene produced by nontreated fruit. However, AVG-treated fruit did soften. Thus, even reduced rates of ethylene being produced by these fruit appear to be sufficiently high to trigger firmness loss.

There have been a number of reports where AVG-treated fruit have emerged from storage with greater firmness. With time and repeated use, the firmness benefit of AVG on fruit emerging from storage will be more clearly defined.

CARRYOVER EFFECTS

Previous reports have shown that preharvest application of AVG may result in carryover effects (Greene, 1983; Williams, 1981). These include increased L/D ratio, increased fruit set, increased vegetative growth, and greater bud break. In these studies, the concentration used was considerably higher than would be allowed on the present label, and the applications were made within a week of normal harvest, a time much later than is suggested on the label. Therefore, the likelihood of any carryover effects following applications of ReTain made according to the label, as it reads now, are remote at best.

Literature cited

Autio, W.R. and D.W. Greene, "Effect of growth retarding treatments on apple tree growth, fruit maturation, and fruit abscission," *J. Hort. Sci.* 69 (1994): 653-664.

Bramlage, W.J., D.W. Greene, W.R. Autio, and J.M. McLaughlin, "Effects of aminoethoxyvinylglycine on internal ethylene concentrations and storage potential of apples," *J. Amer. Soc. Hort. Sci.* 105 (1980): 847-851.

Byers, R.E., "Controlling growth of bearing apple trees with ethephon," *HortScience* 28 (1993): 1103-1105.

Clarke, G., W. Shafer, and B. Devisetty, "ABG-3168: A new, naturally-occurring plant growth regulator for the apple industry," Proc. New England Fruit Meeting of the Massachusetts Fruit Growers' Assoc. 102 (1996): (in press).

Greene, D.W. , "Effect of chemical thinners on fruit set and fruit characteristics of AVG-treated apples.," *J. Amer. Soc. Hort. Sci.* 108 (1983): 415-419.

Greene, D.W. , "AVG: A new preharvest drop control compound for apples," *Proc. New England Fruit Meeting of the Massachusetts Fruit Growers Assoc.* 102 (1996): (in press).

Greene, D.W., W.J. Lord, and W.J. Bramlage, "Mid-summer applications of ethephon and daminozide on apples. II. Effect on Delicious," *J. Amer. Soc. Hort. Sci.* 102 (1977): 494-497.

Ketchie, D.O., and M.W. Williams, "Effect of fall application of 2-chloroethylphosphonic acid on apple trees," *HortScience* 5 (1970): 167-168.

Looney, N.E., "Growth regulator usage in apple and pear production," In: *Plant Growth Regulating Chemicals,* Vol. I., edited by L.G. Nickell. Boca Raton: CRC Press, 1984

Shafer, W., R. Fritts, and B. Devisetty, "A commercial formulation of AVG for use on apples," Proc. Washington State Hort. Assoc. 91 (1996): 169-171.

Shafer, W., G. Clarke, J. Hansen, D. Woolard, B. Devisetty, and R. Fritts, "Practical applications of aminoethoxyvinylglycine," Proc. Plant Growth Regulation Society of America 22 (1995): 11-15.

Unrath, C.R., "Drop control in apples-NAA to AVG," *Using Plant Growth Regulators in Orchards for Profit, 1996 PSU Fruit School,* edited by W.C. Kleiner and G.M. Greene. University Park: The Pennsylvania State University, 1996.

Walsh, C.S., "The relationship between endogenous ethylene and abscission of mature apple fruit," *J. Amer. Soc. Hort. Sci.* 102 (1977): 615-619.

Williams, M.W., "Carryover effect of ethephon on fruit set of Delicious apples," HortScience 10 (1975): 523-524.

Williams, M.W., "Response of apple trees to aminoethoxyvinylglycine (AVG) with emphasis on apical dominance, fruit set, and mechanism of action or fruit thinning chemicals," *Acta Hort.* 120 (1981): 137-141.

Glossary

ABSCISE—the natural separation of plant parts. "Abscission" is the noun.

ABSCISIC ACID (ABA)—a complex natural growth inhibitor, thought to be the principal inhibitor in the dormant (resting) stage of buds.

ABSCISSION ZONE—the zone at the tip of the stem or across the base of the leaf petiole where cells are altered and facilitate fruit and leaf abscission.

ACC (l-aminocyclopropane-1-carboxylic acid)—a close precursor of ethylene.

ADVENTITIOUS—refers to structures arising not at their usual sites, as roots originating on stems or leaves instead of on other roots, buds developing on leaves, stems, or roots instead of in leaf axils on shoots.

ANTHER—structure in flower that contains pollen anthesis—opening of the flower

ANTHESIS—the expanded or full-bloom stage of flowers.

ANTHOCYANIN—any class of water soluble pigments, including most of those imparting red or blue color to leaves, fruits or flowers.

APICAL—meristematic cells at the tip of the stem or the root; region of initiation of the primary tissues. On stems, also known as shoot apex.

APICAL DOMINANCE—apical bud exerts an inhibitory influence upon the lateral (axillary) buds, preventing or slowing their development.

APOPLASTIC TRANSPORT—transport through the cell wall network as far as the casparian strip, then through the symplasm.

ASSIMILATES—products of assimilation; e.g., photosynthates and nutrients.

AUXIN—a collective term for a group of plant bioregulators associated with actively growing plant parts of the plant, particularly the terminal bud on a shoot. Promotes cell enlargement. Responsible for apical dominance. The most common form is indole-3-acetic acid (IAA). NAA is a synthetic formulation.

AVG (amino ethoxyvinyl glycine)—a growth regulator which blocks ethylene production.

AXIL—the angle between a petiole and the stem to which it is attached.

AXILLARY BUD—a bud in the angle (axil) between the leaf petiole and the stem. May be a vegetative bud, fruit bud, or a mixed bud.

BA (benzyladenine)—a synthetic cytokinin.

BIENNIAL BEARING—bearing heavy crops one year and little or none in the following year. Example: Baldwin apple.

BOURSE—the thickened base of an inflorescence in apple and pear; the flower cluster base; axillary buds on the bourse give rise to new shoots (bourse shoot) or new spurs (bourse bud).

BRACT—a specialized leaf or leaf-like part, usually at the base of a flower or inflorescence.

BRINDLE—a thin lateral shoot 4 to 12 inches long, usually terminating in a flower bud.

CARBOHYDRATES—metabolic active compounds, such as sugars, made up of carbon, hydrogen, and oxygen.

CARPEL—a modified leaf forming the structure enclosing the seed.

CARTENOID—any of a number of orange-red or yellow pigments, similar to carotene found in leaves, fruits, and flowers.

CHLOROPHYLL—the green pigment in plants that absorbs light at the outset of photosynthesis.

CHROMOSOME—a unit within the nucleus that contains genetic information.

CLIMACTERIC—a sharp rise in respiration just before ripening.

CROSS POLLINATION—the transfer of pollen from the anther of one plant to the stigma of a flower of another plant.

CUTICLE—a waxy layer coating the outer wall of epidermal cells.

CYTOKININS—a class of plant bioregulators which can be found in most parts of the tree, but typically associated with roots and root growth. Promote and regulate cell division and enlargement. Two naturally occurring cytokinins are zeatin and kinetin. Benzyladenine is a synthetic cytokinin.

DARD—short lateral shoot up to four inches long with a terminal flower bud.

DIFFERENTIATION—the process of developmental change from an unspecialized cell to a specialized cell.

DIPLOID—containing two sets of chromosomes (normal for vegetative tissues; see *haploid* and *triploid*).

DRUPE—a fruit derived entirely from an ovary, one-seeded, with an exocarp, fleshy mesocarp, and a stoney endocarp (as peach, cherry and plum.)

EFFECTIVE POLLINATION PERIOD—period of time during which pollination can result in fruit set.

EGG CELL—haploid cell within the ovule that becomes the zygote and embryo following fertilization.

EMBRYO—portion of seed that develops into seedling.

EMBRYO SAC—the cell in the ovule that produces the egg and in which the embryo is formed following fertilization.

ENDOCARP—the inner layer of the pericarp, ripened ovary or fruit, as the pit of a peach.

ENDOGENOUS—produced from within; originating from or due to internal causes.

ENDOSPERM—portion of seed that nourishes the embryo and is consumed by it during development.

EPINASTY—abnormal growth of leaves or stems, often twisted or misshapen; leaf droop. Caused by exposure to certain growth regulators.

ETHEPHON—a synthetic plant bioregulator which produces ethylene.

ETHYLENE—the principal ripening plant hormone for fruit.

EXOCARP—the outer layer of the pericarp, ripened ovary or the fruit coat, as the peel of an apricot.

EXOGENOUS—arising or coming from an external source (as does an applied chemical).

FERTILIZATION—the union of the male cell with the egg. In tree fruits, the pollen tube penetrates the embryo sac, where one male gamete unites with the egg to form a zygote.

FILAMENT—the stalk on which the anther is attached.

FLOWER INITIATION—initial microscopic changes in which a vegetative bud changes into a reproductive bud; in fruit trees, this occurs during the growing season prior to flowering.

GIBBERELLIC ACID (GA$_3$)—gibberellin A$_3$, one of a related group of plant hormones found in fungi and higher plants. Produced in actively growing areas, promotes cell elongation.

GREASINESS—wax or lipid build up on the surface of some apple cultivars (malus domestica Borkh.) usually after extended storage, which makes them slippery to touch and reduces their aesthetic appeal.

GROWTH REGULATOR—any of several classes of natural or synthetic chemicals that in some way regulate plant growth.

HAPLOID—containing one set of chromosomes, as in pollen grains and ovules (see *diploid* and *triploid*).

HORMONE—a substance produced in minute amounts in one part of the plant and transported to another part where it evokes a response.

IAA (indoeacetic acid)—naturally occurring auxin.

IBA (indobutyric acid)—synthetic auxin.

INCOMPATIBLE—cultivars that produce viable pollen, but are incapable of setting fruit when cross-pollinated.

INTERNODE—the area of the stem between two nodes.

L/D RATIO—length to diameter ratio. Used to determine fruit shape.

LATENT BUD—a bud, usually concealed, more than one year old, which remains dormant for an indefinite period. Under certain conditions, such as severe pruning, a latent bud may grow.

LEAF AREA INDEX (LAI)—the total leaf area of a plant or plants divided by the land area covered by the plants.

LIGHT—the visible portion of the spectrum. The term is sometimes incorrectly used to include the ultraviolet and infrared portions as well.

MALIC ACID—organic acid found in various plant juices.

MERISTEM—actively dividing cells of undifferentiated tissue, as cambium or the tips of a growing shoot or root.

MESOCARP—the middle layer of the pericar, the edible flesh of a peach between the exocarp (skin) and the endocarp (pit).

METABOLIC SINK—the final destination of metabolites produced in other portions of the plant and used in growth and development.

METABOLIC SOURCE—the source of metabolites produced within the plants utilized in plant growth and development.

MIEOSIS—cell division which reduces the number of chromosomes in the cell by half. Essential process to form pollen and the egg.

MITOSIS—cell division where the chromosomes first become doubled longitudinally before separating, so that each of the two resulting new cells contain the same number of chromosomes as the original cell. Essential process for growth.

NODE—the point on a stem from which buds and leaves arise.

NUCELLUS—tissue in the ovule and seed that surrounds the endosperm and embryo.

OVARY—part of the flower that contains the ovule and develops into the fruit or a portion thereof.

OVULE—structure within the ovary that becomes the seed.

PARTHENOCARPIC—requiring no pollination to produce fruit; seedless fruit arising from this process.

PERFECT FLOWER—having both male and female parts.

PHEROMONE—chemical produced by insect that attracts opposite sex.

PHLOEM—specialized cells, exterior to the cambium through which carbohydrates and nutrients move through the plant; typically away from the site of production. The principal food conducting tissue of vascular plants.

PHOTODEGRADATION—the breakdown of a product or compound due to exposure to light.

PHOTOSYNTHATES—products of photosynthesis.

PHOTOSYNTHESIS—the process by which all green plants intercept solar light energy and utilize the energy for the uptake and conversion of carbon dioxide (CO_2) and water (H_2O) into sugars with high energy phosphate bonds.

PHOTOSYNTHETIC ASSIMILATES—assimilates from the leaves, including photosynthates that are necessary for the growth of plant parts that cannot photosynthesize and for some parts that photosynthesize only at low levels, such as some stems and fruits.

PHYSIOLOGY—the function or activities of living systems.

PISTIL—consists of an ovule-bearing base (or ovary) supporting an elongated region (or style) whose expanded tip (or surface) is called the stigma. The ovule gives rise to the seed. The mature ovary (with or without seeds) becomes the fruit of stone fruit and the core of pome fruits.

PLANT BIOREGULATORS (PBRs)—chemicals other than plant nutrients that influence or direct natural plant growth and development phenomena in a beneficial manner. Examples of PBR effects include termination of seed and bud dormancy; promotion or suppression of shoot growth, flowering, and fruit set; advancing or delaying fruit ripening; improving fruit quality.

PLANT GROWTH REGULATORS (PGRs)—see Plant Bioregulators (PBRs)

POLLEN TUBE—a filament containing male sex nuclei, growing from a pollen grain and delivering the nuclei to the egg in the ovule.

POLLEN—haploid spores produced by the anther.

POLLEN INSERTS—containers of pollen placed on the hive alighting board that bees must walk through.

POLLINATION—the transfer of pollen to the female stigma.

POLLINATOR—agent of transfer of pollen, usually an insect.

POLLINIZER—cultivar supplying pollen.

POME—the fruit derived from the fusion of the ovaries, calyx cup, and floral tube, produced by the apple, pear, quince, and other members of the sub-family Pomoideae.

PRECOCITY—relative earliness of cropping in young trees. (Golden Delicious is precocious, Northern Spy is not.)

RECEPTACLE—the modified or expanded portion of an axis that bears the organs of a single flower or the florets of a flower head.

REGULATED DEFICIT IRRIGATION (RDI)—Technique for managing irrigation of fruit trees, which conserves water during periods of tree and fruit growth.

RESPIRATION—the process by which oxygen and carbohydrates are used to produce energy, with oxidation products, carbon dioxide and water, given off.

RINGING—removal of ring of bark from limb or trunk to stimulate flowering and/or fruit set.

ROOT INITIATION—initial microscopic changes that occur when a new lateral root is produced.

SCORING—cutting the bark around the circumference of a limb or trunk to stimulate flowering and/or fruit set.

SELF-FRUITFUL—cultivar that will set a commercial crop of fruit without cross-pollination.

SEPALS—encloses the flower in the bud. They are usually small, green, leaf-like structures below the petals (collectively, the calyx).

SPERM NUCLEUS—haploid nucleus in pollen tube that unites with egg cell to form zygote.

STAMEN—the male portion of the flower that produces pollen; a stamen consists of an anther and a filament.

STIGMA—portion of the pistil where pollen germinates.

STOMATA—plural of stomate.

STOMATE—small openings or pits in the epidermis of leaves, bordered by specialized cells called guard cells, through which water vapor and gases pass. Water vapor is lost through the stomates in the process of transpiration, oxygen is taken up or absorbed in the process of respiration, and carbon dioxide is absorbed in the process of photosynthesis.

STYLE—portion of pistil through which pollen tube grows to reach ovary.

SURFACE TENSION—that property, due to molecular forces, by which the surface film of all liquids tends to bring the contained volume into a form having the least superficial area.

SYMPLASTIC TRANSPORT—transport through the cytoplasm of each cell all the way to nonliving xylem.

TETRAPLOID—having four sets of chromosomes.

TRANSLOCATION—the physical movement of water, nutrients, or chemicals, such as an herbicide or elaborated food, within a plant.

TRANSPIRATION—the loss of water vapor from plant surfaces, chiefly through the stomata of leaves.

TREE ROW VOLUME (TRV)—a method to determine the amount of spray volume needed for thorough coverage of an orchard canopy, specific for different tree sizes or orchard systems.

TRIPLOID—cultivar with three sets of chromosomes, that lacks viable pollen and therefore must be cross-pollinated.

VISCOSITY—the thickness of a liquid, measured by its resistance to flow.

VOLATILE—1) property of liquids which allows it to change easily from a liquid to a gas; 2) a biochemical compound in the gaseous state which is responsible for odors and flavors in fruit.

VOLATILITY—volatile quality or state.

VOLATILIZATION—the evaporation or changing of a substance from liquid to vapor.

WATERCORE—a condition of apple fruits in which the inner tissues become water-soaked.

XYLEM—the woody portion of trees, interior to the cambium. Translocates water and nutrients.

ZYGOTE—single diploid cell, resulting from union of sperm nucleus with egg cell, which develops into embryo.

GOOD FRUIT GROWER

Professional growers throughout the world recognize *Good Fruit Grower* magazine as one of the most comprehensive and authoritative periodicals in the industry.

First published in 1946, the magazine has been an essential part of their operations for a half century. A not-for-profit, grower-owned business, its sole purpose is the education of deciduous tree fruit growers, irrespective of region or nationality.

In recent years, Good Fruit Grower has expanded its educational offerings by teaming with university experts to produce high-quality, low-volume books that present in detail subjects vital to the industry.

Pest management and identification, high density orchard systems, tree fruit nutrition, pollination, and irrigation and water issues all have been covered extensively in separate books. By reading the magazine and using the in-depth manuals for reference, growers remain competitive in the increasingly complex tree fruit industry. Each year, we add a title or two to our catalog to keep it comprehensive.

Readers interested in either a subscription to GOOD FRUIT GROWER *magazine or a current listing of Good Fruit Grower book titles may contact us as follows:*

GOOD FRUIT GROWER
105 S. 18th Street, Suite 217
Yakima, WA 98901-2149
Phone: 509-575-2315
Toll-free: 800-487-9946
Fax: 509-453-4880
E-mail: growing@goodfruit.com
Electronic Magazine: www.goodfruit.com

❧

Tree Fruit Physiology: Growth and Development

Book design by Donna K. Walker
Cover design by Elizabeth Gail Kotlarz
Typefaces: Hiroshige and Frutiger
Printed and bound by Thomson-Shore, Dexter, Michigan
on 60-lb. Joy White offset acid-free paper